HEAVENLY MANSIONS

St Faith's, Stoke Newington, after damage by a flying-bomb, 1944. *See p 238*

JOHN SUMMERSON

HEAVENLY
MANSIONS

and

other essays on architecture

W · W · NORTON & COMPANY

New York · London

To Prudence and Terence
Godparents of
Robert, Edward and Timothy

Library of Congress Cataloging-in-Publication Data

Summerson, John Newenham, Sir, 1904–
Heavenly mansions and other essays on architecture / John
Summerson : foreword by Kent Bloomer.
p. cm.
Originally published: London : Cresset Press. 1949
Includes index.
ISBN 0-393-31857-5 (pbk.)
1. Architecture. I. Title.
NA2563.S8 1998
720—dc21 98-38745
CIP

W. W. Norton & Company, Inc., 500 Fifth Avenue, New York, NY 10110
http://www.wwnorton.com
W. W. Norton & Company Ltd., 10 Coptic Street, London WC1A 1PU

0 9 8 7 6 5 4 3 2 1

PREFACE

AN ESSAY is an attempt, and the ten essays in this book are attempts to illuminate certain widely different aspects of architecture which have interested me. None of the essays is a formal or final treatment of its subject and in some I must confess to trespassing on ground where my passport, as historian and critic, is not exactly valid. I offer no apology for this; architecture, past, present and future, is indivisible and a writer on the subject must pry as best he can equally into Gothic niches and the offices of practising architects. Both have some bearing on the architectural thought of tomorrow.

Some of the essays have been read as papers and a few published as articles. All have been revised and expanded, if not entirely re-written. Essay No. 1 was read as a Sessional Paper before the RIBA in 1946. Essay Nos. 2, 4, 6, 8 and 10 were delivered as part of a course at Bristol University under the Perry Bequest in 1947. Essay No. 9 was, in substance, read before the Architectural Association in 1941. Essay No. 7 was read at the Courtauld Institute in 1945 and published in the *Architectural Review*, whose editor has kindly allowed me to reprint it. Essay No. 3, the longest and the oldest, was awarded the RIBA Essay Medal for 1936 and printed at the time in the Institute's *Journal*; it is reprinted here with the Institute's permission.

I am indebted to the courtesy of the following for the use of illustrations. To Mr Arthur Gardner for Plate VIII; to the LCC for Plate XXXVI; to the editor of the *Builder* for Plate XXXIX; to the RIBA and the Trustees of the British Museum and of the Soane Museum for permission to reproduce prints and drawings in their possession; to Mr George Melly for allowing the reproduction of his drawing by Picasso; to M. le Corbusier for similar permission in respect of the drawings given in Plate XLII and on p. 193; to Mr Mowbray Green for Plate XXIV; and to Mr Denis Clarke-Hall for the plan by him on p. 208. Acknowledgments for assistance in inquiries connected with several essays are given in the appropriate places in the text, but I would like especially to thank Mr Henry Gandy, Dr Eric Gandy and other members of the Gandy family for their generous help in connection with Essay No. V.

Sir John Soane's Museum　　　　　　　　　　　　　　J. S.
March 1948

CONTENTS

THE ILLUSTRATIONS

FIGURES IN THE TEXT

HALF-TONE PLATES

FOREWORD TO *HEAVENLY MANSIONS*

ALL OF the writings in *Heavenly Mansions* will be over fifty years old in 1998, the year of their reissue by W. W. Norton & Company. Most were written shortly after World War II in the context of a devastated and impoverished Europe, by an Englishman of letters clearly concerned with the potential, perhaps the renewal, of the human spirit. The ten essays constitute a passionate book about architectural history loaded with analysis, wit, and a nuanced criticism of the architecture rising out of the ashes. All too often, such critical and passionate writings about something as volatile and as political as architecture become relics, or at least quaint, after a half-century, and thus useful primarily to the researcher as evidence of an earlier way of thinking, while of less interest to the contemporary architectural public or young designer anxious to get on with today's world. In some respects, this book is dated. Many of the original historical "facts" in *Heavenly Mansions* have become common knowledge within the modern architectural academy, which has benefited from a massive outpouring of books on architectural history in the last quarter-century. Yet in most respects the book is as refreshing as, and possibly even more prophetic than, the day it was written. How can that be?

First of all, Sir John Summerson's great strength was in putting history to work as a measure of human potential. Although he wrote about architecture and architects from the twelfth to the twentieth centuries, he seems at all times to be identifying architecture as a creative cultural phenomenon, indeed as a poetic phenomenon with expressive powers equal to painting, music, and literature. To attempt to explain architecture in such broad terms would be to invite reaction from a constituency concerned only about the practical rather than the greater world of architecture. In the process of explaining architecture, Summerson naturally stood up against any doctrine that might obfuscate or diminish its capacity to represent extraordinary visions, visions that could be rooted in antiquity, modernity, science, or art. His writing, therefore, is essentially about the way architects think about the world and is best understood in the light of his view of architecture as one of the humanities.

His capacity to cover so much historical and critical material in remarkably plain, almost lyrical English is also extraordinary. Each essay is quite short and succinct, rarely much more than twenty pages. In places the essays read like mystery stories with plots full of surprises, humor, and pathos. Each of the architects and each of their settings are portrayed as familiar, indeed often peculiar and quirky, as Summerson manages to unfold the circumstances behind some of the most memorable and influential works of great architecture and town planning. His humanist approach makes this book appealing to general readers interested in architecture as well as practicing designers or planners.

I did not read any of the essays during my student years in architecture. In the late fifties they would have been regarded by most "progressive" schools as somewhat irrelevant to a radically new architecture devoted to the economic standardization of function and shelter. Moreover, seven out of the ten essays focus on architecture built before the twentieth century, and thus engage a body of old architectural ideas of marginal interest to the orthodox "modernist." Of course Summerson knew, surely more than most of us, that we could never be medieval again, or even Victorian for that matter. But he does propose that the workings of the medieval Renaissance and Victorian mind can be studied in order to teach us how to think about architecture.

I recall discussing the use of history in the teaching of architecture with the architect Charles Moore in 1966. He and his partners had just completed several small houses in California into which they had placed four-posted aedicules, a term they had discovered in the first essay, entitled "Heavenly Mansions: An Interpretation of Gothic." The essay identified the aedicule as a "little building" whose function was ceremonial, like a shrine standing over the statue of a deity. Such little houses, according to Summerson, could be tiny and cozy, or immense and heroic, while always enclosing a singular spirit. He characterized a Gothic cathedral as a great pile of aedicules, which suggests a pile of "heavenly mansions" and thus a pile of spirits. The modern California architects had seized on the aedicule as an ideal small space to be inserted in a larger space like a house within a house, capable of psychologically enlarging and expressing a sense of center. So successful were their "aediculized" houses that they made a pilgrimage to London and thanked Summerson for providing such a wonderful idea. The great scholar listened with amazement and questioned why they had chosen to use a form that had gone out of fashion in the thirteenth century!

Of course Summerson clearly wanted his study of the past to play itself out in the future. Indeed, he believed that man can form no picture of the future except by reference to the past. That belief was fueled by a refreshing impatience with contemporary architectural ideology and the rational systems of design that were formulated to produce good and progressive architecture. In his second essay, "Antithesis of the Quattrocento," he acknowledged the importance of the rules and numbers implicit in Alberti's *Ten Books of Architecture* (considered generally to be the first theoretical treatise on Western architecture), but contrasted Alberti's rationalism with a close look at the poet Francesco Colonna's Renaissance poem entitled "Hypnerotomachia" (the dream-love-strife of Poliphilus). In the poem "a lover searches for perfect union with his mistress" and dreams of flight into an enchanted forest where he encounters an ancient octagonal palace in which he consummates his search for love. To Summerson, both Alberti and Colonna were smitten by the myth of an ancient Golden Age in which the authority of classical architecture was to be revived both rationally and romantically as the basis for the next four hundred years of Western practice. Summerson was not simply observing an opposition between ways of thinking, but insisting that both men were driven by a search for knowledge lost and buried in the past, a body of knowledge much greater than they thought existed in the present world they were busy creating.

All of Summerson's chosen architects and their works are presented as marvelously imperfect and the muddled products of their time. Imperfection is part of their wonder as they reveal the playful, perhaps even the necessarily neurotic, side of brilliance in its capacity to represent human nature and human aspiration as well as its subjugation to the conflicts inherent in society at any one moment.

Summerson devoted nearly half the text in *Heavenly Mansions* to English architecture. His comments on English architects are the least theoretical and the most psychological. The thirty-six-page essay on Sir Christopher Wren, written in 1936, is the longest and the oldest. In my opinion, it is the only tentative piece in the book. Summerson seems to have been struggling with the problem of Wren's propensity to bring science, engineering, and the "tyranny of the intellect" into the foreground of seventeenth-century design, issues he would develop more thoroughly in *Sir Christopher Wren*, published in 1953. He seemed to be much happier when he wrote about "John Wood and the English Town-Planning Tradition." John Wood the elder pioneered the urban type of plan called the "Circus," a more or less round or oval grouping of town houses with their façades facing inward to a public greensward. This type was by all accounts a great success in the tradition of town planning and appeared over and over "from Bath to Piccadilly, from Exeter to Edinburgh." Like Alberti and Colonna, Wood, albeit designing in the eighteenth century, thought he was recreating the marvels of ancient Rome. When he invented the Circus he might have thought he was building something like the Roman Colosseum, even though he turned it inside-out, ran a street through it, and populated it with houses rather than spectators. "Had he been more of a scholar," Summerson writes, "an exact knowledge of the extent and nature of the Roman Colosseum would probably have extinguished the suggestiveness of the romantic half-knowledge which was his inspiration."

Romantic half-knowledge! This is Summerson at his best, acknowledging both sides of thought at once, in which the intellect and the imagination fight it out, so to say, in the mind of the architect. In such a mind the imagination is future-oriented, creative as we say today, while the intellect is more likely to be fueled by the past manifest in the writings and scientific methods fashionable during the time in which the idea is being produced. Perhaps John Summerson was actually a natural psychologist capable of unraveling the mysteries of the truly creative person.

But *Heavenly Mansions* is basically about the art of architecture and thus about the architect as an artist. In his fifth essay Summerson records the agony and poverty of J. M. Gandy (1771–1843), a brilliant mind who sometimes languished in debtors' prison and other times lived in squalor. Unable to practice much—although he managed a few rather undistinguished buildings—Gandy took to drawing and painting visionary architecture, some so visionary that his images forecast a sort of rural modernism that was to appear after World War I! He also painted fantastic landscapes and fabulous crypts. What Summerson reveals is a passionate artist escaping his oppression twice, first through the frame of a painting, and from there into the romantic garden and grotto of nature. Such an escape, according to Summerson, is no less the work of an architect.

Another English architect, William Butterfield, practicing in the mid-nineteenth century, is driven by "the Glory of Ugliness," which Summerson manages to assess by comparing Butterfield to one of Dickens's characters angrily thrashing about in a joyless London, and by observing Butterfield's disgust with a prissy good taste emblematized by curtains drawn over sooty windows to close out the ravages of an industrial behemoth. Summerson identified Butterfield as a man who could look around and see the city as it was, and proposed that his architecture was as powerful as it was responsive to its poetic and material context.

The one architect that Summerson assaults outright is the French rationalist, Viollet-le-Duc. He does not deny for a moment that Viollet was anything less than "the last great theorist in the world of architecture" responsible for many of the basic tenets of architectural modernism. In short, Viollet proposed, and attempted to prove by his analysis of great Gothic architecture, that a building efficiently engineered and economically and logically composed would produce "good architectural performance." Such a thesis anticipates the twentieth-century slogan "form follows function," as adopted by those anxious to reduce the concept of form to the efficient organization of an object or a building. Summerson argues that Viollet simply did not prove his point. Indeed, nearly a century of architecture guided largely by Viollet's type of materialist theorizing has failed to evidence the virtues promised by such extreme rationalization.

The final part of *Heavenly Mansions* moves into the twentieth century to modernism, to Le Corbusier, to the "fear" of ornament, and finally to the birth of the preservationist movement. By this time, assuming a careful attentiveness to the words and details of the first seven essays, the reader has been brilliantly introduced to the way great architecture reflects the human spirit by a historian who believes "it is time for the architect to take a new and more positive view of his functions, to learn to study not merely minimum requirement, but maximum possibilities; to learn not only how to economize space but how to be extravagant with it . . . to learn not only to use space but to play with space."

Summerson was knighted for his many accomplishments in the history of art. His enduring book *Classical Language of Architecture*, based on a BBC series, was published in the sixties; books published in the seventies dealt with Victorian London, Georgian London, and John Nash; his last book, entitled *The Unromantic Castle and Other Essays*, was published in 1990. The latter part of his life included the directorship of the Soane Museum, a marvelous late-eighteenth-century private house—museum designed by the architect Sir John Soane, with art, architectural drawings, and artifacts he had collected. Yet, of all his works, Summerson wrote towards the end of his life that "the only one of my books likely to outlive me for any considerable period" would be *Heavenly Mansions.*

Kent Bloomer
New Haven, Connecticut
1998

Heavenly Mansions

AN INTERPRETATION OF GOTHIC

THERE IS a kind of play common to nearly every child; it is to get under a piece of furniture or some extemporized shelter of his own and to exclaim that he is in a 'house'. Psychoanalysis interprets this kind of play in various ways.[1] I am not, however, concerned with such interpretations except in so far as they show that this particular form of phantasy cannot be dismissed merely as mimicry of the widespread adult practice of living in houses. It is symbolism—of a fundamental kind, expressed in terms of play. This kind of play has much to do with the aesthetics of architecture.[2]

At a later stage, the child's conduct of the game is transferred to a new plane of realism; he constructs or uses dolls' houses and insists on a strict analogy between his own practices and those of adult life—the doll's house must be an epitome of an adult's home. But whether the child is playing under the table or handling a doll's house, his imagination is working in the same way. He is placing either himself or the doll (a projection of himself) in a sheltered setting. The pleasure he derives from

[1] For a Freudian interpretation of this form of play, see *Social Development in Young Children*, by Susan Isaacs, 1933, pp 362–365. Dr Isaacs describes 'cosy places' but stresses their 'defensive' character rather than their formality.

[2] The relation of play to art is too large a subject to be entered here. Jung, in *Psychological Types* (tr. H. G. Baynes) p 82, emphasizes that its importance does not end with its interpretation as symbolism. 'All creative work is the offspring of the imagination and has its source in what one is pleased to term infantile phantasy.'

it is a pleasure in the relationship between himself (or the doll) and the setting.

None of us ever entirely outgrows the love of the doll's house or, usually in a vicarious form, the love of squatting under the table. Camping and sailing are two adult forms of play analogous to the 'my house' pretences of a child. In both, there is the fascination of the miniature shelter which excludes the elements by only a narrow margin and intensifies the sense of security in a hostile world. Less direct but even more common is the liking for models and houses in miniature. Many of us remember the enormous popularity of the Queen's Doll's House, shown for charitable purposes between the wars. The tiny cottage presented by the people of Wales to Princess Elizabeth exercised a similar appeal. The concept of the diminutive in building exercises a most powerful fascination. The 'little house' is a phrase which goes straight to the heart, whereas 'the big house' is reserved for the prison and the public assistance institution. Pleasure-houses of any kind often take their names from diminutives. 'Casino', 'bagatelle', 'brothel', are all diminutive words. The 'love-nest', 'love in a cottage', the 'little grey home in the west', the 'bijou residence'—all such hackneyed phrases serve to remind us how deep is the appeal of 'the little house'.

, But we must be careful to keep separate two different manifestations of this appeal. There is the 'cosiness' of the little house; but also its ceremony. It is the 'cosiness' which psychologists underline in their interpretation of its symbolism. But for us the ceremonial idea is more important—the idea of neatness and serenity within, contrasting with wildness and confusion without. The ceremony of the child's house, like its cosiness, is found again in adult play—that grave form of play which is intertwined with religious and social customs. The baldachino, the canopy over the throne, the catafalque over a tomb, the ceremonial shelter carried over a pope or bishop in a procession—these are not empirical devices to exclude dust or rain but vestiges of infantile regression such as we have just observed.

It is precisely this feeling for the ceremony of the little house which links all that I have been saying with the development of architecture. The Latin word for a building is *aedes;* the word for a little building is *aedicula*[1] and this word was applied in classical times more particularly to little buildings whose function was symbolic—ceremonial. It was applied to a shrine placed at the far end, from the entrance, of a temple to receive the statue of a deity—a sort of architectural canopy in the form of a rudimentary temple, complete with gable—or, to use the classical word, pediment. It was also used for the shrines—again miniature temples—in which the *lares* or titular deities of a house or street were preserved.

I am not going to trace back the history of the aedicule, but I suspect it is practically as old as architecture itself, and as widespread. The incidence of the aedicule in some Indian architecture, for instance, is very striking.[2] This miniature temple used for a ceremonial, symbolic purpose may even enshrine one of man's first purely architectural discoveries,

[1] Arch. Pubn. Soc., *Dictionary of Architecture*, s.v. Aedicula. It is curious how little currency the word has gained, either in its Latin or anglicized form. Viollet-le-Duc sometimes uses *édicule,* but there is no entry under the word in his dictionary. The OED quotes only Gell's *Pompeiana,* 1832. There is an excellent article s.v. Edicula in the *Enciclopedia Italiana,* 1932.

[2] RIBA *Journal,* 3rd ser., Vol 54, No 8 (May, 1947), p 387. J. Fergusson, in his *History of Indian and Eastern Architecture,* 1876, p 285, says that 'every-where . . . in India, architectural decoration is made up of small models of large buildings'.

a discovery re-enacted by every child who establishes his momentary dominion under the table.

Now, the aedicule, from a remote period, has been used as a *subjunctive* means of architectural expression. That is to say, it has been used to harmonize architecture of strictly human scale with architecture of a diminutive scale, so that a building may at the same time serve the purposes of men and of a race of imaginary beings smaller than men. It has also been used to preserve the human scale in a building deliberately enlarged to express the superhuman character of a god. Perhaps this should be put another way: the aedicule has been enlarged to human scale and then beyond, to an heroic scale, losing its attribute of smallness and 'cosiness' but retaining and affirming its attribute of ceremoniousness. This concept will become clearer as we proceed.

The aedicule becomes of considerable importance in Hellenistic and Roman architecture. Its use as a shrine, recorded on coins and other objects, like the shop-sign shown in Plate I, was not its only use. The shrine *idea* was woven into the development of architecture—both temple architecture and domestic architecture. A striking instance of this is the interior of the Temple of Bacchus at Baalbek (Plate II) where we see not only the shrine or *adyton*—in this case a quite substantial 'temple within a temple'—but a liberal use of aedicules to provide settings for statues both in the shrine itself and in the main structure of the temple.[1]

This example, dating from the 2nd century AD, is obviously over-ripe and complex, reflecting a late stage in a long tradition. But it does show, better than any other surviving temple

[1] Krencker, von Lüpke and Winnefeld, *Baalbek; Ergebnisse der Ausgrabungen*, etc. Berlin and Leipzig, 1923, from which the restoration (Plate II) is reproduced.

interior, how the aedicule became interwoven with temple architecture, so that the full-scale order is laced or counterpointed with diminutive architecture of purely ceremonial significance.

So long as the aedicule is used as a setting for statues its use approximates to its original function as a shrine—a function which it preserved, as we shall see, right through the Middle Ages. But at some period—I cannot say when—its use was extended to give ceremonial importance to an opening—a door or a window. It then became virtually two-dimensional, a frame or portal, suggesting that the opening which it embraced was one of special significance. This special significance, however, was in due course afforded to so many doors and windows that the aedicule became nothing more than a trite, everyday decorative feature. As such it re-emerges early in the Italian renaissance and as such it has been employed hundreds and thousands of times in this and every other country since the end of the 16th century. The Georgian door-case is an instance familiar to everybody, so familiar that it never occurs to us to consider such a thing as being anything so pompous as an aedicule or to connect it with that remote period of architectural history when the miniature temple really possessed some emotional significance, still less to that remoter period when its use was reserved for the shrine of a deity.

But the history of the aedicule in classical architecture is not a subject I want to pursue any further at present. So let us return to the more general consideration of aedicular architecture— the 'little house' with which we began. For obvious reasons, the construction of miniature architecture is rather uncommon; in fact, it is practically limited to the nursery, except in so far as it has become a part of the ornamental systems of various styles of architecture. However, the *representation* of miniature architecture is quite another thing; and one of the most interesting recurrent themes in the history of art is this practice of representing, in paintings and illuminations, an architecture of the fancy—an architecture, very often, which could not be built. Roman mural painting often consists largely of this sort of confectionery. That it is older than Rome is obvious, but the remains of Roman cities yield the richest evidence. The wall-paintings of Pompeii,[1] in particular, have rendered this kind of art famous and given it the name by which it is popularly known —'Pompeian'. Pompeii is rich in well-preserved mural paintings, ranging in date from the 1st century BC up to the destruction of the city in AD 79. They have been classified in four styles, and in each successive style, aedicular architecture takes a more prominent place till in the fourth (latest) style it absorbs the whole interest of the composition. The main characteristics of this fanciful architecture are that it is completely open and incredibly thin—a mere scaffold-architecture, so reduced in mass that it appears to hang in the air. It consists of irrational and purposeless buildings—colonnades, pergolas and paper-thin walls which enclose nothing. Where there are figures, they are sometimes grouped in a theatric tableau borrowed from classical drama, but more often they are single figures—each posed in an aedicule and reminding one a little of the innocent ceremony of the child under the table—that symbol of architecture to which I referred at the beginning of this essay.

Now, at this point I am going to introduce, quite abruptly, the thesis I wish to submit—simply by asking you to compare two architectural compositions. One is a 1st-century wall-

---

[1] L. Curtius, *Die Wandmalerei Pompeiis*, Leipzig, 1929, illustrates the example given in Plate III, which comes originally, however, from d'Amelio, *Dipinti Murali*. For further illustrations, from Pompeii and elsewhere, see F. Wirth, *Römische Wandmalerei*, 1934.

painting at Pompeii (Plate III). The other is the south porch of Chartres Cathedral (Plate IV), built about AD 1250. You will notice that these two compositions, separated in time by more than a thousand years, have a very great deal in common. Both are divided into three bays. In both cases the divisions between the bays are open and extend upwards into aedicules, containing figures. In both, the main openings are crested with gables or pediments. In both, the supporting members are fantastically thin. In short, the porch at Chartres is, in principle, a loyal realization of the Pompeian project!

I admit that to fortify my case I have chosen these examples carefully. The north and south porches at Chartres are, of all the architectural works of their age, the most classical in proportion, distribution and detail—appropriately so, since Chartres was, in the 12th-13th centuries, pre-eminently the seat of classical studies. I admit, too, that the Pompeian example is chosen because, in its main lines, it is a rather felicitous counterpart of the Chartres porch. But, even so, the comparison is sufficiently striking to set one searching for threads with which to link these two works of art together. Can there possibly be any *historical* threads? Or must we refer the resemblances to a basic psychology shared alike by the artists of classical Pompeii, those of medieval Chartres and the child under the table? I believe that there are historical threads, but I do not think that they could have spun their way through a thousand years of history but for the primitive and universal love of that kind of fantasy represented by the aedicule—the 'little house'.

When the Chartres porches were built, Pompeii lay forgotten in its tomb of ashes—even the name of the place had disappeared from human conscience. Obviously, no influences from Pompeii itself can ever have found their way into the medieval world. But the art of Pompeii was an art widespread in the Roman empire and it is only a freak of history which has made the buried city its most conspicuous exemplar. The character and themes of Roman decoration were adopted by Christian artists in many parts of Europe. In the Byzantine Empire, aedicular structures are found in many mosaics—those of Salonika for instance, and of Damascus. In the Carolingian renaissance of the 8th–9th centuries the aedicule appears in many objects, such as, for instance, the Gospel of S Médard-de-Soissons in the Bibliothèque Nationale,[1] in doors, shrines and plaques, and also in what little architecture of that age is left to us. It must also have appeared in the stucco work used on the walls of churches but which has almost entirely disappeared.[2]

Carolingian art provides, no doubt, the most important link between the classical world and the Romanesque revival of the arts in the 11th century. But Romanesque art is, as Deschamps[3] says, the most composite of all arts; there were innumerable contributors to its creation, nor must we forget the main stock —the First Romanesque—on which these contributions were grafted. The First Romanesque of Lombardy had already adventured into arcaded west fronts (like Pavia and Lucca) which are, in effect, aedicular fantasies, and the First Romanesque of France and Spain has its arcaded apses, pilaster-strips, bands and corbel-tables consisting of suspended arches. In the Romanesque churches of Languedoc and Burgundy the aedicular idea is ever-present; in Provence it links up directly with the Roman use of the aedicule; in Poitou and the west generally it begins to

[1] R. Hinks, *Carolingian Art*, 1935, pp 155–6, discusses themes common to Pompeian and Carolingian art.

[2] A. W. Clapham, *Romanesque Architecture in Western Europe*, 1936, pp 14 and 23.

[3] P. Deschamps, *Romanesque Sculpture in France*.

be articulate in a specially picturesque way on west fronts; in Normandy and England it is all ready for the next move—the creation of Gothic.

It has been satisfactorily shown, by Mâle,[1] Lasteyrie[2] and others, that the re-entry of figure-sculpture into architecture in the Romanesque churches of the 11th century was conditioned by the sculptors' familiarity with metal-work, manuscripts and other objects of art: the technique of architectural sculpture, up to the Gothic revolution in the middle of the 12th century, shows clear evidence of such a derivation. But so far as I know, nobody has developed the corollary of this—namely, that the aedicular architecture of Romanesque churches may have been reinforced or given renewed vitality from the same source.

Romanesque architecture is, as I have said, composite; it is an aggregate rather than a synthesis. It preserves much that is Roman—the round arch, the barrel vault and, in some parts of France, the principle of the pilaster and Corinthianesque carving. But to this is added something—something which distinguishes this architecture as Romanesque. This is not simply a matter of ornament—of characteristic sculptures and mouldings. Nor is it a matter of structure, the empirical quest of a satisfactory vaulting system—this quest is, in fact, curiously independent of stylistic development. It is more radical than all this; it is something resulting from a profound desire to escape from the remorseless discipline of gravity, a desire to dissolve the heavy prose of building into religious poetry; a desire to transform the heavy man-made temple into a multiple, imponderable pile of heavenly mansions.

[1] E. Mâle, *L'Art Religieux du 12e siècle etc.* 2nd ed., 1924.
[2] R. de Lasteyrie, *L'Architecture Religieuse en France à l'Epoque Romane*, 1929, pp 196–201.

What is behind this compelling ambition I do not know; to answer that question one would have to approach the subject from a different angle, exploring the psychological atmosphere of Romanesque church-building as it arose from changing social conditions. But two things are sufficiently obvious. First, that the ambition to dissolve architecture from the substantial to the insubstantial did exist; and, second, that this ambition was aided and inspired by a feeling for that frail, picturesque aedicular architecture which, through the various channels I have mentioned, had been handed down from the theatre, house and tomb decorators of Rome.

I have said that Romanesque represents an incomplete synthesis. By this I mean that the aedicular architecture is never wholly identified with the structural carcase. It was introduced in various ways, easily enumerated. First, there is the ornamental shaft, tall and thin, like a literal enlargement of the fancywork of Pompeii. Sometimes it is applied to the wall, sometimes it is sculptured in the wall itself. Sometimes it pretends to support one end of an arch, sometimes a vaulting rib; sometimes to support a corbel-table, sometimes a wooden roof; sometimes it does not pretend, and supports nothing. Second, there is the arcade, a decorative, repetitive combination of shaft and arch—a motif so often allied with the representation of figures that Foçillon[1] has adopted *l'homme-arcade* as an expression; and, most important, there is the vaulting, of which I shall have more to say in a moment. All these features are found in the Romanesque architecture of France and England, but they do not really lift the architecture off the ground. They have the gaucherie of some would-be aviator who, by fixing wings to his shoulders and looking up to heaven, hopes he may find himself flying. In Romanesque, it is always the grave, sombre

[1] H. Foçillon, *Art d'Occident*, 1938.

rhythm which appeals to us; the aedicular scaffolding grafted on to it is rarely moving and often tiresome and bizarre.[1]

Romanesque is puzzling, ambiguous, incomplete. The point of all its business eludes one. Then, suddenly, the creation of Gothic explains everything. Some extraordinary men—some among Abbot Suger's masons at Saint Denis, some elsewhere— saw precisely how to arrive at a true synthesis of the warring elements in Romanesque. They were followed by others and within a hundred years the whole of the first and decisive chapter of Gothic had been written.

The nature of Gothic architecture has been expressed in many formulas, but almost all, since Viollet-le-Duc, are based on technical rather than aesthetic premises. These premises may be perfectly correct, but to give them primacy in an exposition of Gothic architecture is to perpetuate the 19th-century fallacy that architecture is a matter of structure *plus* adornment. Viollet-le-Duc, by analysing French Gothic in terms of equilibrium, made it seem that this was so; but you have only to examine Viollet's own personal background[2] to see why it was necessary for him, in his time, to see Gothic in this way. His method was to break down the Gothic problem from outside, to expose it in the terms which his age and his temperament dictated. His method has dominated the exposition of Gothic ever since; but I venture to suggest that for us, in our time, the rationalistic, non-psychological method is inadequate. And (in view of the fact that Gothic is taught in the schools) positively harmful and misleading because it prompts modern analogies of the most absurd kind. And, further, I suggest that the point where the

---

[1] As, for instance, in the maddening repetitions of Norman arcading in some English Cathdrals, e.g. Peterborough and Ely.

[2] P. Gout, *Viollet-le-Duc; sa vie son oeuvre sa doctrine* in *Revue de l'Art Chrétien*, Supp. III, 1914. See also Essay No VI in this book.

Gothic reality is most easily grasped is precisely in this concept of aedicular architecture, this recaptured inheritance of what let us boldly call 'Pompeian' art.[1]

The creation of something new in the arts invariably means the turning upside-down of some uneasy equilibrium, the making of an adjunct into an essential, a parasitic growth into a main stem. So it was in the passage from Romanesque to Gothic. In Romanesque, the aedicular episodes are ornamental: *merely* ornamental—parasitic. But the creators of Gothic seized upon this incidental 'Pompeian' idea and made it capital. In doing so they created, and at the same time solved, certain structural problems as well as other undefined problems of space and proportion. If we study Gothic in this light—as the evolution of an idea—we shall find that both the technical and the aesthetic aspects fall into place and become readily understandable from our 20th-century standpoint.

As everyone knows, one of the most striking innovations in Gothic is the universal adoption of the pointed arch in place of the round arch. The reasons for its adoption have often been summarized in terms of statical expediency, but there is plenty of evidence to show that it was a matter of deliberate choice— a matter of taste. The pointed arch, with the cusp and one or two other things,[2] were stolen from Arab art across the Pyrenees. It was used here and there, in a casual way, in Romanesque work, for the novelty of the thing, and then seized upon as an essential by the creators of Gothic. It was seized upon as essen-

[1] William Burges was probably the first to draw a parallel between Pompeian painting and Gothic architecture. He used to say that Early French Gothic had more in common with Greek and Pompeian than with the later phases of medieval architecture.

[2] Emile Mâle, *Les Influences Arabes dans l'Art Roman* in *Revue des Deux Mondes*, Nov. 15, 1923.

tial, *not* because it was materially essential, but because the pointed arch struck that note of fantasy which was what the mind of the age desired. It wilfully destroyed the discipline of the round arch, which had become an incubus and a bore and stood in the way of the realization of the free 'Pompeian' church of the future.

The pointed arch was, of course, structurally convenient; but this matter of convenience has been over-stressed. I repeat that Gothic *created and simultaneously solved* its problems. The notion of the Gothic system solving the Romanesque problem is, from the point of view of structure, unreal. We are told that the pointed arch rendered possible the high, brittle structures of the 13th century. But this is not strictly true; structures just as high and just as brittle could have been constructed on a round-arched system. Certainly, the pointed vault exerts a smaller outward thrust against the walls; but in such a very slight degree that one cannot conscientiously see any compulsion in this circumstance. It is convenient, as the builders of Durham early discovered, to use pointed transverse arches in a vault, thereby facilitating the use of semicircular diagonals while retaining a level ridge. But here again it is no more than convenience; and it cannot be seriously maintained that in these great ceremonial buildings the ancient, superb discipline of the round arch was disrupted merely for the sake of a limited degree of technical convenience.

No. The pointed-arch system was, I believe, adopted for this reason: it had an air of fantasy—perhaps, dare one guess, of Oriental fantasy[1]—which went along with the realization of the 'Pompeian' idea. It is impossible, of course, to reconstruct

---

[1] Mâle, in the article already quoted, speaks of 'cet éternel Orient qui a fasciné le moyen-age' in relation to some features in churches associated with the pilgrim routes to Compostella.

the associations which focus round a given form at a given time; but for some reason the pointed arch became attractive in itself at the same time that the aedicular idea had been fully deployed as the subjunctive architecture of the Romanesque. So the whole architectural situation was turned upside-down. Instead of the aedicule serving to adorn the structure, the structure was made the slave of the aedicule. And as a supreme gesture of enslavement, the round arch was broken.

An examination of the great cathedrals of the 12th–13th centuries shows how the aedicule took charge of the new situation. This theme of pure fantasy, once released from bondage, was free to range through all gradations of stature[1] from the heroic to the minuscule. In the naves of the great cathedrals, for instance, we find it performing with easy success the function which the Romanesque had already visualized and painfully attempted in the churches of Caen. At Lâon and Nôtre Dame (Plate v), an aedicular cathedral, composed of shafts and ribs, springs from the capitals of the sturdy nave columns, which form, as it were, a link with the past, the old prose basis from which the Gothic fantasy takes wing. When we come to Amiens we find that the shafts spring from the floor; the sense of a Romanesque basis has vanished and the whole conception, from floor to vault, is aedicular. Aedicular in this sense: that the miniature sky-architecture of the Pompeian paintings has been *realized*—re-enlarged, as it were, to the scale from which the painters may be supposed to have reduced it.

In this aedicular architecture of the grand order, it is to be observed that the ribbed vault plays a most conspicuous and

[1] I deliberately use 'stature' and not 'scale', because one of the fundamentals of Gothic is the preservation of a single scale throughout the structure, in contrast to the classical method by which a combination of two orders represents a combination of two scales.

dramatic part. It is the rib, rather than the vault as a whole, that captures the eye, the rib which flies away from the shaft above its diminutive capital and joins its fellows in a boss at the very summit of the building. Now, this rib is often supposed to be an essential part of the structural scheme of Gothic architecture. It is supposed, in some mysterious way, to canalize the forces latent in the vault and carry them safely down into the buttressed pier. But this is a *post facto* rationalization. The commonsense truth is that the safety of the vault does not depend on the rib, but on the coherence of the vault as a whole, just as it does in any groined vault of the 17th century. The researches of Victor Sabouret[1] and Pol Abraham[2] have established this beyond dispute. If a vaulting rib is smashed by a projectile, the adjacent part of the vault does not necessarily collapse; and if the abutments of a vault are weak it is not necessarily the ribs which start to crack. The rib is simply an ornamental reinforcement of the angles of the vault; the fact that it projects from the vault is of no structural importance whatever. It could just as well be bonded into the severies, retaining a flush face right up to the arris. No; the vaulting rib, like almost everything else in Gothic architecture, originates in an aesthetic intention. The ribbed vault, in fact, may be compared with the airy pergolas which make their frequent appearance in the fantasy-architecture of Pompeii.

From the master-order constituted by the nave shafts and vaulting-ribs, the aedicular scheme descends in a gradation of inferior orders. Thus, a secondary order is provided by the

[1] *Les Voutes nervurées, rôle simplement décoratif des nervures*, in *Le Génie Civil*, March 3, 1928.

[2] *Nouvelle Explication de l'Architecture Religieuse Gothique* in *Gazette des Beaux-Arts*, 1934, p 257. Abraham has devoted a whole volume to the criticism of Viollet-le-Duc's theory: *Viollet-le-Duc et le Rationalisme Mediéval*, 1934.

shafts of the nave arcade, which control the stature of the entire chevet and its chapels, each one of which becomes a paraphrase of the apse itself. The triforium has its own order, so has the clerestory ; the towers rise in stages, order above order. Each portal has its own complex of orders, ranging from the grand aedicules which provide the gables for the arches, to the lesser terraced aedicules which canopy the prophets and martyrs ranged along the jambs. The whole cathedral resolves itself into these aedicular orders, sometimes pertaining to and articulating the structure itself, sometimes confusing and even contradicting the structure. And from first to last, all effort strains at one objective—the destruction of mass, the creation not so much of upward flight, as of suspension in space, the creation of an architecture wholly independent of the exigencies of gravity.

Having proposed the aedicule as the psychological key to Gothic, it remains to test the proposition in relation to some of those characteristics which are no less essential to a complete view of the Gothic phenomenon. Of structure, I have already said something, but perhaps I should recapitulate. I believe that it was the 'Pompeian' idea which *sanctioned* the Gothic system. It sanctioned the rupture of the round arch and arrogated the resulting flexibility of plan to its own purposes. Nowhere is the 'Pompeian' character of Gothic more expressive and lovely than in those instances of apparently improvised vaulting necessitated by the junction of old work with new or by adaptation to an awkward site. Here the scissor-like flexibility of the pointed arch performs all sorts of antics—antics which would be perfectly ridiculous if we did not take them in the spirit in which they are meant—the spirit of a 'Pompeian' perspective.

Precisely the same aesthetic sanction converted the flying-buttress from a pathetic makeshift, an admission of defeat, to a romantic and beautiful component of the system, a fairy via-

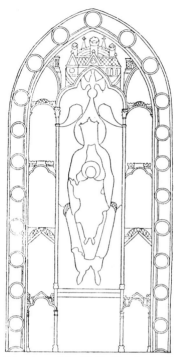

FIG. I. Diagram of the 'Belle Verrière', Chartres

duct having a ridiculous affinity with the conceits in some of the stucco panels in the Naples Museum.

Again, Gothic mouldings develop under the sanction of the aedicule. They represent a device by which the onset of gravity, of inert mass, is dissipated at those places—chiefly openings—where it would normally be most felt. The wall surrounding an opening is disintegrated into a cluster of thin members whose articulation is stressed by the deep undercutting between them; each of these members represents or betokens an aedicular unit which, in early work, is fully expressed in terms of base, shaft, capital and archivolt. The mouldings of capitals are profiled so as to defeat the impression that they are carrying weight; the

17

upper moulding, salient and deeply undercut, gives a shadow suggesting suspension rather than support. Unrelated to the aedicular idea, Gothic mouldings can become meaningless; they do so where the idea is obscured by an excess of vanity on the part of the mason—as, for example, in the Angel Choir at Lincoln—where the mouldings nearly defeat their own end.

The evolution of tracery is, I suspect, closely related to the use of aedicular designs in early stained glass. For instance, in the Belle Verrière of Chartres (Fig. 1), dating from the middle of the 12th century, the aedicule within which the Virgin is seated and the lateral aedicules, containing censing angels, unite to form a structure wonderfully prophetic of the tracery of the next century. And so one could go on. The aedicule unlocks door after door.

The aedicular system stands complete, perfectly realized, in the first quarter of the 13th century. From the middle of the century onwards it is underlined, stressed and even exaggerated, notably by the liberal use of ornamental gables, sometimes in a rather mechanical, inharmonious way, as who should say, 'don't forget that this arch is not just an arch but also a shrine'. This kind of mannerism reaches its peak in a church like Saint-Urbain at Troyes (Plate VI)—perhaps one of the most technically perfect of all French churches—where all the windows are gabled, the apex of each gable thrusting through the pierced parapet of the church.

It is during the first half of the 13th century that one of the major implications of the aedicular system is gradually unfolded. The aedicule is, in essence, a shrine. The Gothic cathedral is, therefore, a multiplication of shrines. As we have seen, these shrines—aedicules—are disposed in a series of orders, descending from the master-order which controls the bay-unit and the vault. The stature of the orders is diminished in the

PEGARD.

FIG. 2. Soissons Cathedral, south transept. From Viollet-le-Duc's
Dictionnaire Raisonnée

aisles, again in the clerestory and triforium and once again on the purely ornamental plane. It is here that it joins hands with the sculptor; these last aedicules are inhabited not by the human users of the cathedral but by supernatural beings carved in stone. Here, in fact, the aedicule returns to its proper stature and proper function—here it is once more the 'little house'. Indeed, it is perhaps more logical to regard the whole cathedral as an *ascent* from this, the normal aedicular scale—than to regard the ornamental aedicule as a reduction from its grand relations who have grown big and been married to the structural carcase of the building.

Anyway, it is on the ornamental plane that the aedicule is employed for the identical purpose for which it is used in manuscripts, ivories, enamels and reliefs, namely to provide a framework, a *mise en scéne*, for iconographical exposition. Already in Romanesque buildings, this idea had been exploited, especially in west fronts (e.g. Angoulême) and portals. But in Romanesque work the sculpture is stylized and the aedicule is a dead form—or rather a chrysalis-form whose potentialities are hidden. The Gothic artists brought to life not only the sculpture but likewise the aedicule itself. Hence, the porches of Chartres, one of which we have already examined; hence also the great portals of Amiens, Bourges, Rheims and Lâon.

The porches of Chartres are wholly exceptional in their perfect fusion of classical and Gothic form. The great portals of the other cathedrals are differently conceived. As they are not self-standing but grow from the main structure of the cathedral, they have to struggle for their aedicular independence. Thus, at Amiens (Plate VIII) the conflict between the descent of the massive western buttresses and the upthrust of the aedicular architecture of the porches is grotesquely painful unless one acquiesces in the artists' pressing invitation to forget all about gravity and mass and accept the aedicular scheme and that alone—a scheme without gravity, suspended in the air. To help you to this illusion they have done everything in their power. They have made the aedicular frontispiece fantastically top-heavy, with huge pinnacle-formations at the summit and no base-mould whatever except a trivial offset near the ground, as if to declare with maximum emphasis that such architecture as this does not rest on the ground: does not need foundations (the Rheims artist, who carved hanging tapestries round the base of the portal pressed this point even further!). To defeat the potential onset of gravity in the buttresses they have sunk roses and quatrefoils in them, as though casually to suggest that the masonry surface is a mere veil. And to emphasize once again the *suspended* character of the composition they have contrived deliberate discords where the gable-eaves meet the buttresses, suggesting that the gables, which might seem too substantial if they seemed to rest on the frail structure beneath, are themselves suspended from the clouds and have just been drawn into place by the flying monsters straining from their lower angles. Has any Baroque or Rococo architecture ever set out to contradict the structural elements of a façade with such determined insolence?

It is in these great porches and portals, as I have said, that the aedicular scheme is harnessed to the purpose of the iconographers and sculptors. Just as the architecture of the Pompeian murals provides the setting for scenes and personages drawn from classical myth and drama, so these portals provide the setting for those iconographic arrangements which, as Emile Mâle showed, in his great books, are no arbitrary or sentimental groups but schematic expositions drawn from the theological and encyclopaedic literature of the Middle Ages.

Let it be understood that in this interpretation I claim no

discovery concerning Gothic. The identification of the aedicule as the leading theme is suggested here only for its convenience in the understanding and exposition of Gothic architecture. Its convenience is considerable, for it seems to illuminate not only the Gothic fabric itself but Gothic architecture in relation to other architectures and, likewise, Gothic architecture in relation to other aspects of medieval life and thought. It now remains to elucidate some of these relationships.

First, let us re-examine the relationships of Gothic to classic architecture. At the beginning of this essay we glanced at the part played by the aedicule in antiquity—its function first as a shrine, then as a portal, and its development in the 'aedicular' architecture of Pompeian wall-paintings. We then rediscovered the aedicular principle in 12th-century France, finding a strikingly close parallel between certain later Pompeian murals and the porches of Chartres. Admitting this parallel to be wholly fortuitous, there is still an identity of spirit between the two manifestations which is sufficiently remarkable. One is prompted to ask if there was not some kind of 'renaissance' in the 12th century which made it possible for the vestigial memories of Roman decoration to coalesce once again into a nearly classical form of expression. The answer to such a question is unambiguous. There was such a renaissance, and in other spheres of 12th-century life its reality is easily recognized and has long been admitted by historians. C. H. Haskins, in 1927, made the renaissance of the 12th century the subject of an important book,[1] covering literature, jurisprudence and science, but not extending to the visual arts. He succeeded, however, in showing that the general advance in intellectual achievement characteristic of the 12th century was pretty clearly in the nature of a renaissance

[1] C. H. Haskins, *The Renaissance of the Twelfth Century*, 1927 (new ed. 1939).

—a second and stronger wave of classical resurgence than the first wave which belongs to the age of Charlemagne.

In literature the term 'renaissance' is easily justified by an enormously vigorous cultivation of the classics in the Cathedral Schools and the outpouring of new classical poetry, both religious and secular, often adhering closely to classical models. Hildebert of Le Mans, for instance, perhaps the greatest of medieval latinists, who worked at the end of the 11th and beginning of the 12th century, was the author of a famous elegy on Rome[1] which reminds us that, as Haskins says, Rome was to the men of the Middle Ages 'the great fact in their immediate past'.[2] The Middle Ages were, indeed, haunted by Rome and the classical world; in a sense, the *quattrocento*, with its real, objective renaissance, laid the ghost by finding it flesh and blood after all. The Middle Ages possessed a traditional recollection of Rome but did not know Rome; the only threads which they held firmly in their hands were literary threads—textual threads. The architecture and sculpture of Rome were, except in Italy itself, hidden from them. But, even so, the tradition of Roman splendour in the visual arts was an element in the medieval mind which cannot be ignored.

So it is reasonable to see the architecture of the 12th century as to some extent a kind of renaissance; or, more accurately, perhaps, as a filling-in of the architectural category to balance other categories in which the connection with the ancient world was more definite and actual—the categories of language, poetry, jurisprudence and the sciences. It is, after all, not the presence of monuments or texts which creates a renaissance; it is the psychological atmosphere of an age, and its 'will to form',

[1] Beginning *Par tibi, Roma, nihil, cum sis prope tota ruina.* Quoted in full by H. O. Taylor, *The Medieval Mind*, 1911, Vol 2, p 191.

[2] Haskins, op. cit., p 117.

which makes it possible for these things to play their part. The mental orientation of the 12th century tended towards the classical; hence the renewed study of the classics and the writing of classical poetry, and hence, too, the creation of an architecture in which affinities with antiquity are recognizable.

It would be difficult, I believe, to find in the Latin literature of the 12th century any specific expressions of admiration for the architecture or sculpture of ancient Rome. On the other hand, there are evidences, here and there, of a general admiration—a secular, non-aesthetic admiration—for its nobility and wealth of materials. Suger, the rebuilder of St Denis, considered obtaining columns for his Abbey church from the Baths of Diocletian and was only deterred by the dangers and difficulties of transport.[1] And Suger was always ready to acquire Roman antiquities for his treasury—witness the antique porphyry vase, now in the Louvre, which he 'converted' into an eagle by the addition of bronze head, wings and talons. Suger's aesthetic appreciation of such things was, perhaps, limited; on the other hand the classical world meant much to him—he could recite long passages from Horace by heart.[2] To him, as to so many of his contemporaries, Rome constituted an enormous factor in the historic past—a factor from which it was impossible (unless one was a St Bernard) to withhold a certain reverent admiration.

To think of the 12th century as having witnessed a ' renaissance' is greatly to modify the customary view of Gothic and classic art as 'opposites'; and in fact this habitual antithesis is in many ways highly unsatisfactory. It is a too obvious conclusion drawn from *prima facie* impressions. The silhouettes of art-history which automatically take shape in the individual mind

[1] E. Panofsky, *Abbot Suger*, 1946, p 91.
[2] Panofsky, op. cit., p 13.

can never be veritable 'traces' of the disposition of events; they are merely local and subjective simplifications. And it is probably nearer the truth to think of the whole flow of European art as a classic stream, distorted for a period from its course, than to think of an opponent 'will to form', breaking in during a Gothic interval and disappearing again with the exhumation of antiquity during the *quattrocento*. The Gothic interlude is, indeed, apparently separate and self-contained; but it is really the same European classic stream flowing under changed conditions, undergoing an extravagant metamorphosis whose effects lasted for some four hundred years.

A thesis precisely the opposite of this is the one so brilliantly expounded by Wilhelm Worringer[1] who sought to define Gothic as the great flowering of that northern 'will to form' which is already latent in the primitive interlaced ornament of the barbarian races, and which is in its very nature opposed to classicism. Instead of seeing the Gothic cathedral as a prodigious but temporary distortion from the norm of classicism, he sees certain forms of later classicism (especially the Baroque) as 'Gothic in disguise'—an assumption of classical forms by peoples in whom the inorganic, abstract 'will to form' was deeply ingrained. This point of view is so precisely antithetical to the one I have been adducing that there is no difficulty whatever in harmonizing the two, for we have here, quite simply, exterior and interior impressions of the same phenomenon. If the 12th century witnessed a 'renaissance', the movement was shaped by the immensely powerful psychology, into which it penetrated, a psychology which you may call, if you will, the psychology of northern man as opposed to that of his Mediterranean counterpart.

To marry these two points of view is, I think, to balance up

[1] W. Worringer, *Form in Gothic*, trans. H. Read, 1927.

the Gothic phenomenon very fairly. Worringer is impressed by the 'chaos' of Gothic—'a deliberate chaos of energy developed in stone'; and he observes that 'this super-logical, transcendental effect' arises from a 'logical work of multiplication', and it is this nervous passion for multiplication which stamps the Gothic cathedral with that same fervid, restless character which he finds in early Germanic bronzes and the interminable inter-lacings of many 8th-century manuscripts. This multiplication in Gothic architecture is, as I have tried to show, essentially the multiplication of the aedicule motif. Now Worringer, very naturally, arrives at the aedicule right at the end of his exposi-tion; having started with a broad hypothesis concerning the northern will to form, the detailed character of the Gothic system only comes under observation in the final analysis of architectural method:

> Gothic man seeks to lose himself not only in the infinity of the great, but also in the infinity of the small. The infinity of movement which is macrocosmically expressed in the archi-tectural structure as a whole expresses itself microcosmically in every smallest detail of the building. Every individual detail is, in itself, a world of bewildering activity and infinity, a world which repeats in miniature, but with the same means, the expression of the whole .... The crown of a pinnacle is a cathedral in miniature, and anyone who has sunk himself in the ingenious chaos of a tracery can here experience on a small scale the same thrill in logical formalism as he ex-periences in the building system as a whole.[1]

Thus Worringer, approaching our subject from a very dif-ferent starting point, states his appreciation of the aedicular

[1] Worringer, op. cit., pp 165–6. Quoted by permission of G. P. Putnam's Sons, Ltd.

system as an *effect*, whereas we have been studying it as a *cause*. Our approach has been that of the architect; Worringer's is that of the art-historian. Our approach has, I think, illuminated one side of the problem which Worringer does not touch; for in the notion of the aedicule as something belonging intimately to the classical world, but which was revivified in the creation of Gothic, we find an expression in terms of architecture of that paradoxical renaissance of the 12th century which in other aspects of medieval life can be fully substantiated. Thus, Gothic architecture, however striking may be its individuality and however great may be the temptation to *oppose* it to classicism as the embodiment of a different principle, is truly a continuation and development of the classical line, a metamorphosis of classicism, temporary and unstable, seeking its way back to permanence and stability as soon as the great creative crisis of the 12th–13th centuries had spent itself.

Our theme could be pursued into several other spheres, notably into scholasticism and into the political philosophies[1] of the Middle Ages. Moreover, the declension of Gothic through the 13th, 14th and 15th centuries could be interpreted exactly in the terms which we have employed. From the great west façade of Strasbourg to the simplest East Anglian screen, with thin buttresses to each mullion, the aedicule persists as the basic unit of design. Already by the middle of the 13th century, however, the vivid articulation becomes blurred. The shafts fall into decorative groups, attach themselves to columns and end at last as merely the salient members in rhythmic sequences of mouldings. Tracery dissolves into the

[1] Mr Howard Colvin has drawn my attention to a striking passage in O. Gierke, *Political Theories of the Middle Ages*, trans. F. W. Maitland, 1900, pp 7 and 8, where an analysis of medieval social philosophy can be paraphrased sentence by sentence as an analysis of Gothic architecture in terms of the aedicular theory.

flowing harmony of the curvilinear. Silhouettes of towers no longer strain upward with defiant, inelegant force; the stages are nicely modulated in anticipation of the height to be attained. Gradually, Gothic is emptied of the sense of effort and daring—and chaos; it becomes relaxed, sensuous and conventional. This is not a decline in any pejorative sense, but a declension: a slow wending back, stage by stage, to the classic norm. During this process the aedicule becomes the oft-repeated unit in a purely decorative system, its last and humblest role being that of the cusped panel which covers so many thousands of square yards of 'Perpendicular' walling.

But to develop all this is beyond the scope of this essay. I have been concerned to demonstrate two things only. First, that the idea of the aedicule or 'little house' is an idea of fundamental importance in the aesthetics of architecture. Second, that this idea, applied to the study of Gothic architecture, tells us much about that architecture and something about its relationship to the other architectures of the world.

II

Antitheses of the Quattrocento

THE OLDER text-books describe the renaissance as a 'rebirth of classical culture'; but this phrase, too partial in its application, has tended, since Burckhardt's time, to be superseded by a description insisting more on the synthesis of a new view of life in which the revival of classical art, literature and learning is only an incidental part. And yet, in architecture certainly, if one searches for the magic spring, the touchstone of Renaissance creativeness, one finds it in this world *revival*.

Children's stories traditionally begin 'once upon a time'. Those four words cast a spell; they divide the period of known and experienced time from a period indefinitely remote when things happened very differently and not always in what we choose to regard as a natural manner. Fables of the marvellous and the impossible have a setting detached from ordinary time. And there is one fable, the simplest of fables, which the human race seems always to have cherished—the fable of the Golden Age. It is the belief that there was a time when man led an idle, amiable, carefree existence, without passion, without curiosity. For us, the familiar versions are the classical reign of Saturn and the Biblical Garden of Eden. But the notion of a Golden Age is almost universal and is, moreover, easily transposed from the fabulous to the not-quite-fabulous and thence, sometimes, to the real. The idea that man has lost something which he may at some future time hope to regain; the idea that somewhere a treasure is buried which he may hope to recover; these ideas have no necessary relationship to historical situations but are part of the mythology of mankind and have formed themselves in a way which we must leave the anthropologists to determine and the psychologists to explain. But they do, in a curious way, become woven into our notions of history.

The importance of this recurrent idea in the development of civilization is this. Man can form no picture of the future except by reference to the past. And just as an unconscious dread of the world of space lures him back towards the security of the womb, so his fear of events in time drives him back to the same archaic existence when life was without care and without ugliness. But again, just as the idea of spacial regression recoils and asserts itself positively in forms of play and forms of art, so the idea of regression in time recoils and crystallizes in the conception of an earthly or heavenly state of bliss. The strength and importance of this myth throughout human history cannot be exaggerated. Of its importance in quite recent times very much could be said; its importance in the development of the Renaissance, especially in its architecture, it is now my intention to consider.

The Renaissance was the occasion on which the myth of the Golden Age was overtaken by objective thought. I do not mean this literally, although it may be nearly literally true. The specific legend of the 'former age' interpreted by classical writers, was passed down through the Middle Ages notably through the medium of Boethius' *Consolatio Philosophiae* where it is embodied in a short poem; and the medieval fondness for the legend eventually lost itself in the wider knowledge of the classics which dawned throughout Europe in the 15th and 16th centuries. Thus the old legend in its classic dress does actually span the distance between the classical world and that of the Renaissance. But I am using this phrase 'the Golden Age' in a broader sense—meaning the unspecifiable epoch to which the imagination travels for consolation and refreshment. In the

Middle Ages, such romantic retrospection probably confined itself within the outlines of scriptural history, except in so far as the classical version of the story was available. An Italian poet[1] of the 14th century did not hesitate to equate the classical Golden Age with the Garden of Eden in a Dantesque allegory of human life. But it was about the year 1300 that the ruins of Rome began to exercise, in Italy, a deeper fascination than any purely literary tradition could do. For nearly a thousand years those ruins had excited only dim emotions and been objects sometimes of aversion and fear, sometimes of an obscure veneration. But then came a phase of melancholy liking and it was gradually discovered that by the exercise of intellectual effort it was possible to link them with real men and events and definite periods of time. They became part of the historical picture which the Renaissance painted for itself in the liveliest colours and which it believed to be a more or less faithful representation of Ancient Rome. Obviously it was not. The Ancient Rome cherished by the Italians of the 15th century was a fiction—a myth deftly fused with ascertained fact and with the measurement of distance in time and space. But with this imaginary picture the whole fabric of Renaissance life and art is closely interwoven, so closely that it is impossible to assign priority to either of those two motives which combined to make it actual—either, that is, the regressive motive, the search for beauty and consolation in a dream of a Golden Age, or the assertive motive, the making of the dream into a concrete image, knit into the experience of the 15th century.

The Renaissance has been described[2] as 'man's discovery of himself and of the world', but these discoveries were dependent on a third, the discovery of a Golden Age which (it was pos-

[1] Federigo Frezzi. See J. A. Symonds, *Renaissance in Italy*, 1898 ed., p 146.
[2] By Michelet.

sible to believe) *had really existed* in the shape of Imperial Rome. In a sense, the Italian's discovery of Rome was the discovery of himself for, to a great extent, he recreated Rome in his own image. But it was his confidence in the real existence of Rome which enabled him to have confidence in his own creativeness. On that sense of historic reality he leaned while he wove the fiction which we, looking back, recognize as part of the reality of his own age.

In the architecture of the Italian Renaissance we can read all this very clearly, for architecture, of all the arts, had the most direct and literal relation to the ruins of Rome. And those ruins were by far the most moving part of the Roman legacy. Just why ruins can be so moving is a subject which I shall discuss in another essay,[1] but quite apart from their character as ruins they had the virtue of undoubted authenticity. There could be no question of corrupt texts or faulty transcriptions. There they stood, on the exact spots where antiquity had raised them, the shadows striking just as they did under the rule of Augustus or Vespasian. In the atmosphere of the 15th century these ruins were, I imagine, even more evocative and full of hidden life than, say, Fountains Abbey is to us, and one reads without surprise of the humanist, Pomponius Laetus, who was so moved by them that he would stand before them as if entranced, or would suddenly burst into tears at the sight of them'.[2]

The effect of the ruins on the earliest Renaissance architects we can only guess. Filippo Brunelleschi, the first architect to measure the ruins of Rome and to make practical use of his results, has left us no personal account of his famous journey or of his feelings about what he found there. Vasari, however, tells

[1] Essay No X.

[2] J. Burckhardt, *The Civilization of the Renaissance* (Phaidon edition) pp 168–9.

us how he became 'capable of entirely reconstructing the city in his imagination, and of beholding Rome as she had been before she was ruined'. After Brunelleschi we meet the theorists, the writers about architecture, and here we are admitted more freely to the mind of the Renaissance. Here, we can see it at work and learn much. It is of some of the earliest of the Italian writers on architecture that I want now to speak and of two famous works in particular. First, Alberti's *De Re Aedificatoria Libri Decem*, written before 1450. Second, Francesco Colonna's *Hypnerotomachia Polyphili*, written in 1467 and printed in 1499.[1]

These two books are absolutely different in character and show us two entirely different aspects of the Renaissance attitude to ancient architecture. Alberti's approach is, from beginning to end, objective. Colonna's is no less emphatically subjective. And yet, if we study Alberti we find the subjective aspect of the Renaissance piercing the intellectual armour-plate at certain points. Whereas in Colonna we find his dreamy romance punctuated by intellectual excursions of the most objective kind. Alberti was, of course, by far the greater of the two men. Colonna, apart from his book, is nothing but a name.

Leon Battista Alberti was born in 1404, the illegitimate but favoured son of a family of rich Florentine merchants. His intellectual and athletic aptitudes were both extraordinary and were developed with lavish care. He was educated in the law, travelled for a few years in France, Belgium, and Germany and returned to Italy at the age of twenty-eight. A severe illness

[1] Both these works are admirably described by Anthony Blunt in his *Artistic Theory in Italy*, 1450–1600. For Alberti, see R. Wittkower, *Alberti's Approach to Antiquity in Architecture*, in *Journal of the Warburg and Courtauld Institutes*, Vol iv, 1940–41.

seems to have interrupted a career which might have led to a bishopric, and he turned his attention from the law to the arts and sciences. As a writer he was enormously prolific. His works include the *Trattato della Famiglia*, dealing with the domestic virtues in general and the history and destiny of the Alberti family in particular; several dialogues; plays; essays on the arts; poems; and a series of *novelle* in which he declares himself a well-informed though not necessarily experienced misogynist. He was a painter and a musician, though none of his studies in these arts have survived. But posterity remembers him chiefly as an architect and as a writer on architecture and it is with these capacities only that we are now concerned. Alberti, like so many great Tuscans, spent a great part of his life in exile. When at last he saw Florence, Filippo Brunelleschi had built the great Cathedral dome, the Innocenti and the Pazzi Chapel. It was to Brunelleschi that he dedicated his treatise on painting—in effect, an exposition of the laws of perspective. At forty-two he began his own first important building, the transformation of the old church of S Francesco at Rimini, for Sigismondo Malatesta. Leaving this unfinished after four years he produced his greatest written work, the *De Re Aedificatoria Libri Decem*.[1]

This work is the theoretical corner-stone of the architecture of the Renaissance and, as such, of immense value to anyone who hopes to understand that architecture and all its many subsequent ramifications throughout Europe from the 15th to the 19th centuries. One would not, I think, read it for pleasure; but as a document it is of the greatest interest.

The *De Re Aedificatoria* is obviously modelled on the work of

[1] The best general account in English of Alberti and his work is still that contained in J. A. Symonds' *Italian Renaissance* series, published in 1875–81. For Alberti's literary work see *Italian Literature*, Pt 1, pp 159–189; for his place as a humanist, *The Revival of Learning*, pp 247–249.

Vitruvius, whose ten-book treatise on architecture, written in the reign of Augustus, is the only work on the subject which has survived from classical times. It is modelled on Vitruvius, but in a proud, arrogant way. Alberti is always the master and he does not hesitate to transpose Vitruvius' material to applications quite foreign to the meaning and intentions of the ancient author. Like Vitruvius, however, Alberti offers us a comprehensive survey embracing town-planning, design, construction and professional practice. His contents range from aesthetics to the composition of mortars and from questions of etiquette to questions of sewerage. The debt to Vitruvius is not avowed and, throughout, the author sustains a tone of personal authority. He sifts facts, explores traditional knowledge, ransacks ancient authors and dismisses what he considers superstition; although sometimes cautious where he is not sure, he doubly underlines whatever he believes to be practical, reasonable and right. Nowhere is there a trace of sentiment or romantic feeling —indeed the whole organization of the work is hard and abrupt, and the tenth book ends gracelessly with a chapter on repairs. One feels that Alberti is using his intellect in an arrogant but a defensive way and that he is trying not to raise, but to lay the ghosts of ancient Rome. Or, to put it another way, he is trying to present a case perfect on its own merits, resting at no points on *a priori* assumptions regarding the glory of the beauty of the Roman world.

How far does Alberti succeed in this aim? In the technical field—in the chapters on masonry, timber, the raising of weights, the sinking of wells—his objectivity carries all before it. But when he comes to aesthetics it is different. He must start somewhere. He is determined, however, not to hang upon the authority of Rome but to announce principles whose validity is self-evident. Here Vitruvius is no help for he was the servant of tradition; but Alberti seizes some of his dicta and uses them in his own way. After several incidental skirmishes with the subject of beauty he tackles it seriously in his ninth book, telling us that 'there are three things principally in which the whole of what we are looking into consists: the *Number* the *Finishing* and the *Collocation*'. He proceeds to explain these expressions. Of the first he says that 'some numbers are greater favourites with nature than others, and more celebrated among learned men'; and he quotes sanctions of one sort or another for every number from two to ten. These sanctions may seem to us rather odd.

Thus Five is 'worthily dedicated to the Gods of the Arts'; Nine is important as the period of gestation, counted in months; Ten is the most perfect according to Aristotle; and so on. By Finishing, his second heading, he means ratio and here he takes the unexpected course of developing an analogy with music. 'The same numbers which please our ears please our eyes'; so he sets forth a series of ratios based on the intervals of the Pythagorean scale. Finally, under Collocation, by which he seems to mean proportion, he declares that 'it is much easier to conceive when it is ill done than it is to lay down exact rules for the doing it'; it is 'chiefly to be referred to the natural judgment'.

Obviously (to us) this treatment of the subject is not entirely adequate. The numerical sanctions are so many tautologies. The analogy with music simply amounts to the transference of an established convention in one art to the purposes of another.[1]

---

[1] Pythagoras, in the middle of the 6th century BC, invented (or introduced from Egypt or Persia) the rationalized musical intervals familiar today. He discovered that a vibrating string, stopped at its centre, produced the 'octave'; that the same string stopped at two-thirds of its length produced the 'fifth', and at three-quarters, the 'fourth'. Taking the interval between fourth and fifth as a unit ('one tone') he found that exactly one-and-a-half

And the third term, which might be expected to embrace the whole subject of modular design, is confessed to be incapable of exposition. Further, Alberti himself hastens to explain that, over and above these three factors is the dominant factor of *Congruity*, 'which runs through every part and action of Man's life, and every production of Nature herself'. By this phrase he may possibly mean what we would describe as 'style'. The truth is that Alberti has accepted architecture as one of the intellectual problems of his time, posed, in the first place, by the ruins of Rome and in the second by the Brunelleschian revival; and he is bent on reducing it to theoretical terms, just as Vitruvius had done, but in the light of his own experience. He evidently persuaded himself that he had done so, for he tells us how often his own sketches failed to conform to the discipline (presumably the musical ratios) which he imposed, and how they had to be remorselessly revised.

Alberti did not make classical architecture his avowed starting-point; he writes always simply of *architecture*, as an abstract proposition. But the avowal is all the time imminent, and, sooner or later, Alberti has got to meet the challenge of the *orders*. The five orders—or, to narrow the hierarchy to its ruling triumvirate, the three orders: what are they? An 'order' of architecture consists of columns, together with the beam resting on them and the eaves of the roof above that—the repeating

tones were required to fill the intervals between 'first' and 'fourth', and 'fifth' and the 'octave'. Now the 'octave', 'fifth' and 'fourth' have been discovered intuitively at many different times and places, such discoveries representing, no doubt, an intuitive adumbration of the intellectual concepts expounded by Pythagoras. It cannot of course, be represented that there is greater sensuous pleasure in a 'fourth' or 'fifth' than in the same intervals augmented or diminished. And the same applies in architecture, to the rectangles representing these and other ratios (e.g. the 'golden cut'). The sole value of these ratios is that they are intellectually fruitful and suggest the rhythms of modular design.

unit of a temple portico or colonnade. But not just any column, beam and eaves: an order is a special form of this combination, with all sorts of idiosyncrasies of proportion and ornament for which it is impossible to assign any material reasons. But unless, say, a Doric order possesses these idiosyncrasies—unless it has a certain kind of base, a certain kind of capital and certain curious grooved tablets called triglyphs, in its frieze, it is simply not a Doric order. There is, to be sure, a little latitude allowed in respect of proportion and omissions, but very little. The same applies to Ionic and Corinthian. Each is an elaborate and (seemingly) quite arbitrary aggregate of architectural detail—just as arbitrary as those rules of Latin grammar which forbid one to ask why it is a certain and indisputable fact that *sine, tenus, pro* and *pre* 'take the ablative' and cannot nor ever will take anything else. The parallel with grammar is a good one. Grammar is a crystallization of usage. And so are the orders. The reason why there are three principal orders is, roughly speaking, that in different areas of the ancient world different usages prevailed in the art of temple building. Greece developed the Doric order; Asia Minor the Ionic; of the Corinthian order all we know about it is that it occurred occasionally in Greece in many different forms and was the last of the three to crystallize. Under the Roman Empire these local usages all found their way to the capital and became part of the grammar of Roman architecture. How strict and systematic this grammar became is shown by Vitruvius, who gives us the rules as he received them, unquestioningly.

Now, these orders—these dialects, forms of usage—are liable to cut mercilessly across any theoretical consideration of classical architecture as an affair of absolutes. Either they must be accepted as language is accepted by a poet, clothed with their own historic colours, or they must be utterly banished from any

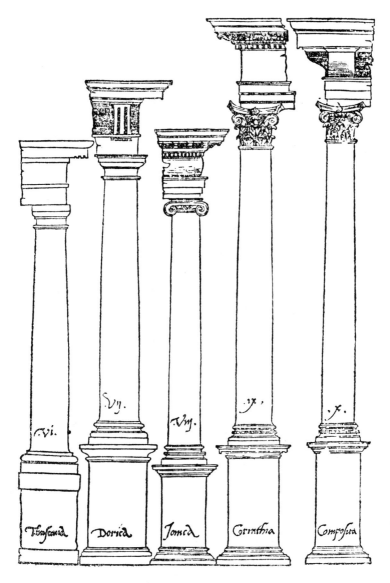

FIG. 3. The Five Orders, from Serlio

theory claiming to be fundamental. But Alberti in his philosophy, although he is straining all the time at fundamentals, does
neither the one nor the other. Or, rather, he accepts the orders
for the brief and insufficient reason that, *'from an imitation of
Nature'* the ancients 'invented three manners of adorning a
building and gave them names drawn from their first inven-
tors'. In other words, the orders are sanctioned by Nature,
upon the ultimate principle (in Alberti's scheme) of Congruity,
though the credit for their discovery must lie with the architects of the classical world.

Alberti never comes nearer than that to admitting himself a
'revivalist' and the sustained independence of his point of view
is perhaps the most astonishing characteristic of his book.
Loaded as he is with classical erudition, he employs it only as an
arsenal of old experience to be used critically and with reserve.
Even Vitruvius, so soon to be enthroned as an oracle, is used
merely as a source and by no means an infallible source at that.

If we turn from Alberti's writings to his executed works we
find very much the kind of architecture we should expect such
a man to produce. It is a very far cry from Brunelleschi's mar-
riage of a Roman revival to *trecento* problems; it is architecture
on which intellectual concepts are coldly and deliberately imposed. Take, for instance, the church of S Francesco at Rimini
(Plate x) where the west front is based on the theme of a Roman triumphal arch, a triplicate version of an arch existing in
Rimini itself. Alberti may or may not have been attracted to the
theme as a symbol of triumph over death (the sarcophagi of Sigismondo and Isotta were intended to be placed in the lateral arches)
but the interpretation has the character of a design *thought* rather
than *felt*. The variation in the width of the centre and side arches
gives rise to ambiguities in the relations of the attached columns,
to the piers against which they stand and also very conspicuously

in the placing of the spandrel ornaments, and although on closer inspection one discovers the spacing of the whole composition to have been precisely thought out, the discovery does not resolve the slight awkwardness at first apparent but, in fact, reinforces the impression of a preconceived idea painfully and assiduously elaborated.

Alberti's later works show as clearly the sinister force and persistence of the man's mind. The front of S Maria Novella was, according to Dr Wittkower[1], retrospective and archaeological in intention: an attempt to complete the building as its 14th-century beginners might have wished, but with modifications inspired by the proto-Renaissance of the 12th century as well as by antique examples. It is, in fact, a very curious compromise, baffling in its diffuseness. Yet, the Alberti discipline is there and Dr Wittkower has shown that the whole composition fits with extraordinary accuracy into a combination of squares and rectangles whose relations are of the simplest.

At S Sebastiano, Mantua (begun 1460) and S Andrea (begun 1472) in the same city, Roman formulas are directed with unflinching zeal to purposes which must, at the time, have seemed fantastically alien to their nature. Both the west front and the interior of S Andrea (Plate IX) derive from the triumphal arch motif, as seen in the example at Ancona. The design is cruelly ironed out in the course of being adapted to the west front of a broad church but rather more gently used in the bay design of the interior. In both, the mechanical nature of the transfer is unmistakable; though in the interior, as also most notably in the side elevation of the Rimini church, the Alberti doctrine does give us a spacing and rhythm which seems intuitively and not merely intellectually right.

Finally, there is the famous application of pilaster orders to

[1] *Journal of the Warburg, etc.*, loc. cit.

the façade of the Rucellai Palace in Florence—aesthetically
a pointless experiment, a piece of pure empiricism, an intellectual gambit; but, for all that, an experiment which succeeding
centuries accepted and humanized—and justified.

I am not disputing the enormous importance of these buildings as pioneer works in the progress of Renaissance architecture.
I am only concerned to show that this is intellectual pioneering
and not intuitive invention. Intellectual discovery can only
proceed by crude analogy—by transferring existing fixed concepts to situations susceptible of change; and unless a new
synthesis has been intuitively foreshadowed, the process may
result only in a sum of additions. Such a result may have its
value; it may stimulate others to creation. I believe something
of the sort was the case with the works of Alberti.

If we were to read Alberti and Alberti alone we should find
the greatest difficulty in understanding what was really happening at the birth of Renaissance architecture. The adoption of
Roman forms seems utterly heartless in a context so coldly
intellectual. There must, surely, be another side to the picture—
and, of course, there is. But we shall not find it in the Florentine
intellectual, the ecclesiastical lawyer with all the learning of the
age at his command. We shall find it, rather unexpectedly, in
the prose-poem of a young Venetian monk belonging to the
next generation—a man who built nothing and only described
the buildings which form the illustrations of this work.

Francesco Colonna, the author of the *Hypnerotomachia
Poliphili*, discloses his identity in an anagram provided by the
chapter-headings. The grotesque Greco-Latin title, signifying
'the dream-love-strife of Poliphilus.', foreshadows that esoteric
perversity which colours the work. The *Hypnerotomachia* is
medieval in form; it is the story of a dream in which a lover
searches for perfect union with his mistress. Falling asleep,

Poliphilus finds himself in a strange landscape where there are no living creatures and where, in spite of a mild and fragrant breeze, not a leaf stirs. Hence he passes into a dark forest, where panic seizes him and he runs aimlessly till he sinks into an exhausted sleep, dreaming himself into a remoter landscape where he finds every imaginable tree, some bearing wonderful fruit (Fig. 4). He is frightened by a wolf, but it turns away without molesting him. Then, in the distance, he sees, between two hills, a vast building—a great stepped pyramid rising from a massive base and surmounted by an obelisk. He walks towards it, but it seems to recede, so vast is its scale. Eventually, he comes closer and is able to examine the building in detail. He finds it is half-ruined and incredibly ancient; he marvels at the immense wealth and labour which must have been bestowed on it. So fine are the joints of the masonry that a needle could not pass into them. He is awed and a little frightened. He shudders at the silence, broken only by the sound of lizards moving across the face of the marble. But he retains sufficient presence of mind to give us a minute description of this strange monument; and he even finds and records the architect's name, engraved in Greek characters on the plinth.

Looking about him, Poliphilus finds all kinds of other buildings and sculptures, all ruined but all retaining an exquisite finish. So fresh and constant is the wind in this dreamland that not a cobweb is suffered to defile the fair face of the workmanship, which is so smooth, he says, that it might have been modelled in wax. There is a triumphal arch which Poliphilus carefully measures, deducing from it the secrets of proportion employed by its ancient builders. There is a statue of an elephant with an obelisk on its back. And everywhere are sculptures, inscriptions and hieroglyphs which Colonna transcribes and translates for us with pedantic care.

FIG. 4. Poliphilus and the Wolf. From the *Hypnerotomachia*

But his adventures have hardly begun. Strolling through the triumphal arch he encounters a terrible dragon (Fig. 5) and flies for his life, entering a dismal labyrinth. From this he at last emerges near a beautiful fountain which he carefully describes. He meets five nymphs who are the five senses. They console him and bring him to an octagonal building which is their bathing-place. With exquisite embarrassment he shares their immersion. He is introduced to the court of Queen Eleutheri-lides, whose palace furnishes more material for description. Eventually the scene changes and in a new landscape, even more charming and spring-like than the last, he is approached by a nymph whose loveliness requires several pages of minute description; delicate in person and dress, diaphanous, star-

FIG. 5. Poliphilus flies from the Dragon. From the *Hypnerotomachia*

spangled like Botticelli's Primavera. She turns out, of course, to be Polia herself and the rest of the work is devoted to the progress of the two lovers through a variety of ceremonies, some of a mildly erotic character, all rich in archaeology, a journey to Cytherea and their final union blessed by the Goddess of Love herself.

From one point of view, the remarkable thing about this remarkable book is the author's intense awe-struck nostalgia for the ancient world and its monuments. The picture he presents consistently evades the archaeologically authentic; it is based on considerable knowledge of ancient authors and monuments, but this knowledge merely serves to feed an imagination which breeds its own ruined masterpieces, its own

45

system of hieroglyphics, its own liturgies and its own curious blend of Greek and Latin diction. The spirit of the book is thoroughly medieval and the climate of Colonna's dreamland is very much, as Mr Blunt observes, that of the *Roman de la Rose*. But unlike any previous dreamland, Colonna's contains architecture which can be measured in every detail and which even discloses methods of design which, having been employed by the ancients, could be employed again by a generation, which, with humility and diligence, recognized the treasure lost and found. The *Hypnerotomachia* shows us, as it were, the reverse side of the Renaissance medal—the romantic, haunted, introverted side; the side which is so easily overlooked in the usual assessment of the Renaissance as essentially objective, scientific and extravert.[1]

The precise difference between Alberti and Colonna is this. Alberti takes hold of the notion of antiquity as it has taken shape in his mind and rationalizes it mercilessly, overhauling the entire structure—nearly (but not quite) down to its foundations. Colonna, on the other hand, approaches *his* classical world obliquely. For him, the picture is almost too delicate to touch. Psychologically, Colonna is easier to understand than Alberti. For all his twisted quasi-scholarship, he is simpler. There is no impassible gulf fixed between the *Hypnerotomachia* and William Morris's *News from Nowhere*. Alberti, on the other hand, is really difficult. His is a massive intellectual performance which at certain vital points fails to convince. For instance, where Colonna seizes the simple notion of the module and plays with it as a beautiful toy, Alberti constructs that elaborate but nearly meaningless theory of ratio which seems to have given

[1] In architecture that is. In painting, we constantly find ourselves in the atmosphere of the *Hypnerotomachia*. Giovanni Bellini's *Earthly Paradise* is an obvious example.

him, as a designer, even more trouble than it gives to his critical reader.

What can we learn from the co-existence of these two opposite points of view in 15th-century Italy? In the first instance, the fact that Alberti and Colonna were two wholly different types of person. That is obvious. Alberti was one of those tough, energetic thinkers in whom intuitive capacity is somewhat limited. Colonna on the other hand, was not a thinker; feeling and intuition dictate his attitudes all the time. Such a man would be incapable of putting on a performance like the *De Re Aedificatoria*; Alberti, equally, would find incomprehensible and childish, Colonna's record of subjective experience. The difference between the two types stands likewise, perhaps, for the difference between the mental climates of Florence and Venice. To Florence certainly belongs all that we think of as most robust and energetic in the early Renaissance; while from Venice comes a vision less clear, less decisive, and veiled, as the Florentine Renaissance was not, with a sense of the romantic distance in time, of the ancient world.

But the main point is this. The two books stand for two widely different aspects of the Renaissance, both of which are essential to an understanding, not only of the architecture of that age, but of the whole progress of classical architecture since—of Mannerism, Baroque and of the Greek and Roman revivals. Should we regard these two points of view as complementary—as having sprung together from the circumstances of the 15th century? Or should one or the other have precedence as the originating attitude? Let me return for a moment to my description of the Renaissance as 'the moment at which the myth of the Golden Age was overtaken by objective thought'. If the implications of the aphorism are correct I think there is no doubt which of the two books gives us farthest access into the mind of 15th-century Italy. It is Colon-na's. Alberti's is admittedly the more monumental, the more masterly, and in a dozen ways the more important. And it is the earlier (having regard to the birth-dates of the authors) by a whole generation. But, whereas Alberti's objectivity stands out from his period in the most striking and phenomenal way, in Colonna we see intellectual curiosity still in the womb of the Middle Ages. Reading Alberti, one has the impression that in his mind something is being assiduously repressed. What that something was, it seems to me, Colonna reveals. Quite simply, it is romance—the sense of myth. And it is that, I believe, which lies nearest the heart of the Renaissance conception of architecture.

Now our consideration of two aspects of the Renaissance mind is, as I have said, of importance for the appreciation of later classical building. The names both of Alberti and Colonna echo through architectural history—Alberti's by far the most resonant, but Colonna's surprisingly persistent.[1] But it is not so much the names but the points of view which they represent which are perennially important, and whenever we look at a classical building—whether we are in Florence, in Paris or in London—those two points of view will certainly haunt us.

From Alberti derives, I think, much that is forbidding and repellent to the layman in these matters. Many people believe themselves incompetent to look critically at architecture—especially classical architecture—because they feel that they are not 'in the know'; that there are deep secrets, 'rules of propor-tion', canons of design, inaccessible to the untrained mind. Much of that mystagogy belongs to the tradition of Alberti and the many treatise-writers who followed him. If you cannot

[1] Sir John Soane (1753–1837), for instance, possessed three copies of the *Hypnerotomachia*, one of which he annotated.

feel your way into classical architecture as you do into a fairy-story you must be content to amuse yourself, if you can, with the gymnastics of architectural grammar. If you are unwilling to accept the five orders as the gift of a myth, delightful and glorious *fundamentally* because they derive from an old, forgotten world, then you must argue yourself into believing that, somehow or other, they embody absolute values of proportion and ornament; and that argument is difficult in the extreme. Strangely enough, however, that is just the argument to which every respectable architect in the 16th, 17th, 18th, and most of the 19th centuries subscribed. Although in his works he might expose a very different attitude, the doctrine to which he subscribed was that the orders embodied basic and absolute aesthetic values—as basic and absolute in their way as the 39 articles. The creative architects in the classical tradition have always been those who, while accepting the rules, have had something of Colonna's feeling for their fairy-tale origin; the monsters of classical architecture have usually been those who have 'worked' the rules as an intellectual mechanism. Since the rules are the same in both cases it is impossible to distinguish the two types except after prolonged familiarity with their works in their particular historical context. But I believe that, for most of us, the approach to classical architecture in general is immensely facilitated if we take both these aspects into account and in the right sequence—if, that is to say, we accept the orders, with all their rules and trappings, as antique treasure-trove, as the buried legacy of a Golden Age, and from that point go on to consider and criticize the building as an intellectual creation. Although classicism is often equated with realism and objectivity, nearly all classical art since the Renaissance contains that romantic infection which it is fatal to ignore. And in England, a country with fewer Mediterranean contacts than most European nations, our classicism is often haunted by Roman ghosts. I will not develop that theme here, because John Wood's creation of Bath, the subject of another essay in this book, supplies the perfect illustration of it.

Neither Alberti nor Colonna are much read today and I do not know that I would advise any publisher to give them to the world in a popular edition. But there they stand, at the gateway of the Renaissance, the two opposite principles contained in that, as, I suppose, in all great historic movements. Alberti, the man of rules, insistent on the concrete, the absolute, the present. Colonna, the dreamer, never formulating, but only discovering and recording the Golden Past, refracted in his own imagination. The two types have moulded architectural history ever since, but have rarely stood out so clearly embodied as in the two celebrated books to which I have here alluded.

III

The Mind of Wren

I

A CANDID approach to the architecture of Wren is difficult because of the almost superstitious esteem in which his works are held. Everything with which his name is associated is held to be of such inestimable merit that to discover in them an element of inconsistency, of failure to achieve an integral artistic result, is to invite suspicion as a deliberate detractor of an unquestionably great figure. But in this essay my object is to bring some definition to that too vague 'greatness' which, in Wren's achievement, we all acknowledge.

The splendour of Wren's intellectual powers no one has questioned, or ever can; the range, subtlety and strength of his mind are as impressive to us as to his contemporaries. But we must remember that architecture, except in its purely technical aspects, requires from its exponents something besides strength and quality of intellect. In the act of designing an imaginative aspect is implicit, and it is this which makes architecture one of the arts and not merely one of the simpler branches of technics. Both intellect and imagination, intuitively co-ordinated, are necessary to design, and the quality of a design depends on the measure of completeness in this co-ordination. I am not going to suggest at this stage in what degree Wren failed to achieve this completeness. But I believe that he did fail, in a greater degree, perhaps, than we care to admit, and I believe that this failure can be traced back into the social growth from which his mind developed. The failure is, in fact, an historical phenomenon of much interest, and one which can be detected in many regions of English culture of the period. Most relevantly we can trace it in the philosophical writing of John Locke, Wren's exact contemporary, whose theory of knowledge exhibits, as I hope to show, just that unsatisfactory relationship between intellect and imagination which is betrayed in the works of the architect. Wren was, beyond doubt, better equipped intellect- ually than Locke (to whom both the arts and the higher mathe- matics were closed books) and it is for that reason that he has never, like Locke, been removed from the very high pedestal of admiration on which his contemporaries placed him. But, indeed, there should be no question of pedestals. The object of history is not to assess comparative merits but to clarify our perceptions as to how certain ideas, attitudes, and institutions have come into being. In the life and work of Wren is discern- ible the pattern of his epoch. If, in the conceptual currency of today, it is desirable to elucidate that pattern with the help of such relative terms as 'failure' and 'success', it is merely re- acknowledging Croce's axiom that 'all history is modern his- tory', and that the only objectivity which we can achieve is the sincere interpretation of the concepts of another age in terms of those of our own.

2

We cannot easily come at a clear presentment of Wren's mental development without following a chronological thread, and the main facts of his early life must be summarized. He was born in 1632 at East Knoyle, Wiltshire. His father was rector there at the time, but soon afterwards became Dean of Windsor in succession to his brother Matthew, the new Bishop of Nor- wich. Dr Wren's family was considerable, but Christopher was the only boy to survive; of his three elder sisters, Susan is the only one of whom we know anything, while of his younger sisters nothing is recorded. The mother seems to have died when Christopher was about thirteen.

After leaving Knoyle, the family must have lived partly at Windsor and partly at Great Haseley, Oxfordshire, where the living was held by Dr Wren concurrently with his Deanery; during this period Christopher was tutored by a clergyman. He was physically delicate, but his mental development was rapid and vigorous, and at nine he was strong enough to be sent to Westminster.

The beginning of the story is, then, in the sphere of Carolean churchmanship. The new Dean of Windsor, and his elder and more famous brother, the Bishop of Norwich, later of Ely, were, during Christopher's boyhood, men of late middle age, whose childhood had been passed in the mercantile environment of Elizabethan London, an environment from which their intellectual abilities and ambitions had severed them. Their place in the established order was fixed by education rather than by birth or wealth. They were part of the consolidated structure of Church and State which the Elizabethans had reared on the foundations of the earlier Tudors, but which was soon to be undermined by the very merchant class in which the two Wrens had been nurtured.

The English Church under Charles I was founded on faith and scholarship; faith in the authority of the Bible, and scholarship in the interpretation of the Early Fathers. It was an elaborate structure, insular and double-faced. To Catholic criticism it replied in the cool terms of Protestantism; to the Puritans it turned the haughty and intolerant face of Catholicism. It was in a high degree authoritarian. If the Puritan revolution had failed radically, we should have had in England a State religion as inflexible as that which the counter-reformation forced upon 18th-century France. Such a Church, self-contained and lacking the moral support of international and immemorial vassalage, needed a lively intellectual nucleus—a Jesuitry, as it were, to fan the flame of orthodox criticism and feed it from untainted Patristic sources. It was men like the Wrens, working in the tradition of Lancelot Andrewes and his disciple Laud, who fulfilled this function; and it was in this atmosphere of intellectual conservatism that Christopher's inclinations towards learning were formed.

It was an atmosphere in which medievalism and humanism were, somewhat artificially, mixed. We can picture Dr Wren, in his tiny mullioned rectory at Knoyle, devising the dedicatory inscription which adorned its walls. The Latin has the scholarly, idiomatic flavour of the New Learning, although its piety is Gothic; the date is supplied in tortuous Jacobean cryptogram. Of mathematics and music Dr Wren had some knowledge, he was an antiquary of precise and intelligent observation, and had even concerned himself with the theory, and in some small measure the practice, of architecture. But every interest was coloured with the fundamental conservatism of his profession and faith.

Christopher arrived at Westminster in 1641 or 1642, and under the rule of Dr Busby received that rigorous schooling in Latinity without which no one could hope to cross the intellectual threshold of the 17th century. While he was at school his sixteen-year-old sister, Susan, married a clergyman named Holder, a young man of ability in mathematics and music. Holder took a warm interest in his young brother-in-law, and introduced him to a wider and less strongly coloured conception of intellectual life than he had hitherto known. After leaving Westminster Christopher spent some three years in

London, and then went up to Oxford, at the age of 17, as a Gentleman Commoner of Wadham College.

To reach manhood in the late 1640's must have involved much heart-searching, especially to anyone with a mind as strong and as early mature as Christopher Wren's. Looking back at the period from our detached modern vantage-point, its outlines seem comparatively simple, and we see a great revolutionary movement just entering on its central crisis. But when we come down to detail and try to see things as they must have appeared to an Oxford student of the time, the pattern of events becomes less positive. We must not imagine the social revolution of the 17th century as a battle between defined classes of people, all of whom knew exactly what was happening. It was a struggle within a closely integrated society with few class barriers, and the intensity of the struggle created lines of conflict running in various and often surprising directions. The feudal pyramid of social and economic obligation was still present, though its outlines were blurred and its bulk rapidly dissolving; a new shape of things, in which the seed of industrialism was already sprouting, was sapping its stability, in preparation for the ultimate collapse of 1688. The situation is reflected in the mental constitution of the time, and, consciously or unconsciously, in the mind of each individual; but the reflection is a refracted image, and often the conflict which is economic in origin is manifested as one of religious faith or scientific doubt. The greatest fissure created on the mental plane is that between Anglican and Puritan, and this conflict, in turn, set up minor situations and produced remoter fissures. We have only to recall that Milton's *Comus* and Prynne's *Histriomastix*, both products of Puritan minds, were produced in the same year, to understand in what diverse directions the conflict was manifested.

While Wren was at Westminster, the acts of violence which preceded the Civil War took place. Strafford was executed and ten bishops, including Wren's uncle, Matthew, now Bishop of Ely, were put in the Tower. Then came Edgehill, the Cornish rising and the Royalist defeat at Marston Moor; then Naseby, and the execution of Laud. Wren must have been in London when Fairfax's army, refusing demobilization, marched on the city. In the year that he went to Oxford, King Charles was beheaded.

By implication of his environment, both at the Windsor deanery and to a less extent at Westminster School, Wren was committed to the Royalist and conservative cause. Had he been of different calibre in mind and body, and living a year or two earlier, he might have been a hard-fighting cavalier, or a Royalist diplomat. As it was, his physique and family background tended to make him a thinker rather than a fighter, and a thinker could not easily espouse a cause with as little substance to it as cavalier loyalism. To cut the knot by embracing Puritanism was impossible to a man of his upbringing, and, besides, Puritanism, like Royalism, meant in some degree a surrender to enthusiasm. This, above all, was impossible to a mind like Wren's.

The resolution of the conflict, for Wren as an individual, lay in an altogether different direction. It was to be found not in the political crucible of London but in the academic routine of Oxford, where, under a surface sometimes ruffled by political faction, the time-honoured routine of scholastic learning set the place for a tranquil but industrious mode of life. Thomas Sprat, in whose lucid and revealing pages the nature of 17th-century opinion is most easily gauged, speaks of the 'men of philosophical minds, whom the misfortunes of the Kingdom, and the security and ease of a retirement amongst gown-men' had drawn to the university, and observes that from these arose 'a race of young men provided against the next age, whose minds . . . were invincibly arm'd against all the inchantments of enthusiasm'.[1]

To a scholar who saw nought but 'inchantments of enthusiasm' in the rival loyalties in Church and State only one course was open, namely, to follow learning for its own sake, compromising delicately with political situations as they arose. It was not really a question of avoiding the issue, for the ultimate issue, to such a man, was not so much between King and Parliament, Bishop and Presbyter, as between the New Learning and the old, between Science and the remnants of Scholasticism. The revolution was working itself out on the intellectual plane.

Seventeen-year-old Wren, arrived at Wadham, immediately ranged himself with the champions of the New Learning. The actual curriculum of the university must have been irksome to him since it was of a purely scholastic nature, consisting mainly of the classics, logic and Aristotelian dialectics. Far more important were the friendships made with older men who were in a position to strike out into new fields and new methods of study. These men, since they gave Wren his real intellectual starting point, deserve some attention. Chief among them was John Wilkins, Warden of Wadham. 'Lustie, strong-grown, well-set, broad-shouldered',[2] Wilkins was an excellent leader; he had at one time been private chaplain to the Prince Palatine, but adapted his politics to the Cromwellian situation and was instrumental both in averting Parliamentary interference at the university and in organizing the group of men in whose hands the New Learning was beginning to gather strength. When

[1] T. Sprat, *History of the Royal Society*, 2nd ed., 1702, p 53.

[2] J. Aubrey, *Lives*, Ed. 1898, p 301.

Wren came up to Wadham, Wilkins was thirty-five, but even so he was the eldest of the circle. Of the others, Wallis, the mathematician, was thirty-three, Seth Ward and Ralph Bathurst, both future Bishops, were thirty-two and twenty-nine respectively, while Thomas Willis, the physician, was twenty-eight. Within five years of Wren's arrival, Lawrence Rooke, Jonathan Goddard and Robert Boyle, all round about thirty, joined the number, while young Thomas Sprat, the eventual historian of the group, matriculated in 1651.

This famous group of brains, the eventual creators of the Royal Society, was drawn from widely different regions of society, and their politics were both various and variable. Wallis, for instance, decoded messages for the Parliament, but won credit at the Restoration for having withheld some of the information thus obtained. Ward started as a violent anti-covenanter, later took the oath to the Commonwealth, but returned to his old views when occasion allowed. Goddard was Cromwell's confidant and physician, held in high honour by the Roundheads. Bathurst and Willis, both deep-dyed Royalists, lay low during the troubles, confining themselves to non-controversial research. Sprat wrote in praise of Cromwell but 'turned about with the virtuosi' and earned a bishopric under Charles II. Wren seems to have avoided any political commitments. He graduated in 1650 and was elected a Fellow of All Souls three years later. In 1657 he succeeded Rooke as Gresham Professor of Astronomy, and left Oxford for London, to take up residence in Sir Thomas Gresham's old palace in Bishopsgate. At this miniature university, with its pleasant arcaded courtyard, like a transplanted fragment of Oxford, Wren worked for the better part of four years; then, in the year after the Restoration, he returned to Oxford as the new Savilian Professor of Astronomy.

At this point we must consider the difficult subject of Wren's scientific achievements. It is difficult because so diffuse. He was in touch with every branch of research and contributed something important to most of them; but none of his work ever crystallized into a monumental and epoch-making result. As a boy the theory of the sundial engaged his imagination, and this led him at once to mathematics and astronomy. At the same time he devised a 'pneumatic engine' of some kind, and this opened up to him the line of research in which Boyle eventually achieved pre-eminence. In his early Oxford days he helped Sir Charles Scarburgh with his anatomical work, while a little later he took the initiative in experiments relating to blood transfusions and vivisection. All the time he was producing inventions with an industrial application, many of which are curiously prophetic, but none of which have, or ever had, any real importance.

It is important to remember that to the scientists of Wren's time philosophical sanction for scientific work was still something new. John Wallis tells us, for instance, that even mathematics, the most abstract and respectable of the sciences, 'were scarce looked on as academical studies, but rather mechanical— as the business of traders, merchants, seamen, carpenters, surveyors of lands and the like'.[1] The philosophers, in fact, took over the data compiled by generations of mercantile brains, examined and correlated them on the high plane of 'philosophical' thought. In return, they felt obliged to keep the industrial application of new discoveries constantly in view, 'to assist familiarly', as Sprat has it, 'in all occasions of human life', and in Wren's case this obligation was especially pronounced. It was this, together with a strong visual interest in experimental research, forcibly instanced by his love of model-

[1] J. Wallis, *Account of Some Passages in His Own Life*, quoted in DNB.

making (Plate XI) which made the passage from science to architecture so easy.

Nevertheless, his work in astronomy was far from negligible. Sir William Dampier-Whetham[1] mentions him as one of the handful of scientists who forged the essential link between Keplerian and Newtonian astronomy. Newton himself considered Wren to be one of the three best mathematicians of the time.[2] He followed up Descartes' work on moving bodies and suggested to Boyle a means for testing the Cartesian hypothesis that the moon exerted pressure on the atmosphere; a suggestion which led to the invention of Boyle's barometer.

The one region of thought which Wren seems to have skirted respectfully and never entered was that of pure speculation. In this respect he was, no doubt, inhibited by the strong predisposition of his class to allow to the Bible and the Christian faith an axiomatic and unquestioned authority. One imagines that his general outlook took its bearings from Descartes; for Descartes' god, being impersonal and mathematically remote, was easily attachable to the traditional forms and beliefs of an English churchman, while being eminently acceptable to a scientific mind. With the stark materialism of Hobbes, Wren could have had no sympathy (he did, as a matter of fact, correspond with Hobbes, though on a purely scientific topic); he is far closer in general outlook to Locke, whose typically English empiricism provides, as we shall see, a striking parallel with his own architecture.

3

In the spring of 1660 came the Restoration, and with it a delirious recoil from twenty years of tension and uncertainty.

[1] *History of Science*, 2nd ed., 1930, p 167.
[2] *Parentalia*, p 136.

There was a general reshuffling of responsibilities in favour of those who could present a clean bill of loyalty. Philosophy was shown (with only moderate plausibility, to be sure) to have been 'always loyal in the worst of times',[1] and the young King proved to be keenly interested in the New Learning. The nuclei which had formed at Wadham and Gresham Colleges were reorganized with the addition of some assured Royalists like Lord Brouncker and Sir Robert Moray, and Charles placed himself at their head. Wren drew up a rather pompous preamble for the Charter, and the Royal Society was incorporated in 1663. The Restoration showed Wren in a particularly favourable light. His uncle, released after eighteen years of imprisonment, was an heroic and venerable figure; his father had died an unshaken loyalist and Wren was able to hand over to the new Dean of Windsor the precious archives which had been in his keeping. Wren himself had become involved in no transactions which could possibly cast a shadow on his loyalty, and he was exactly the type of man to whom an important appointment should go. The King, moreover, took a personal interest in his work, and bestowed his model of the moon among the treasures of the royal cabinet. In 1661 Wren was appointed assistant to Sir John Denham, the new Surveyor-General.

The nominal distinction of the post was far less than its actual importance. Denham, a literary gentleman and diplomat, to whom Charles owed substantial obligation, over and above the reversion granted by his father, was ineffective as an architect. John Webb, Inigo Jones's assistant and relative, should really have had the post both on the scores of loyalty and experience, but was rather unfairly passed over, though he subsequently did Denham's work for him at Greenwich and elsewhere. Wren immediately became the dominant brain and the man to

[1] Sprat, op. cit., p 59.

whom everyone looked for leadership in the sphere of architecture.

Now Wren's emergence into the architectural world at this precise moment is of great significance. It is essential to think of him not as an individual but as one of a group of minds among which a certain state of tension existed, a tension set up as the result of a revolutionary crisis. We can compare the situation with that of the Court intelligentsia under Charles I. This had produced Inigo Jones and his school, but had disintegrated under the stress of the civil war, with the death of the King, and later of Jones himself. Neither Pratt nor Webb, still less Denham, had the personality to effect a re-establishment. Therefore, it was natural that the succession should pass to a quarter where tension was highest—namely, the Royal Society group.

Wren's was a perfect specimen of the Royal Society type of mind, a fact which qualified him well for any Government appointment. In his capacity of Assistant Surveyor, it is primarily as a responsible 'Civil Servant' that we must think of him. His qualifications as a designer were secondary. There was, let us remember, no architectural profession, no definite body of men styling themselves 'architect'; the term had a very special, and highly intellectual, significance. Building was carried on under the supervision of artisans calling themselves masons, bricklayers, or carpenters, and such men worked to a code handed down from the Middle Ages and merely modified by successive generations of craftsmen. London consisted almost entirely of the work of such men. 'Architecture' was a very different thing. It was best understood in Italy, and gentlemen who had been to Italy, and even those who had not, were expected to know something about it. But, however much they knew they made little use of their knowledge, unless it was to adorn their mansions with what Evelyn, with true Royal

Society hauteur, calls 'busie and Gothic triflings in the compositions of the Five Orders'.[1]

It is probable that nearly every member of the Royal Society had a fair smattering of architectural knowledge and could have filled the surveyorship without discredit. For Wren, it had been only one of many intellectual diversions, and in a list of exhibits at a Wadham Assembly, in 1660, certain 'new designs tending to strength, convenience and beauty in building' figure inconspicuously among such things as astronomical and anatomical models, agricultural devices, musical instruments, engines of war, and an instrument for writing double.

4

Now Wren's interest in architecture turned upon two clearly separable issues. In the first place he was a man of science, anxious and able to place the whole of building technique on a new plane, opening out the subject to correspond with the broad scientific theories which were established in his mind. In the second place, he was a classical scholar with all the glowing enthusiasm for the logic and structural fitness of the Latin syntax which the 17th century, more than any other, was able to enjoy. If we wish to understand Wren's early works (and without doing so we cannot properly understand any of them) we must keep these two aspects constantly in mind.

Let us turn at once to Wren's first important building, the chapel at Pembroke College, Cambridge, built at the expense of his uncle, the aged Bishop. Here is a strictly rational building, a plain oblong, brick box with pitched roof, ceiled internally, the whole being turned into Latin by the application

[1] J. Evelyn, *An Account of Architects and Architecture*, in his translation of Fréart's Parallel, 1664.

of a Corinthian order. The windows are very large, with correct classical adornments, and panels below them. On the west gable is a small eight-sided lantern with a cornice, lead cupola and weather-vane.

The modern eye immediately seizes on this terminal lantern as the one feature in the building which suggests an imaginative touch. Closer examination, however, reveals it as a supernumerary unit rather out of key with the design as a whole. The ultimate appraisal of the building must be this: it is constructed with a great deal of thought and expressed in sound Latin; but in conception it is unimaginative.

'Unimaginative' is perhaps too vague. 'Unpoetical' is more exact since it implies the absence of that deft, intuitive, co-ordination of thought and imagination which is exactly what is missing in Pembroke Chapel. That there was nothing poetical in Wren's point of view at this critical and formative period of his career must certainly be admitted. He was working as an empirical philosopher, against the background of Latinity which his environment provided as the starting point for all the arts. This attitude, collectively represented by the Royal Society, was thoroughly anti-poetical. The imagination was regarded with the utmost suspicion, and consciously thrust aside as the enemy of truth. The imaginative strain in Elizabethan thought, for instance, and in the work of a man like Sir Thomas Browne, was generally despised. The approved point of view crystallized in the calm prose and limited common-sense philosophy of Locke who was not in the least interested in art and obviously despised poetry.

Wren's second building of importance, the Sheldonian Theatre at Oxford (Plate XII), is a very highly wrought classical production, but here, just as in Pembroke Chapel, the idiom of the architecture must be placed on the totally unimaginative plane of an academic Latin essay, a production comparable, let us say, to Wren's elaborate inaugural lecture at Gresham College, or his long Biblical interpretation, in hexameters, of the signs of the Zodiac. The idiomatic composition of classical elements obviously had a great appeal to the architect and his like-minded contemporaries; one might compare the compact disposal of a return cornice with a neat use of the ablative absolute. But the sense of novelty which invested this sort of thing is lost to us, and one fails to recognize in the Sheldonian any appreciation of the values of mass, spacing, and linear texture which Inigo Jones had, long previously, shown to be of the essence of classical design. Technically, of course, the Sheldonian is full of originality, especially as regards the roof, with its ingenious trusses whose composite bolted tie-beams suggest a background of research of which we know little. But all this is hidden from view, and the grammarian's hood conceals the brain of the mathematician.

5

It is very difficult to determine to what extent Wren ever really broke away from the limitations of this non-imaginative approach to the arts. In his formative period (say up to the age of forty) he was at the very centre of the movement *against* imaginative expression, a movement which went much farther in this country than anywhere else in Europe. It was not easy for a Royal Society man to escape from the tyranny of intellect, and when the movement in the reverse direction began it was to a great extent literary, arising from the cultivation and development of wit rather than from any of the visual arts.

Wren's literary proclivities are, in this connection, of some importance. In his own writings he gives no clues, but in *Parentalia* there are two brilliant letters addressed *to* him by

Sprat in 1663 and these give, by reflection, a valuable picture of Wren the theatre-goer and literary dilettante. Wren himself was an ineffective letter-writer; his letters indicate the impatience of literary grace which is often found in company with first-class brains. Sprat, on the other hand, who wrote beautifully, keenly appreciated his friend's mental capacities, and one of the letters is confessed to be a résumé of a conversation between the two. The tone of the letters is gay and supple. From one of them we learn that Wren was, as we should expect, an intense admirer of Horace. We may, perhaps, assume that he shared Sprat's admiration for Cowley's lively conceits. But more illuminating is the analysis of the nature and function of wit contained in the second letter and avowed to be a reflection of Wren's own thoughts on the subject. Wit, the sole imaginative outlet of the philosophic mind, was beginning to assume immense importance. 'The Age in which we live runs . . . mad after the Affairs of Wit,' wrote Sprat.[1] In wit was embodied just that immediate, intuitive perception which was so firmly repressed in the Royal Society mentality. 'Its chiefest Dominion is in forming new Significations, and Images of Things and Persons. And this may be so suddenly practised, that I have known in one Afternoon, new Stamps, and Proverbs, and Fashions of Speech raised, which were never thought of before, and yet gave Occasion to most delightful Imaginations.'[2] Wit became the imaginative descant of the age, emerging now in the disciplined prosody of Dryden's satire, now in the rich humanity of the comedy of manners. And let us remember that it was to a great wit that the leadership of English architecture passed when it left the hands of Wren; in Vanbrugh, dramatist first and architect afterwards, the imagination

[1] Letter to Wren, *Parentalia*, p 102.
[2] *Ibid.*

broke down its literary confines and flooded into architecture.

The literary world of Wren's time was dominated by the towering figure of Dryden. But although his life and Wren's have many points of contact (he was a parson's son, a Westminster boy, a Fellow of the Royal Society, and within a year of Wren's age), their parallel achievements are curiously unrelated. The truth is that poetry never received the set-back, at the revolution, which architecture did; nor was it intellectualized by being placed under the scrutiny of the New Learning. To the pervading sense of crisis it responded with satire and panegyric and a new formalism which cleared the air of metaphysics, but among the poets there was hardly any of that intense 'brave-new-world' conviction which we find among the scientists and philosophers.

Dryden himself was indeed almost responsible for a re-emergence of the imaginative approach, and it would in some ways be easier to link him pyschologically with Vanbrugh (thirty-four years his junior) than with Wren. It was he who humanized the passionless drama of Davenant, who drew attention once more to the romantic beauties of the Elizabethans, and who believed that 'an heroic poet' should 'let himself loose to visionary objects'.[1] But all the time he was, of course, fundamentally loyal to, and in a sense frustrated by, the rigid formalism which caged the imagination within a framework of metre and rhyme instead of making it, as Coleridge and Wordsworth were to do a century later, the veritable mainspring of poetic creation.

6

The chronology of Wren's career and the events which led up to the assumption of his greatest responsibilities after the

[1] *Essay of Heroick Plays* (prefixed to *The Conquest of Granada*), 1670.

fire of 1666 have no direct bearing on our purpose and are, in any case, familiar. It is well known that when his astronomy lectures and the preliminary discussions regarding the rehabilitation of Old St Paul's were interrupted by the plague of 1665, he took the opportunity of paying his one and only visit abroad. He left London for Paris in June. We know little about his visit, except what he himself tells us in a long letter to an anonymous friend. But what we do know together with obvious inferences drawn from the state of affairs at the time make this interlude of the greatest historic importance.

The presence of an Englishman in Paris in 1665 is in any case a circumstance of interest. Since the Middle Ages France and England had drifted far apart, and when Louis XIV and Charles II started their parallel reigns in 1660 the social structures and outlooks of the two countries were strikingly different. The English, who had repudiated the Roman Church and executed their King, did not find themselves in sympathetic accord with a nation which was heading for an anti-Protestant coup, and where a feudal nobility was impregnably entrenched. A nation of small landowners, moreover, socially organized on a basis of country wealth and country residence, was bound to have a very different outlook from one in which both wealth and social life were concentrated in towns.

It was natural that the urban organization of France should produce a more coherent and richer culture than the scattered countryside economy of England. In Paris, the Court provided a world of personalities, politics and culture round which the whole of France revolved; at the centre was Louis, the inaccessible, glorified sovereign of Versailles, a very different figure from English Charles, with his rambling half-medieval palace at Whitehall, whose galleries were open to the humblest of country squires. The machinery of Louis' Government was in the hands of Colbert, who, at the time of Wren's visit, was conducting a tremendous drive for order and efficiency; on the one hand reforming the fiscal system, on the other reorganizing industry and regimenting the arts. Architects and painters, sculptors and designers, were dragooned into Government service, and their talents directed towards a colossal parade expressive of the Louis regime.

Englishmen, in their rough, vigorous, and slightly squalid island setting, watched the Colbert parade with no enthusiasm and some degree of contempt. Sprat, for instance, while allowing Paris to be a great intellectual centre, found it all the worse for 'being the seat of gallantry, the arts of speech and education', and Wren voiced the same opinion when he criticized the ascendancy of feminine influence in politics, philosophy and the arts. If French taste found a following in England it was among courtiers and fashionable women rather than among professional men and the intelligentsia. Criticism from the French side, when it was not bluntly hostile, was puzzled. The French found the English lazy and boorish, but somehow unaccountably ingenious and poetical. M. de Sorbière, one of the few articulate French visitors of the period, described the English as a nation which, 'under the rose, is of a very irregular and fantastical temper'.[1] And if Sorbière found English manners lacking, their country houses contemptible, and their tobacco habit excessive, he had to admit that nothing could be 'more civil, respectable and better managed' than the meetings of the Royal Society.

As an 'interested observer' in the Paris of 1665, it is clear that Wren's English assurance never for a moment deserted him. He found much to admire and much to emulate, and his

[1] S. Sorbière, *A Voyage to England*, 1667, p 63 (Sorbière's visit took place in 1664).

sojourn of about six months gave him an opportunity of getting something more than mere travellers' impressions. Yet the essential world of Racine, of Poussin, of Sevigné, never captured his allegiance, or even, one suspects, his real appreciation. He remained the calm English scientist, well aware of his debt to Monsieur Descartes, keenly alive to the quality of French thinkers like Pascal and of the achievements of contemporary French architects and painters; but still virtually unconscious of the emotional colour, the latent romanticism, which is the glory of French art of the later 17th century.

French culture in 1665 had reached a stage to which contemporary English culture might have been comparable had there been no revolution, had the Carolean monarchy and the Laudian Church been consolidated, and the magisterial system been superseded by a privileged land-owning aristocracy. Architecture, under such circumstances, would have developed in the direction which Inigo Jones and his school defined, and a tradition of taste would had been established too firmly to be deflected by any access of intellectualism. Instead of Wren, we might have had an English Mansart, and instead of the St Paul's we know, we might have had a structure more conservative, perhaps, in general form, but having the stylistic subtlety to which Jones's works were tending, but which English architecture never properly attained till the time of Chambers.

To gain a further impression of Wren's English mind outlined against the French cultural scene, it is worth considering for a moment the position of painting in the two countries. In England, painting meant portraiture purely and simply; historical and genre painting was imported, largely from Holland, but took no root. France, on the other hand, already had a great school of classical painting. Nicholas Poussin died in the year that Wren visited Paris; Claude was painting in studious retirement at Rome; Le Brun was working in the Louvre, soon to be followed in the same work by Mignard. Now, if we look at the kind of work which Poussin and Claude were doing we shall find not only that it was much concerned with the representation of architecture but that it embodied an emotional, even a romantic, reaction to classic forms very distinct from anything which an English scientific mind could conceive. Nothing could be more foreign to Wren's latinity than the haunted Roman castles of Claude (of whom, by the way, he would hardly have heard in 1665) or the luminous ruins of Poussin. His expressed admiration for historical painting extended, one imagines, no further than an appreciation of the purely technical achievements of men like Poussin and Le Brun. And it is significant that his admiration is expressed not in his own words but in a florid quotation from Fréart, appended as a postcript to the Paris letter.

7

Wren returned to London, as English as he had left it, in November, 1665, and immediately took up the old subject of St Paul's. It is to the history of the cathedral that we must now give our attention, tracing the evolution of the design in the light of our analysis of its architect's intellectual development.

Wren's proposals for the restoration were of a moderate nature and thoroughly practical. He proposed to provide the interior with a Roman skin to match Inigo's exterior. The old vaulting, however, being a danger to the stability of the nave, he proposed to remove, replacing it with a light brick vault, 'very geometrically proportion'd to the Strength of the Butment' and covered with stucco. The choir was to remain Gothic. The middle part of the church, where the tower, that

'Heap of Deformities', rose above the crossing of nave and aisles, he considered to be so ugly and decrepit that demolition was the only thing. The immediately adjoining bays in nave, choir and transepts were likewise to be taken down, and the whole central area remodelled to support a dome: 'A form of church building,' noted Evelyn, 'not as yet known in England, but of wonderful grace.'[1] The future crown of London's sky-line emerges for the first time in these words: 'I cannot propose a better Remedy (for the crossing), than by cutting off the inner Corners of the Cross, to reduce this middle Part into a spacious Dome or Rotundo, with a Cupola, or hemispherical Roof, and upon the Cupola (for the outward ornament) a Lantern with a Spiring Top, to rise proportionately, tho' not to that unnecessary Height of the former Spire of Timber and Lead.'[2]

Wren's insistence, at this early stage, on the desirability of a domed space is significant. We can sense his impatience with the purely formal values of the new architecture and his ambi-tion to come to grips with scientific issues. How little his sen-sibility to the use of architectural forms had as yet developed we can see from this pre-fire design (Plate XIII), whose dome is, in effect, an elongated edition of Bramante's proposal for St Peter's, known to him, no doubt, through the many editions of Serlio; the 'spiring top' is in the nature of a huge stylized pineapple. The whole design is curiously artificial in char-acter; we can imagine Wren piecing the classic elements together as he would piece together a hexameter and being mildly surprised at the happiness of the result. A letter[3] which he wrote to Dean Sancroft about this time indicates the trend of

[1] *Diary*, August 28, 1666.

[2] Proposals to the Commissioners, 1666, in *Parentalia*, p 129.

[3] *Bodleian*, Tanner 145, No 115. Reprinted in *Wren Society*, XIII, p 44.

his thought: 'Carmina proverbialia,' he says, 'sounds better to most Eares than Horace, and wee have fewer Judges of a Latine style in building than in writing, but I hope you will go to the charge of trew latine . . . ' Again, the satisfaction of the scholar exercising his mind in problems of prosody comes out in his confession (in a later letter)[1] that even if the designs are not adopted, 'I shall not repent the great satisfaction and pleasure I have taken in the contrivance, which aequalls that of poetry or compositions in Musick'.

In September, 1666, the great fire rendered all previous discussions regarding St Paul's of little account, and attention was for the moment diverted to the possibility of rebuilding the whole of the burnt-out area on a new plan. This interlude, with its disappointing end, is familiar history. Eighteen months passed before Wren's mind was once more brought to bear on St Paul's. A pathetic attempt on the part of the church authorities to case up those parts of the ruin which were not too far gone proved vain labour, and in April, 1668, the architect was sent for from Oxford. Three months later he was instructed to prepare an entirely new design, 'handsome and noble, and suitable to all the ends of it, and to the reputation of the city, and the nation, and to take it for granted, that money will be had to accomplish it'.[2]

The idea of a domed area continued uppermost in his mind, but the problem of what position it should occupy in a cathedral plan seems to have offered no obvious solution in spite of the many precedents afforded by Italy and France. If we can trust the evidence of the two City plans of 1666, it seems that Wren's first conception was of a domed east end with a nave running westward. With the First Model of 1670-2, portions

[1] *Bodleian, ibid.,* No 117. Reprinted in *Wren Society,* XIII, p 45.
[2] Sancroft to Wren, *Parentalia,* p 133.

of which have recently been identified in the cathedral library,[1] this arrangement was reversed; the design then comprised a domed hall at the west and a nave running east. This arbitrary reversal, implying a doubt that there could be any one inevitably right relationship of form and function in a cathedral, is characteristic of what we may call Wren's empirical method of design. We have already emphasized, as an attribute of the contemporary mind, a conscious (but in reality, of course, only apparent) independence of judgment, a sense of detachment manifesting itself in the latest phase of the New Learning, and giving the proper psychological atmosphere for empirical philosophy. To transfer this concept of empiricism from philosophy to design is not difficult. Empirical design may be expressed as the antithesis of imaginative design; empiricism involves a conscious selection of formal relationships, imagination an unconscious selection. As a philosophic concept, empiricism implies the formation of judgments in the light of previous experience rather than of established principles; in other words, it implies an *arbitrary* approach. In transferring the concept from philosophy to design it is this arbitrariness which is the striking thing, though the real point is that in certain kinds of thought and certain kinds of design we recognize a common quality which can only be accurately expressed by the use of the same word in both contexts.

Wren's empiricism is apparent not only in the arbitrary approach to the cathedral problem as a whole but in the character of the design itself in so far as we can deduce it from the fragmentary model and from Sir Roger Pratt's critical notes.[2] Pratt, of course, being an architect trained in the taste and technique of the Inigo Jones tradition, took a vigorous dislike to

[1] Illustrated and discussed in *Wren Society*, XIII.

[2] R. Gunther, *The Architecture of Sir Roger Pratt*, 1928, p 213.

Wren's arbitrariness. He objected to the abrupt, elongated plan, to the use of porticoes without reference to the relative importance of the entrances they sheltered (two of the three porticoes applied to the western vestibule appear to have sheltered no entrances). He objected also to the lucarnes ('How ungracefully and weakly do the Lucarnes stand which are over the Portico of the East end'), to the ornaments of the windows in the loggias, and to the colonnades of the dome. Pratt was assessing by standards of taste a design whose real standards were purely intellectual. It was a case of intuitive criticism being applied to empirical design, a situation on which nothing but a critical stalemate could ensue.

This First Model, though approved by the King and 'applauded by persons of good understanding',[1] raised much controversy. It raised, in fact, two distinct schools of opinion. On the one hand there was the clerical view that it was no cathedral at all since it had neither transepts nor aisles. And there was the view of the 'conoisseurs and criticks', who had seen St Peter's, and who hoped for something more impressive, a closer rival to the Papal basilica. So Wren, 'in order to find what might satisfy the World ... drew several sketches merely for discourse-sake.' For the connoisseurs he struck out a highly intellectual study (the 'Great Model' (Plate xiv), a vast cupola rising from a nicely related system of domes and vaults, the whole having something of the satisfying involution of a mathematical theorem. For the parsons, who were even more shocked by this second design than by the first, he designed what was, in effect, a Gothic cathedral with the details latinized (the 'Warrant' Design (Plate xv).)

Now these two designs, produced within a very short time of each other, provide striking evidence of the separateness of

[1] *Parentalia*, p 137.

those two factors in Wren's mentality which we have previously distinguished, the factors associated with Wren the Latin
scholar and with Wren the scientist respectively. But not only
can we link the designs with two aspects of their creator's mind;
we can link each of them with a separate series of influences in
his mental development. Thus, the latinity aspect, as we may
call it, recalls the scholarly, ecclesiastical atmosphere of the
Windsor deanery, the Oxonian curriculum outside the narrow
circle of modern philosophy, and the early essays in Latin versi-
cation. The scientific aspect, on the other hand, is the spiritual
child of a revolutionary epoch, the outcome of an intellectual
struggle taking place in the minds of the thinking minority of
Englishmen; here the link is with the Wadham and Gresham
groups, the anatomical models, and the Royal Society.

We can carry the historical analysis a step further by relating
these two aspects of Wren's mind to the divided mental outlook of his time. As Professor Trevelyan[1] has shown, the Restoration was a double event. The year 1660 saw the restoration
of the monarchy and aristocracy; the following year saw the
restoration of the Anglican Church. Each restored party established a characteristic mental attitude, and these attitudes are
eloquently formulated in Wren's two designs. Rationalism and
religious indifference among the scientifically minded aristocracy find their perfect symbol in the Model Design, whose
absolute symmetry coldly ignores the sense of orientation implicit in any building in which a congregation faces an altar or
a preacher. On the other hand, the Gothic form of the Warrant
Design is counter-revolutionary in character; it symbolizes that
liberal conservatism which did not die with Laud but raised its
head once more to strike the final blow to Puritan worship
from the safe cover of the restored constitution.

[1] *England under the Stuarts*, 16th ed., 1933, pp 332, *et seq.*

The Warrant Design was, of course, the one to receive official approval, and with the issuing of the warrant discussion was closed. Wren decided to give the public no further opportunity of expressing their prejudices, and the final design was worked out by the architect in the narrow circle of criticism provided by the King and the court intelligentsia.

The cathedral as we know it, begun in 1675 and finished thirty-five years later, is totally different from any of the preparatory designs. Wren accepted the inevitability of a cross plan with aisles, but wedded it to the central-area idea which he had developed to the utmost in the Model Design. His preliminary drawings in the All Souls' and St Paul's libraries show him struggling to get rid of the medieval conception of a nave as an indeterminate aggregate of bays not sensibly affected by the subtraction or addition of a single unit, and to give his plan a ruling and inevitable scheme of proportion. As for the superstructure of high nave with low flanking aisles, he might as well have despaired of giving his exterior an appearance much more classical than that which Inigo Jones contrived for the old church recased. However, he compromised to obtain his end, and erected the immense screen wall which serves the triple purpose of masking the flying buttresses, giving additional weight to the aisle walls in their thrust-resisting capacity, and giving to the exterior as a whole an apparent bulk in consonance with the most exalted principles of classical design.

Wren's empirical, arbitrary methods of composition are most clearly seen in the preliminary designs for the cathedral, especially when these designs are considered as a related group. In the finished structure it must be admitted that the strict intellectualism of his earlier maturity has to some extent dissolved, probably as a result of wider acquaintance with French and Italian work, but partly also under the influence of the changing viewpoint of the times. Nevertheless, Wren the empiricist emerges, on the whole, more consistently from the cathedral than Wren the Anglo-Italian Baroque designer.

It has often been justly remarked that criticism of St Paul's is hampered by the aura of pride and affection through which Englishmen regard it. To enjoy it as a work of architecture certainly requires a little more effort than to honour it as an object of sentimental regard; while to appreciate the nature and historical diagnosis of its faults requires an almost painfully open mind.

It is, therefore, interesting to turn to the remarks of a French critic[1] who cherishes no illusions whatever about the merits of our architecture. This gentleman is admittedly hard to please, but we need not follow him either in his unintelligent dislike of sash windows or his contempt for plain brickwork. Nor need we necessarily agree with him when he starts his criticism of St Paul's by remarking that the nave is excessively high and narrow. What follows, however, is important. The radical fault of St Paul's he finds to be the false emphasis, internally, of the colossal dome, which serves merely to cover the crossing of nave and transepts, thus grotesquely exaggerating the function served simply and adequately by the medieval lantern tower. Our critic then points to the central area, where the dome rests not on four massive piers but on eight clusters of rather weak-looking pilasters whose effect is still further embarrassed by the openings into the aisles contrived between them (Plate XVI). Both these criticisms are very much to the point. To the first we can only answer that the false emphasis is a direct result of the conflicting outlooks of the philosophers (the domed-space men) and the ecclesiastics (the Gothic-nave men) and of the parallel conflict in Wren's own mind; to the second we can

[1] Paul Biver, in A. Michel, *Histoire de l'Art*, vi, Part 2.

only repeat that Wren designed empirically, not imaginatively, and that where the identification of structure with decorative ordonnance presented peculiar difficulties, he was inclined to resort to the glaring artificiality seen in the central space of his cathedral.

8

But the element of compromise, of disunity of conception, goes very much deeper than these general criticisms of the composition of St Paul's. It is a strain of inconsistency running through the whole of Wren's work. Sometimes it emerges crudely, as in the less successful City churches; sometimes, as in the library at Trinity College, Cambridge, it can only be faintly detected. But it is always there. It is an essential part of Wren's mind and of the collective thought of his time.

In order to bring our picture of the architect's mentality into sharper focus we must consider its relation to his artistic method and actual views on design. His own summary of aesthetics, printed in the *Parentalia*,[1] and obviously based on a searching analysis of his own technique, provides a good starting point. During the course of the essay we read: 'There are two Causes of Beauty, natural and customary. Natural is from Geometry, consisting in Uniformity (that is Equality) and Proportion. Customary Beauty is begotten by the use of our Senses to those Objects which are usually pleasing to us for other Causes, as Familiarity or particular Inclination breeds a Love to Things not in themselves lovely.'

This statement is a quite remarkable adumbration of an aesthetic generalization widely accepted today. The Ozenfant-

[1] In an appendix entitled *Of Architecture; and Observations on Antique Temples*, etc., p 236, *et seq.*

Jeanneret Purist manifesto[1] of 1921 contains an almost identical formula. But Wren did not mean, perhaps, just what we should like him to mean and the formula can be interpreted in various ways. The brusque division of aesthetic values into two groups is typical of the 17th-century desire for broad explanations of complex phenomena in common-sense terms, and, like most such explanations, it contains psychological error. The error in this case is the false creation of categories which are not, in actual fact, distinguishable. If we admit the basic purity of primary geometrical forms, we have to remember that as soon as two or more of these forms are brought into proximity we are dealing not with mathematical inevitabilities but with issues involving remote and complex associations which can only properly come under Wren's second category of 'customary' beauty, but which are, in fact, excluded from his formula altogether. He obviously believed that (and designed as if) intellectual control could be established over the whole process of design, and he seems to have been largely insensible to formal relationships except in so far as such relationships had a geometrical (i.e. intellectual) basis.

It may seem a little absurd to criticize Wren's works on the basis of his own brief and obviously inadequate theoretical notes. On the other hand, his strong intellectual integrity makes these notes, brief as they are, of special value. His theory is a very good expression of his practice. The important point is that the former claims a double sanction for the latter, and herein the central weakness of both theory and practice can be detected. Of the two sanctions, one is the intellectual or 'geometrical' sanction, affecting the general form, disposition of openings, and so forth; the other is the imaginative or 'customary' sanction affecting those necessary features in the design

[1] *L'Esprit Nouveau*, No 4, Jan., 1921.

which distort it from absolute regularity and symmetry. It must be assumed, moreover, that, 'customary' sanction covers those elements of the classical decorative grammar not 'geometrical' in character, but approved under the general contemporary sanction of antiquity—such features, for instance, as swags, consoles, and the more elaborate sequences of mouldings.

Now, the trouble about this conception of design is that between the two sanctions occurs an awkward fissure where inconsistency is bound to creep in. If an artist allows himself a divided sanction for his results, his standard of rightness must necessarily be insecure. He is avoiding the real issue, which must rest ultimately with intuition. Wren seems to have been aware of this when he assigned a function in the 'customary' category to the architect's 'judgment'. But he was too intellect-ridden to leave it at that, and hastened to add that 'always the true Test is natural or geometrical beauty'; which is no test at all, and is very liable to constitute an excuse. The major faults in the design of St Paul's, for example, may be condoned as complete intellectual solutions of certain problems in design, but they cannot escape condemnation as evasions of the artist's real goal, which is the complete intuitive unification of the intellectual and imaginative factors.

The root of the matter lies, of course, outside the individual mind of Christopher Wren. His approach to design is simply part of a general attitude of mind which his generation produced and to which English empiricism in all its aspects belongs. Wren carried empiricism into architecture just as Locke carried it into philosophy, and Locke's explanation of knowledge contains the same kind of psychological inconsistencies as Wren's architecture. It is hard to pin down any particular portion of Locke's work as exemplifying this, but it may be worth glancing at one of his best-known theses, that of the derivation of knowledge from a process of sensation and reflection. Here, as in Wren's aesthetic, we have the characteristic desire for lucid explanation of phenomena in common-sense terms, and again a highly artificial division into categories is attempted. To *sensation* Locke ascribes our consciousness of a thing being 'yellow' or 'hot' or 'sweet', while to *reflection* he ascribes such ideas as 'perceiving', 'doubting' or 'willing'. Yet it is obvious that the idea of 'heat' can no more be established without reflection than the idea of 'doubting'. Such an inconsistency did not trouble Locke, however, because his anxiety to construct a neat explanatory framework of general validity in relation to current concepts excluded the imaginative perception which would have hindered him in constructing it. Locke's lucid, sympathetic prose, carefully purified from the romanticisms of Lord Herbert or Sir Thomas Browne, carries us past a multitude of such inconsistencies and builds up an imposing philosophic structure as noble and courageous as St Paul's, yet as thoroughly impregnated with inconsistency.

9

I have attempted to sketch in broad outline some leading aspects of Wren's mind and have set forth the evidence chronologically, following the biographical track from Wren's childhood to somewhere about his fiftieth year. Upon the evidence belonging to this period an extremely clear-cut mentality can be envisaged, a mentality dominated, and in a sense distorted, by the abnormally strong intellectual currents of the time. We have examined the relations of Wren's mentality to the major political and philosophical issues of the period, and also to the issues involved in a study of his artistic output. We have, however, so far largely and purposely ignored the evidence of the last four decades of his phenomenally long life, since these could hardly be expected to shed much further light on the 'essential Wren' which it has been our object to identify. Nevertheless, those forty years of post-maturity present important problems, and although their detailed consideration lies outside the scope of this essay it is necessary to indicate their nature and extent.

The leading problem of Wren's later years is that associated with the development of a distinct late manner in which the intellectual hardihood of his early designs gives place to something more emotional and more in consonance with the dramatic generalization of the Baroque. To make this difference clear we need only point to some striking comparisons. Compare the dome of the Great Model with that of the finished cathedral; the tower of St Mary-le-Bow with that of St Vedast, and any of the earlier designs with such pre-eminently Baroque works as the west towers of St Paul's and the great design for Whitehall Palace. The change has been described by one author[1] as a progression from small to larger units of design, thus suggesting the type of reintegration which has been elaborately analysed by Wölfflin in his *Principles of Art History*. It is the change which occurs between the architecture of Bramante and that of Michelangelo, between painting of the time of Dürer and that of Rembrandt. Wölfflin himself calls it a development 'from multiplicity to unity', and summarizes it as follows: 'In the system of a classic (e.g. Bramante, Raphael), composition, the single parts, however firmly they may be rooted in the whole, maintain a certain independence. It is not the anarchy of primitive art: the art is conditioned by the whole, and yet does not

---

[1] Geoffrey Webb, in his introduction to the Nonesuch Edition of Vanbrugh's works. Mr Webb is quoting the expression from Geoffrey Scott, who uses it in analysing the work of Michelangelo.

cease to have its own life . . . In both styles unity is the chief aim . . . but in the one case unity is achieved by a harmony of free parts, in the other, by a union of parts in a single theme.'

This is not precisely the metamorphosis which we find in Wren's work, though it is like it. Inigo Jones had already gone a great way towards Wölfflin's 'union of parts in a single theme' though none of his work crosses the Baroque border-line. But Wren's fresh start was of a very local and special nature, and cannot logically be brought into relation with the main sweep of European art. It must be considered on its own merits. That Wren was not by temperament in accord with the Baroque spirit is perfectly clear; but it is equally clear that in such designs as Hampton Court and Greenwich he was handling classic forms in a loose, unconventional fashion which, allowing for a strong individual trend, can be called by no other name.

There are two directions in which this difficulty of the late Wren manner may be to some extent cleared up. The first consideration must be an examination of credentials. It has been shown in Volume VI of the *Wren Society* that the domes at Greenwich are much more likely to be the work of Vanbrugh than of Wren; and it is obvious that similar probabilities in regard to Vanbrugh and Hawksmore exist in the case of other late works. The second consideration concerns holograph drawings. Here we are on very sure ground, for Wren's style of draughtsmanship is distinct and personal. The *Wren Society* has published his original sketches for Hampton Court (1689) and Greenwich (before 1702) and these give us as clear a view as we could wish of the orientation of the architect's mind as it advanced into old age. The sketches are void of any suggestion of drama; they are the precise, modest statements of a scientific mind (Plate XVII). And yet the *raw material* of the designs is quite definitely Baroque; there are the cartouches and trophies, the giant orders and interrupted rhythms. That the contemporary Italian manner had fascinated Wren ever since he had the tantalizing five-minutes' view of Bernini's design for the Louvre in 1665 is perfectly clear. But it is clear, too, that he looked at this Baroque work with the eyes not of a Baroque artist but of an English intellectual. It fascinated him, but he could not identify himself with it. Hence both the success and the failure of his later work. Success in that he retained that marvellous objectivity which enabled him to make the best possible use of the materials and craftsmen which came to his hand; and failure, in that his work falters between the static unity of the 'high' Renaissance and the dynamic, emotional unity of the Baroque.

If the theory of Wren's mental constitution put forward in this essay were made the basis of a critique of his works, one building would stand out as by far the most satisfactory embodiment of his conception of architecture; that building is Trinity College Library, Cambridge, designed in 1676 (Plate xviii). There we have the 'essential Wren' in epitome; the adventurousness of the empirical approach, with a minimum of psychological inconsistency; and a loving appreciation of the Roman syntax, without artificiality or false compromise.[1]

No other building of Wren's achieves this satisfying synthesis of all his finest qualities. In the City churches, although we can admire his genius as a geometrical, three-dimensional planner, we must confess that often the articulation is confused by insensitive modelling (especially, as Soane[2] observed, in St Stephen, Walbrook). In his towers and spires we can see the triumphs—and the disasters—of a fancy controlled empirically, not intuitively. In St Paul's success and failure are inextricably

---

[1] Both aspects are admirably reflected in the famous letter from Wren to Dr Barrow (*Wren Society*, v, p 32).

[2] In his RA lectures.

woven, although the ultimate grandeur of the whole, as a sheer monument of intellectual self-reliance, is beyond all criticism or praise.

The vein of psychological inconsistency which runs through all Wren's work is no mere falling short, on the part of an individual, of standards which abler men would have attained. Historically, Wren's failure is as significant as his success, for both are the product of that tyranny of intellect which the 17th century established and from which almost every great artist of the 18th century was in conscious or unconscious revolt. It was in England that the tyranny reached its most formidable pitch, with the result that English thought became the fulcrum of European philosophy till the time of Kant. English architecture, while sharing with the other arts the profound disadvantages of intellectual domination, was nevertheless caught up in the ascent of greatness which belonged to the period and one of whose highest peaks was the mind of Christopher Wren.

IV

John Wood and the English Town-Planning Tradition

THERE IS, in the City of Bath, a group of streets of houses whose arrangement and architecture, taken together, represent something unique in the urbanism of Europe. The group consists of Queen Square, Gay Street, the Circus and the Royal Crescent. The planners and architects were, as everyone knows, John Wood the elder, followed by his son of the same name. This combination of street-architecture has been enormously praised, but I do not think it has occurred to anybody to inquire how it came into existence—how the combination formed itself in the mind of the first John Wood and what sources he and his son drew upon for their inspiration. The lives of the Woods have never been written and they never seem to have moved into the limelight of 18th-century gossip. On the other hand, the elder Wood left several printed and MS works of quite imposing dimensions and with the help of these and a knowledge of the architectural events of his period it is possible at least to sketch the 'case-history' of the Bath phenomenon.

The elder John Wood is said to have been born in 1705, a date not well authenticated and, in fact, not credible.[1] For if he *was* born in that year it means that by the time he was 17 he had

---

[1] The only evidence is an obituary in *Bath Journal*, May 27th, 1754, giving his age in that year as 49. The notice in *Gents. Mag.* is probably copied from this.

completed a large country house and a church in East Cheshire[1] and that before he had attained his majority he was already living in London, conducting some business in Yorkshire, fully apprised of the state of affairs in Bath and sufficiently a man of the world to approach two Bath landowners in London with ambitious schemes for speculative development. All the evidence points to an earlier birth-date. Even so, it was certainly a very young man who, in 1727, began the architectural transformation of Bath.

Until lately, we knew nothing whatever about the beginning of Wood's career. But some remarkably interesting evidence has come to light and a suspicion that he must at one period of his life have been active in London has been copiously confirmed, not only by some researches in London itself, but by the disclosure that in the Henry E. Huntington Library in California, USA, there is a collection of papers relating to the Duke of Chandos and his building ventures, in which Wood's London activities are mentioned. I have not had an opportunity of seeing these papers, but Dr Collins Baker, the Director, has very kindly sent me some relevant excerpts from them.

John Wood was evidently a Yorkshireman and the son of a man in the building trade there. He was taken up by a Yorkshire gentleman, Robert Benson of Bramham, who pursued a political career in London, became Lord Chancellor in the Tory Government of 1710 and was raised to the Peerage as Baron Bingley in 1713. Bingley employed Giacomo Leoni to build his house at Bramham, completed (according to *Vitruvius*

---

[1] Capesthorne, for John Ward Esq. I am indebted to Mr Stanley A. Harris of Liverpool for communicating to me his discovery of Wood's authorship of this building. Mr Harris has suggested some excellent reasons for believing that Wood was early associated with Leoni, who besides having been employed by Wood's patron, Lord Bingley, executed two important commissions in the same area as Capesthorne.

Britannicus) in 1710. Later we find him among a group of Tory peers who interested themselves in the London building development constituting Cavendish Square, and this Square, as we shall see in a moment, played some part in John Wood's architectural beginnings.

Wood himself, in his *Essay towards a Description of Bath*, tells us nothing about all this. He does tell us, however, that in the summer of 1725 he was in Yorkshire and it was there that he drew out his first plans for Bath. He knew, evidently, all about Bath. He knew that a subscription had been opened for making the Avon navigable from Bristol to Bath; he knew about the *Improvement Acts* of 1707 and 1721; and he must have realized, too, that under the rule of Richard Nash, already 51 and a Bathonian of twenty years' standing, the city was on the threshold of immense prosperity. But John Wood was not yet Wood of Bath. He was based on London, and I find in the St Marylebone rate-books that a John Wood was living in Oxford Street from 1725 to 1727 inclusive.[1] The house thus rated will have been a stone's-throw from Cavendish Square and, as Wood tells us himself that 1727 was the year that he left London, I think it most probable that this is our man. So he was living in Oxford Street, right between the two liveliest centres of building progress in the London of the time—the Cavendish-Harley estate on the north and the Grosvenor estate on the south. The buildings on these estates—especially the two great squares (Cavendish and Grosvenor) unquestionably provided the source of John Wood's first inspirations in the building of Bath.

On the Cavendish-Harley estate, belonging to the Earl of Oxford, Cavendish Square had been divided, as I have said,

---

[1] In 1725 he pays 5s. poor-rate; this, at 3d. in the £, implies a rateable value of £20 a year. In 1727 he pays 7s. 6d. He was not rated in 1726.

between a group of Tory peers. Lord Bingley, Wood's patron, was one of them, and built a great house there, on the west side. The whole of the north side had been taken by the Duke of Chandos, the famous paymaster-general who at first proposed to build something in the nature of a palace, but later (after the South Sea Bubble) reduced his project to two isolated houses at the east and west corners.[1] Chandos employed many builders and architects, but principally a very able man called Edward Shepherd,[2] whose name is still pronounced by Londoners when they speak of Shepherd's Market. Chandos also employed, probably on the recommendation of his friend Lord Bingley, a much younger architect—John Wood.[3]

In 1727, the names of Chandos, Shepherd and Wood are inextricably involved, both in London and Bath. In Bath, the Duke of Chandos built the group of six houses still known as Chandos Buildings, and here his architect was John Wood— those were his first Bath buildings. Shepherd, the designer of the Cavendish Square houses, was instructed by the Duke to inspect his work at Bath. While in London, on the other hand, Wood, in 1728, was asked for an estimate for 'carrying on and

[1] These houses were not, as often stated, wings of the proposed mansion. I regret having fallen a victim to this error in the first edition of my *Georgian London*, 1945.

[2] d. 1747, not 1745 as in A.P.S. *Dictionary*, where the only biographical notice of him is to be found.

[3] Dr Collins Baker tells me that on Feb. 5, 1726-7, Wood was in London working for Bingley. On April 21, he was 'at Lord Bingley's', evidently in London. In 1728, Chandos, speaking of his employment of Wood, said that he was 'willing to encourage a young Man just coming into the world'. On the other hand, in the same year, speaking of a disadvantageous contract Wood had made for himself, he says, that Wood had 'been so long versed in such sort of business'; though he may have meant to convey simply that he had been 'bred up' from very early years under Lord Bingley.

finishing' one of Shepherd's houses in Cavendish Square.[1] It is obviously all one party. And if the original leases of Wood's Mews, which lie off Grosvenor Square, could be consulted, it would perhaps be found that Wood of Bath, no less than Shepherd, has his memorial in the gazetteer of modern London.

That Edward Shepherd's buildings provided Wood with his first models for imitation seems probable if we cross Oxford Street and examine a speculation in which Shepherd was involved on his own account in Grosvenor Square at exactly the same time (Plate XXI). Here, on the north side, he had taken a number of sites and was attempting what had not been attempted before—to give a row of houses the architectural unity and character which belongs to a palace or a public building. In other words, he was erecting a symmetrical block of houses having in the centre an attached portico surmounted by a pediment. Which is to say that he was doing exactly what John Wood was to do, a very few years later, on the north side of Queen Square, Bath (Plate XXII).

Unfortunately, Shepherd's project in Grosvenor Square was spoilt by his failure to acquire the whole of the sites on the north side; and when his group of houses was built, with the portico a long way westward of the axis of the Square, it failed to make a very good impression. Somebody[2] called it 'a wretched attempt at something extraordinary'. However, the *intention* was of the greatest importance, for here is not only the authentic London prototype of one of Bath's principal monuments, but the first realization of the idea of grouping town

[1] In this same year, according to Dr Baker, 'four several Estimates for Houses in London' are mentioned in Wood's accounts; and he expressed himself anxious to show 'what the Bath Stone wou'd do in Town'.

[2] Ralph, *A Critical Review of the Public Buildings . . . in and about London.*

houses in symmetrical blocks—an idea of basic importance in the whole development of English town-planning.[1]

So it now appears that John Wood, who has always been thought of as a wonderfully original provincial, was nothing of the kind. The architecture he brought to Bath in 1727 was the fruit of at least two years' intensive London experience. Palladian Bath was born in the purlieus of London's Oxford Street.

However, we have only arrived at the beginning of the Bath story and the denouement of Wood's ambitions and genius remains to be traced. He tells us in his book[2] that when he returned from Yorkshire to London in 1725, he brought with him two plans. One was for ground at the north-west corner of the City of Bath belonging to Robert Gay, 'an eminent surgeon in Hatton Garden', Treasurer of St Bartholomew's Hospital and, incidentally, MP for Bath. The other was for ground on the north-east, belonging to the Earl of Essex. Wood seems to have regarded these two projects as alternatives, for in each of them he introduced features which could hardly be duplicated in the same city. These features are very interesting. Perfectly independent of what he was to derive from Shepherd's work, they give us our first insight into Wood's mind, which, we see at once, was not that of a mere superior artisan such as his relations with the Duke of Chandos might make him seem to be.

In each design (he tells us) I proposed to make a Grand Place of Assembly, to be called the *Royal Forum of Bath*; another Place, no less magnificent, for the Exhibition of Sports, to be called the *Grand Circus;* and a third Place, of equal State with either of the Former, for the Practice of

[1] Shepherd's design very likely owes something to Colin Campbell's first design for Wanstead House, as engraved in *Vitruvius Britannicus*, Vol. I, Pl. 22 (Plate xx).

[2] *Essay towards a description of Bath*, 1742, 2nd ed. 1749; reissued, 1765.

medicinal Exercises, to be called the *Imperial Gymnasium* of the City, from a Work of that Kind, taking its Rise at first in *Bath*, during the Time of the *Roman* Emperors.

The immediately striking thing about these proposals is their grotesque impracticability. The Forum one may perhaps indulgently interpret simply as a Square, like Cavendish or Grosvenor Squares (hardly 'grand places of assembly', however); the Circus, 'for the exhibition of sports', bears no conceivable relationship to any known aspect of 18th-century life; while the Gymnasium where the gouty invalids were to practise their 'medicinal exercises' suggests such a quaint picture that one is tempted to wonder if, after all, the date 1705 is not correct for the architect's birth, and these fantastic proposals are not those of a young aspirant just out of his 'teens.

What induced this obviously practical and competent young builder to put forward this trinity of impossibles? Well, presumably, he had been reading. Although nothing Roman stood above ground in his time, he had discovered that Bath was a Roman city; and he had built up for himself a very lively picture of what a Roman city ought to be like. Lively rather than accurate, for Wood's Forum, his Circus and his Gymnasium bear, in their intended functions, as little relationship to ancient Rome as to Georgian England. Vitruvius, whom Wood cannot have missed and with whom he was certainly familiar at a later date, admittedly describes a forum; but he has only a passing reference to circuses (making it clear, however, that the Roman circus was not circular) and on gymnasia he is silent. Vitruvius, in fact, is not the answer, and one searches in vain for some volume sufficiently romantic and ill-informed to have suggested to John Wood the three propositions on which he hung these plans which occupied him in the summer of 1725.

Probably no such book exists, for one indisputable characteristic of John Wood was his extraordinary capacity for inventing history. The man who, seventeen years later, was capable of identifying the mythical Bladud with the mythical Abaris, of making him (them) a disciple and colleague of Pythagoras and the son of a friend of the prophet Haggai, would, at an earlier age, have no compunction in presuming that a Forum was a fashionable parade-ground, a circus a circular amphitheatre in which sports were held and a gymnasium a kind of exercise-ground for hypochondriacs. Wood's historical imagination was staggering. In his *Essay towards a description of Bath* we learn, in addition to this surprising history of Bladud, that Bath was the chief seat of Apollo and that the god in person was wor-shipped there by the Druids who—believe it or not—established a University at Stanton Drew. Such vigorous romancing as this was, however, extremely important in its way. It was the cata-lytic agent which released John Wood's imaginative power. Every scheme he proposed is coloured by the feeling that he is restoring antique grandeur; every Corinthian column he erec-ted was a step towards the restoration of Aquae Sulis, that miniature Rome where philosophy had flourished under the personal aegis of Apollo. I am sure that nothing would have surprised the architect less than to meet a centurion in Gay Street or to find a toga hanging in his front hall at Batheaston.

Wood's original plans, which he brought from Yorkshire in 1725, lay under consideration for a year. He had to visit York-shire twice in the summer of 1726 and it was not till November of that year that he became Robert Gay's agent, empowered to do business with anybody who would build the long street of houses eventually to be known as Gay Street. In 1727, Wood was up to his neck in Bath building schemes. He moved down from London and took up his residence there. He had in hand, apart from the Avon navigation scheme, at least four separate

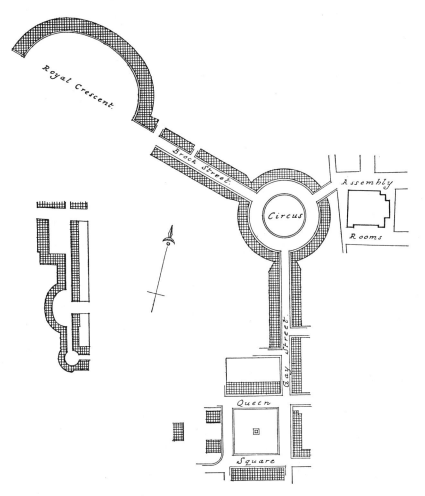

FIG. 6. Queen Square, the Circus and Royal Crescent, Bath, with (left) America Square, the Crescent and Circus, Minories, London, to the same scale

projects—the Gay estate, the Duke of Chandos's houses, an extension for Ralph Allen's house and schemes for a hospital and other buildings commissioned by Humphry Thayer, a Com-

95

missioner of Excise[1] and a friend of both Gay and Allen—and it is interesting to note that these four projects (with the possible exception of the Allen house) were all commissioned *in London*. This underlines the fact that Wood was a Londoner, at least in a limited sense, and not the local product which some writers would have us believe. He descended on Bath fully equipped as a London architect and the architecture he brought to Bath was the metropolitan Palladianism of Lord Burlington and his circle. The houses he built in Bath were, apart from the liberal use of stone, London houses.

Wood came to Bath not only as an architect but as a contractor. He had sent down an army of workmen before him—masons from Yorkshire, carpenters, joiners and plasterers from London and elsewhere and, for the Avon scheme—in which, by the way, he was early concerned—navvies who had been engaged on the Chelsea waterworks. And when he found that Gay was becoming nervous about the effect his speculation might have on his constituents, he threw up his agency and leased some of the ground himself—enough to start building the east side of Queen Square.

Queen Square was the first component of Wood's Bath plan to be built, but it does not represent any of the three features comprised in the Yorkshire plan. Queen Square was an extemporization, strongly reminiscent, as we have seen, of what had lately been happening in Cavendish Square and Grosvenor Square in London. The idea behind the design was, as I have said, the same as Edward Shepherd's—to group ordinary town houses in such a way as to give the effect of a single palace. This idea Wood realized on the north side of the Square, where his fine block of houses with its pedimented centre and end pavilions, its Corinthian columns and pilasters, certainly has

[1] *Gents. Mag.* 1737, p 767.

the air of a palace or even a town hall. The east and south sides of the Square he built in a much plainer style, while on the west side he copied almost exactly what Shepherd had done for the Duke of Chandos in Cavendish Square; which is to say that he built two separate houses at either end of the site, leaving the centre open. This centre was to form the fore-court of a third house, set back from the Square. Chandos, so far as we know, never proposed building a third house in Cavendish Square, though to do so is such an obvious way of completing the scheme that it must surely have been discussed. In any case the lateral houses in Queen Square obviously derive from the London counterparts which Wood knew so well.

Queen Square, begun in 1729, was finished seven years later. Meanwhile, in 1730, Wood became involved, with Thayer, in a building scheme for the Abbey Orchard. This time he produced his project for a Circus, but although it was approved in Bath it was obstructed by some interested parties in London. So the Circus was abandoned for the moment and a Forum proposed instead. This was actually begun in 1739, two years after Thayer's death. The blocks of houses known as South Parade remain today the one executed part of Wood's Royal Forum; and the rather dismal sunk tract of allotments which you see on the right as you go into Bath from the station occupy the intended site of the Forum itself—that 'grand place of assembly' which was to revive the social glories of the city of Apollo.

After 1742, the year in which Wood published his own description of his works in Bath, it is not easy to follow his activities in detail. We know that he built the Exchange at Bristol, the Grammar School at Bath and several country houses and we know that he published books on architecture and archaeology. We know that Gay died in 1738 but that Gay

Street began creeping up the hill in the 1750s and that on February 18, 1754, Wood laid with his own hands the foundation stone of the King's Circus (Plate XXIV). Three months after that great event he was dead.

After nearly thirty years of labour Wood saw two-thirds of his favourite dream coming true. The Royal Forum and the Grand Circus had both been well begun. Only the Imperial Gymnasium had failed altogether to find a place in the realization of the expanded City. It is remarkable what dogged loyalty to an aesthetic obsession will achieve.

If we enter the Circus at Bath with the terms of Wood's Yorkshire project in our minds, the first thing we shall notice is that it is not, and obviously never was, intended 'for the exhibition of sports'. It is simply a residential enclosure, consisting of 33 identical houses, with a circular plot of garden in the middle.[1] However, the circus idea is not limited to the circular plan, for the whole composition is, roughly speaking, a miniature model of a Roman amphitheatre—turned inside out; and it is, of course, obvious that when Wood used the word 'circus', what he meant was 'amphitheatre'. And the amphitheatre which he had in mind, was the greatest of all amphitheatres—the one begun by Vespasian in the 1st century AD—in fact, the Colosseum. Wood never saw the Colosseum. Perhaps he never saw even an adequate representation of it. Indeed, one's impression is that his notion of that vast building was obtained from the cheap engravings and bird's-eye restorations published in Italy and distributed far and wide in his time (Plate XIX). Those restorations, in their careless way, show the Colosseum as a tiny circular building (it is really elliptical), a mere ringlet sited among the other tiny monuments—temples, baths and obelisks—which fill the picture.

[1] This was an afterthought. Originally, the whole area was cobbled.

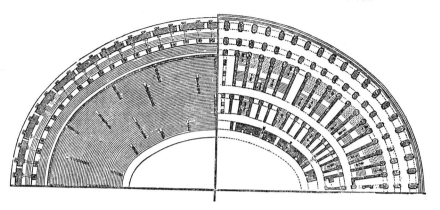

FIG. 7. Half-plan of the Colosseum. From Fergusson's *History of Architecture*

Wood's amiable vagueness as to historical fact allowed him to conjure up a Colosseum which was of quite moderate dimensions and circular on plan. To build such a building in Bath—to fill no matter what function—was one of his ideals. Nor was the ideal relinquished when it dawned on him that the functions proper to such a conception—gladiatorial combats, for example—had no appeal for audiences in an elegant 18th-century spa. Having built eight houses in Queen Square in the guise of a palace, why not build thirty-three more in the guise of an amphitheatre? And since, for a variety of reasons, it was convenient for the houses to face into and not away from the arena, why not simply turn the whole thing inside out? This is what he did, and, of course, the 18th century was sufficiently well informed to recognize it. Hence Smollett, in *Humphry Clinker*, 'The Circus is a pretty bauble and looks like Vespasian's amphitheatre turned outside in.'

To us, the trick seems rather less obvious. But that is only because the circus as a component of urban planning is now

more familiar to us than the antiquities of Rome. But John
Wood's Circus was the first. It was the pioneer of all circuses,
from Bath to Piccadilly, from Exeter to Edinburgh. It introduced this connotation of the word into our language—a connotation, as we have seen, based on a misconception. Had
Wood been less of a scholar he would never have been inspired
to build a circus at all. Had he been more of a scholar, an exact
knowledge of the extent and nature of the Roman Colosseum
would probably have extinguished the suggestiveness of the
romantic half-knowledge which was his inspiration.

The Circus stands on its own merits, a delightful architectural creation. Yet to critics too conscious of its giant prototype
it seemed far otherwise. To Smollett it was 'a pretty bauble';
and Sir John Soane, in 1809, told his Royal Academy students[1]
that although the Circus at Bath 'may please us by its prettiness
and a sort of novelty, as a rattle pleases a child . . . the area is so
small and the height of each of the orders is so diminutive that
the general appearance of the entire building is mean, gloomy
and confined'. And Soane pressed home the criticism by showing
a diagram in which the Bath Circus is sitting humbly in the arena
of the Colosseum (Plate XXIII). But such criticism is, I think,
prejudiced. The Colosseum was built for an audience of perhaps
45,000 people; the Bath Circus for the residence of thirty-
three gentlemen and their families. Comparatively, the Circus
is perhaps a bauble, and a very lovable one; but more
than that—the persistence of the conception in English planning
proves that Wood had created something of considerable value.

But before we go on to consider the repercussions of Wood's
Circus in the century which followed its foundation we must
visit that great monument of domestic planning which adjoins it
—the Royal Crescent (Plate XXV). This was begun by a syndi-

[1] Sir J. Soane, *Lectures on Architecture*, ed. A. T. Bolton, 1929, p 160.

cate in 1767, thirteen years after the death of the elder John Wood, and we shall never know whether the strikingly original idea which it embodies was conceived by the father or the son. Whichever it was, the plan of the Crescent evolved in the most amusing way out of the Circus. I have represented the Circus as a miniature Colosseum made into a circular, instead of an elliptical building, and then turned inside out. The Crescent is likewise a Colosseum; but it has retained its elliptical plan, been turned inside out and then cut in half. The idea of *half-a-Colosseum* will have emerged naturally out of the division of the Circus into segments to admit streets. The restoration of the proper Colosseum curvature was a happy inspiration suggested, perhaps, by the nature of the site. In any case, I have no doubt that that was the process by which the prototype of all architectural crescents came into being. Such was the fecundity of the 18th century's amateur archaeology!

The Crescent, however, echoes the Colosseum only in its plan. The treatment of the elevation is quite different. The three ranks of orders, standing over each other in the Circus, are abandoned and the architect reverts to the ordonnance of the London house, as Inigo Jones had fixed it 140 years before—that is to say, a plain ground-storey acting as the base or podium of an order running through the two upper storeys. Indeed, it is very likely that the design of the Crescent was suggested by Inigo Jones's treatment of the west side of Lincoln's Inn Fields (Plate XXVI), where that architect ordained a continuous parade of Ionic pilasters from end to end and where, in Wood's time, all that was executed of that parade still existed.[1] This treatment

[1] Even if Wood did not see this London work, he would know it from the engraving in *Vitruvius Britannicus*, 1715, vol I, Pl 50. In vol II of the same work, Pl 100, Campbell gives a design of his own, 'in the palatial style', where the same theme is extended to eleven bays.

gives the Crescent a majestic scale, placing it beyond the criticism of those who found the Circus niggling. Soane, for instance, greatly admired the Crescent.[1]

Over and above the individual architectural qualities of these two compositions is a quality which is, perhaps, incidental but which greatly enhances their beauty as a piece of planning—that is, their successful combination in relation to the site and to the rest of the layout to which they belong. Like almost all English planning schemes of the past, the Bath scheme was empirical—an affair of continuous extemporization. Wood's Yorkshire plan must have been exploded the moment he started to build; and from 1727 onwards he can never have looked much farther ahead than the finishing of the particular piece of ground where his men were at work. As we have seen, he seized the opportunity to build his 'forum' in quite another part of the city from that where he had begun Queen Square; and he only made it a 'forum' because he was not allowed to make it a circus. Eventually he placed his circus at the top of Gay Street where it confirms and crowns the whole of that area of Bath. Then, from the Circus, Brock Street and the Crescent jut out like a giant sickle, while the third street which leads out of the Circus—Bennett Street—goes directly to the Assembly Rooms. Thus, the Circus is a rotunda, the hub of a three-spoked wheel whose mobility makes the whole plan hang together. The introduction of a fourth street would have spoiled it by making each of the segments too small, destroying the sweep of the curve and suggesting a rigid, stationary cross-plan—a mere Oxford Circus in fact. The three streets, each leading to entirely different incidents in the whole plan and branching out at angles not easily determined by the eye, give meaning to the Circus without injuring its gravity.

[1] *Lectures*, loc. cit.

This easy, natural, almost casual, planning is really a by-product of the Woods' achievements at Bath; it arises from the collision of intention with circumstance. It is not wholly the Woods' creation, but a creation of the contours, chances and necessities of Bath. Nevertheless, its general applicability was immediately appreciated, at least by one English architect—the younger George Dance. Now, Dance, who succeeded his father as clerk of the works to the Corporation of the City of London in 1767, has every right to be considered next in succession to the Woods in the English town-planning tradition. In a variety of planning schemes—some executed, some unfortunately not—he showed that the particular Bath achievement possessed a general applicability of great value; in fact, it is due to him that both circuses and crescents became *types* and not unique instances.

As early as 1768, Dance had introduced the circus into a plan he made for roads in Southwark and Lambeth, linking up the Thames bridges. Some of these roads he caused to meet in the still existing St George's Circus, where he placed a stone obelisk in the centre (1771). Here, for the first time, the circus was used as a monumental form of crossing; Oxford and Piccadilly Circuses were foreshadowed.

Then, in 1769, the year of the completion of the Bath crescent, Dance was planning, in the true Wood spirit, the area now covered by Finsbury Square. These plans were discarded, but at the very same time (from 1768) he was laying out the most curious piece of miniature town-planning in London—the combination consisting of America Square and the adjoining Crescent and Circus, in a lowly area of the City, just off the Minories. All America Square has been rebuilt, but in the 'Crescent' and 'Circus' (as they are still proudly labelled) some of the original houses survive bearing witness to London's first adoption of the great Bath idea.[1]

Then, still from Dance's hand, followed Alfred Place, off Tottenham Court Road, where two crescents facing each other on the axis of a short, wide street survive now only in the shape of their sites.

Dance's masterpiece as a town-planner would certainly have been the great scheme he designed for Lord Chancellor Camden's property in St Pancras—the area now covered by Camden Town. The plan was engraved, and three copies have survived among the Dance drawings in the Soane Museum. Designed, presumably, soon after 1791, it closely reflects the Bath plan, though adapted to wholly different circumstances. There are two great units. One is a circus; the other is not a crescent, but a crescent multiplied by two, or in other words, a complete Colosseum. And, as if to confirm our suspicion that Wood's original Crescent was a Colosseum -cut-in-half, Dance replacing the missing half actually calls his structure the 'Camden Coliseum'!

The history of circuses and crescents in the towns of Britain would be a curious work and will probably one day be written. Here we are only looking at the outlines of a tradition and must be content with reviewing a few significant examples. We shall find that after their first appearance in Bath the circus and the crescent took rather different courses. The circus never repeated its original success as a great residential focus. Possibly there was *something* in Soane's criticism that it was 'gloomy and confined'; possibly squares have the advantage over circuses of admitting more variety in the treatment of their four sides; and straight walls are, of course, always less costly to build than

[1] I am grateful to Mr T. A. Manning for communicating the results of his research in the City records.

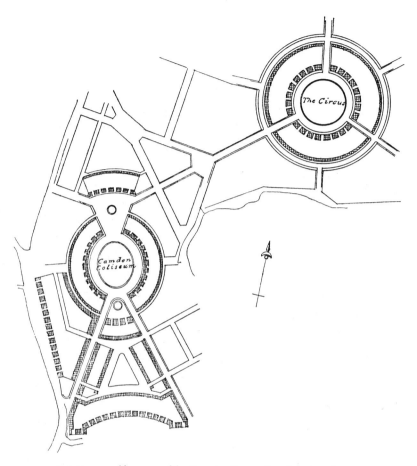

FIG. 8. Proposed lay-out of the Camden Estate, London, by George
Dance the younger

curved walls. Anyway, I can think of no other circus in Britain
in any way comparable to the Bath prototype. Circuses, so-
called, fall into roughly two categories. Either they are, in
effect, double Crescents, like the Camden Coliseum in Dance's
project, or they are circular spaces at the crossing of two main

roads, small in scale and consisting, in fact, of nothing but four curved splays on four corner blocks. Such is Dance's St George's Circus; and such were Oxford Circus and Piccadilly Circus as Nash built them.

The Circus as a double crescent consists usually of two facing segments or ellipses; an excellent example of the latter type was Bedford Circus at Exeter (Plate XXIX), built from 1775 onwards and utterly destroyed by enemy action in 1942; there are others at Greenwich, Edinburgh and elsewhere, but we may dismiss them for now as belonging to the crescent *genus*. The Circus as a crossing is more important. This theme, introduced, as we have seen, by Dance, reached its highest importance when John Nash, in 1811, making his gigantic plan to link up Regent's Park and St James's Park by means of Regent Street, took Wood's idea of the circus and used it in the Dance manner. At three points in this Royal Mile he proposed circuses: at Piccadilly, at Oxford Street and at the Marylebone Road. One of his reasons for these circuses was that they camouflaged the change of character as one crossed from south of Oxford Street to north of Oxford Street or from south to north of Euston Road.[1] This was a selling-point in the plan's favour, as everything depended on attracting fashionable life northward beyond its conventional boundaries. But Nash's circuses, like Wood's, were also architectural show-pieces of some consequence. Piccadilly Circus had panelled elevations in what we think of as the 'Regency' style; Oxford Circus had Corinthian pilasters. And the northernmost Circus, at the crossing of Euston Road, was to be one of the largest things of its kind in existence, with an Ionic colonnade all along the ground floor. The objections to circuses, whatever they were, operated against this one, and when it was half-built the project was modified and the com-

[1] See my *John Nash*, 1935, p 125.

pleted portion christened Park Crescent. As such it still exists (though badly bombed) and its noble simplicity and fine detail make it a close rival to either of the Woods' monuments at Bath.

Thus we see that the original idea contained in the Bath Circus was side-tracked; the circus became, in principle, a development at a cross-roads and was never again built as a great residential precinct. Today it survives in the familiar traffic 'roundabout'.

The crescent proved very much more successful. We have already seen how Dance brought it to London. The greatest rival of the Bath example is, however, the Crescent at Buxton (Plate xxvii), built for the fifth Duke of Devonshire by John Carr of York in 1779–81. Here we have something more than an echo of the Bath prototype. Here is a critical restatement of the theme by an architect as able and learned as the Woods. In describing the Bath Circus, I suggested that the elevational treatment probably derived from Inigo Jones's scheme for the west side of Lincoln's Inn Fields; the motif is, in fact, identical. The Buxton Crescent likewise goes back to the proto-master of English classicism; Carr, however, was thinking not of Lincoln's Inn Fields but of Covent Garden (Plate xxviii). For here are Jones's so-called 'piazzas' of Covent Garden re-edited in crescent form, all as correct in scale and detail as Jones himself could have wished.

The Buxton Crescent, however, stands rather apart from the great army of crescents which sprang up all over the country from about 1780 onwards. They were not always as ambitious or as deeply studied; the crescent, in fact, unlike the circus, got married into the vernacular and became everybody's property. It ceased immediately to be 'half-a-colosseum' and became— well, just exactly what we think of when we use the word

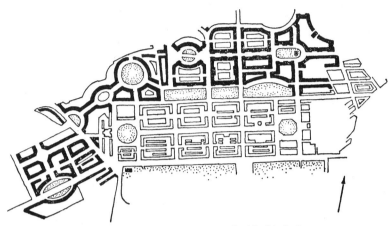

FIG. 9. Edinburgh New Town, showing (in black) the later extensions, planned under the influence of the Woods' work at Bath

'crescent' in an architectural sense, a row of houses set out on a curve. Bath's second Crescent—Camden Crescent, built for the same Lord Camden who sponsored Dance's Camden Town project—is merely a shallow bay of Corinthian houses (1793). Bristol can show a most eccentric variation in Berkeley Crescent—high and narrow, instead of broad and low. The Crescents of Exeter are very slight segments of circles; and perhaps the subtlest of the crescents is the one at Shrewsbury, a tiny row of houses with just the suspicion of a curve. At Brighton the crescent arrived in 1798 and at Royal Crescent in that town we find it interpreted in black glazed brick with bay-windows and balconies (Plate xxx).

After Waterloo, the crescent theme became so popular that few towns are without their examples and no large estate plan was considered complete without one or two such features. At Edinburgh, the three principal extensions of the New Town, laid out from 1815 onwards and shown black in the accompanying diagram, are rich in crescents: they comprise five single crescents and two double crescents as well as a large circus. Here the architecture (mostly by W. H. Playfair, Thomas Hamilton and Gillespie Graham) is incredibly stiff and dour; the siting, in relation to the natural contours, is infelicitous and the junctions between the three lay-outs are hideous. The happy flexibility of the Bath idea has been missed, but there remains, none the less, a certain grandeur about this part of the Edinburgh scene.

Well sited, crescents are irresistible. On steep sites they sink comfortably into the hill-side; by the sea they give a happy suggestion of panoramic vision; and where there is neither hill nor sea they still possess an elegance and humanity denied to the straight terrace or the awesome and too-embracing circus.

The crescent tradition died with those of the square and the terrace. All three were killed by the accession to power of that proud individualism which sees a domain beyond each garden gate and holds that a castle is still a castle even when only semi-detached. The suburbia which Mr Richards has described so well in his recent book[1] had no room for squares or crescents and the gifts of the two John Woods to our national town-planning tradition survived them by less than a hundred years.[2]

But they were and still are gifts of great value. It was not only these two shapes in themselves which exerted their influence throughout Britain, but the way in which they were used. Unconsciously, perhaps, the Woods realized the profound unimportance of symmetry in a town-plan—a lesson which some of our more academic planners have, it seems, still to learn.

[1] J. M. Richards, *The Castles on the Ground*, 1946.

[2] A pathetic remnant of the tradition may be seen at Royal Circus, West Norwood, SE27, where a circus was laid out on a glorious site in about 1860. It must have failed utterly, for the adjacent houses are of the most wretched character and mostly comparatively recent in date. Another mid-Victorian circus, hardly more satisfactory, is Charleville Circus, SE26.

The Woods were at the same time practical and romantic; they had their feet on the ground and their heads in the clouds. They never tried to make Bath into a grand pattern because they knew that the man in the street never sees a town as a pattern but only as a perspective from the point where he happens to be. On the other hand, they knew that buildings, even when they are groups of quite ordinary houses, are capable of that heightened effect which constitutes monumental architecture. The wisdom of the Woods became the wisdom of their age and wherever you find good Georgian planning you find something which is traceable to their creations at Bath.

V

The Vision of J. M. Gandy

WHETHER THE art of architecture may enjoy an existence independent of execution or potential execution is a question which the great draughtsmen of the Baroque age have settled, though not absolutely beyond dispute. The creations of the Bibienas and of Piranesi do expand the art beyond the bounds of probability, though scarcely beyond those of possibility; and it seems as if the art of the architectural fantasy has merely a longer leash than the art which is fettered by convenience, statics and material resources. To retain the characteristics most essential to his *genre*, there are certain things which the creator of fantastic architecture may not do. He may not lose sight of scale. Once that is lost or even rendered ambiguous, his drawings become incapable of communication in architectural terms. Nor may he employ forms which have not some reference (however slight) to our experience of executed architecture; otherwise his work departs altogether from the architectural sphere and must look for its justification either to qualities residing in itself or to its usefulness as a representation of some formal organization which may be sculpture but cannot be architecture. But within these obvious limits the art of the architectural fantasy is valid and has some philosophic importance.

Architecture is a chained and fettered art. Far from being 'frozen music', it is an art constantly attempting to realize in solid, stable form those effects which music is able to conjure up in an instant—effects which succeed each other rapidly during the progress of a musical work. Music can attain the colossal in a way which, in architecture, only the rarest opportunities render even remotely possible. Music can, in a few moments, admit us through vast portals into avenues, courts and halls of infinite extent and variety. Music can suddenly raise up an entire structure and, by the device of modulation, lift it on to a podium, abruptly recess its façades and turn them bodily into the sunshine. Music can etch silhouettes ten times more intricate than those of Dresden or London City, repeat them, increase or reduce them, hurl them into the distance or bring them before us in precise detail. Most of the essentials of architecture—mass, rhythm, texture, outline—are within music's power. Almost, the two arts are the same art, the one able to express nearly everything which the imagination is capable of conceiving, the other bound by the rigours of economy and use.

But has not architecture its own special attributes, which are no part of the world which it is music's function to create and recreate? Certainly it has. Architecture, by virtue of its actual limitations, can exploit our capacity for dramatizing ourselves, for heightening the action of ordinary life; it can increase man's psychological stature to an angel's. All this it does through its irrevocable attachment to function. The dramatizing of movements appropriate to architecture (and impossible without architecture), movements like entering through a door, looking out of a window—mounting steps or walking on a terrace—is something with which music has nothing to do. Here is architecture's special province which on the one hand constricts its movement and on the other intensifies its meaning.

Thus architecture is at once a developed art with functions unique to itself, and a restricted art with potentialities which it can never explore beyond a certain line, dictated by expediency, economics and statics. But when once we remove architecture from the arena of the solid and material, when once we resort to the arena of *representation*, we remove the weightiest and most obvious restrictions on imaginative flight. We are free at least to *depict* those things which architecture might do in certain circumstances—circumstances bounded only by the remotest confines of probability. Here is the sphere of the maker of architectural fantasies. He can make architecture approach towards the freedom of music. He can explore a great margin of territory—nearly virgin territory—capable of yielding architectural treasure, unique and enthralling.

It is curious, at first sight, how little work has been done in this territory and what relatively feeble work it is. With the exception of Piranesi, nobody has produced architectural fantasies which are greatly honoured as works of art; nor can one feel this to be due to a miscarriage of historic justice. The truth is, perhaps, that the fantasy demands too much of one man, for he must be both architect and graphic artist— and yet neither altogether. He must, in the first place, have the power to develop an architectural composition far beyond the region where he is subject to the discipline of function and the test of experience; and, in the second place, be able to portray his design in such a way that the total result will be a single work of art in which architecture and draughtsmanship are inseparably united. It may be argued that the fantasy should logically be a joint work—that the architect should design the building and the draughtsman humbly and loyally portray it. Logical that may be, but the fact remains that no two artists of real power have ever united their efforts in this direction. Every artist desires to achieve finality in his own work. The goal at which the maker of fantasies aims is, inevitably, the final *representation* of his architectural ideas; the handing over to a draughtsman of working drawings of an unbuildable building would, it must be admitted, be a singularly discouraging proposition. A partnership in the creation of architectural fantasies is a possibility: in certain circumstances it might produce art of a high order. But such circumstances have never arisen.

The architectural fantasies which the centuries since the Renaissance have bequeathed to us are not, perhaps, among the greater products of artistic effort, but they have at least the interest of being products peculiar and distinct in their nature, belonging to that category of artistic effort whose scope we have just been trying to define. The Italians reached the greatest heights and Piranesi raised the art of the architectural fantasy to a level of tragic seriousness which has been the inspiration of most who have succeeded him in England, Piranesi's influence was great. Coleridge and De Quincey were among his admirers; architects like Robert Adam, the younger Dance and Robert Mylne knew him and learnt from him; and so did Soane. And the draughtsman whose work is the subject of this essay is in the descent of those who derived from Piranesi and strove, with varying success, to perform on his level.

Joseph Michael Gandy[1] was born in 1771, the son of a man employed at White's by the proprietor of the club, John Martindale. When James Wyatt rebuilt the club-house, Martindale showed him some of Gandy's sketches with the result that Wyatt took him, aged 15, into his office. Becoming a student at the Royal Academy, he received its Gold Medal in 1790, and in 1794 Martindale sent him to Italy, whither he travelled in the company of C. H. Tatham. Competing at the Academy of St Luke he was awarded a special medal, but his

[1] For particulars of Gandy's life, I am greatly indebted to Mr W. H. Gandy and Miss Rosalie Gandy, who kindly lent me a transcript of his letters and other papers.

sojourn in Italy was an anxious one, for the French armies were penetrating into the country and when supplies from home stopped, as a result of Martindale's bankruptcy in 1797, Gandy was in a sad way. Selling his medal and such clothes as he could, he made his way to Florence and there luckily fell in with a King's Messenger, known to his family, who brought him home.

In England, Gandy found his prospects excessively dim. Looking round for employment, he found a place in the office of John Soane, one of the few architects with many commissions on his hands. To Soane he remained constantly indebted for employment of one sort or another and for gifts and loans. He practised independently from about 1800, and in 1803 was elected ARA—a curious election, considering that he had not then shown a single executed work. In 1808 he undertook to tutor Soane's elder son and, in the following year, the two of them went to Liverpool, where Gandy had entered into a partnership. Quarrelling almost at once with his partner, he returned to town in 1810, by which time young Soane had committed himself to an unfortunate matrimonial engagement. In London, Gandy was constantly employed by the elder Soane to illustrate his designs, in those lavish water-colour perspectives of which the Soane Museum contains so many. Living in continual poverty, he declined to declare himself a bankrupt and in 1816 was in the Fleet Prison. But even here he industriously drew and there is no break in the stream of designs flowing year by year into the RA Exhibitions. Between 1789 and 1838 there are, in all, only three years when the catalogue gives no entries under his name. He showed no fewer than 112 pictures.

Of Gandy as a man, we know little, but perhaps enough to place him, roughly, as an individual. The eldest of three brothers who all made some mark in architecture, he started adult life conscious of being under-educated, nervously dependent on patronage, and ever suspicious of intrigue among his contemporaries. He married, probably in 1801, and had a family of nine children, this burden and the poverty it entailed increasing his dependence, his nervousness and horror of criticism. His work, very often and very naturally, seems to constitute an attempt to place before the world a personality very different from its author's—confident, powerful and full of learning. He was introspective, and attracted by religious theories; at one time much moved by the sermons of a non-conformist preacher, he later penned a confession in which his divinity is 'the sacred Aum or Om of all antiquity' and the individual a flying atom in a cosmos ruled by Natural Law, in which absolute Christian values may be descried by the discerning. One divines an uncommon integrity in the man's writings and actions, and his last surviving letters (dated 1837) do not suggest the shipwrecked mentality which one writer has recorded, apparently on hearsay. Portraits rarely tell us much. Suffice it to say than one by Sir William Allan[1] shows a sallow, fleshy face with dark hair and large dark eyes.

Gandy's work may be considered in three parts—the executed buildings, two very curious books of designs and the architectural fantasies. The buildings are the least important. They have little relation either to the designs in the books or to the fantasies and are but a slightly differentiated personal contribution to the architecture of the period. So we may dismiss them in few words.

The first executed building recorded was a boat-house on

[1] In the possession of Dr Eric Gandy, whose kind assistance in my inquiries it is a great pleasure to acknowledge. Dr Gandy has presented one of his ancestor's drawings to the Soane Museum.

Windermere for Sir J. Legard, shown at the RA in 1804.[1] Then came a more substantial commission—the narrow-fronted Phoenix Fire Office,[2] 1805, with façades to Charing Cross and Spring Gardens. Greek Doric and Ionic orders were applied to the ground and first floors of the Charing Cross Front, while in Spring Gardens the Ionic only appeared in pilaster form. The Greek Doric ground floor was to become a favourite theme of Gandy's.

A Public Bath at Lancaster (shown at the RA 1806) was executed and still exists,[3] but the Ball and Assembly Rooms at Liverpool (1810) were almost certainly not carried out.[4] Storrs Hall, Windermere, which he showed in 1808 and 1811, exists and is now an hotel. Gandy seems to have added wings at either end of an old square house and to have joined the wings by a Greek Doric loggia across one front and a verandah across the other. The result is a great blockish house with redeeming effects of recession and shadow. Gandy's familiarity with Soane is perhaps responsible for some features of the design.

In 1817 Gandy showed the Prison at Lancaster at the RA. This, formerly the Female Penitentiary, exists as part of the general rebuilding of the Castle in the Gothic style by Harrison

[1] The drawing exists, but I have not had an opportunity of seeing it.

[2] *Survey of London*, Vol XVI (St Martin-in-the-Fields, Part I). Demolished.

[3] It is No 43 Bath Street. Corry's *Hist. of Lancs*, 1825, rightly states that there is nothing remarkable about the exterior. When Gandy was tutoring young Soane, the latter produced a 'Design for a Public Bath' and showed it at the RA in 1811. The design, slightly eccentric and much scored with incised ornament, was, no doubt, more or less Gandy's. The drawing is in the Soane Museum.

[4] This was perhaps a project connected with the Town Hall, whose interior was gradually reconstructed after a fire in 1700 from designs by Wyatt, executed under Foster.

of Chester, from 1788 onwards. Begun in 1818 and finished in 1821, it is more severe and mason-like than Harrison's work, and has the rather melancholy interest of having been designed, in part, while its architect was himself residing in the Fleet Prison.

In the following year, 1818, Gandy sent to the RA a 'House at Sion Hill, Bath'. This is a very unusual building, known as Doric House, and situated on a steeply sloping corner site. Built for occupation by the painter, Thomas Barker, and containing a picture gallery, its dour Grecian character opposes the elongated elegance of the Bath tradition. The façade to the hill, with its superimposed Doric colonnades (a curious reminiscence of one of the Paestum temples) is certainly original and, like so much of Gandy's work, more than a little funereal.

A villa near Birmingham and a house at Leytonstone both shown in 1819, elude inquiry, but some houses in the Wandsworth Road (1825) still stand (Nos. 238–246), though partly hidden by the shops built later in their front gardens. They are most extraordinary specimens of their ordinary semi-detached stucco kind, inasmuch as they are decorated with the incised frets often used by Soane, but rarely with such insistent effect. A separate house in the same district, No. 363 Kennington Lane, is an even more striking example of this manner and must also, I feel sure, be by Gandy.

Other works by the architect are recorded[1] but they are small; and if they exist they are not likely to add much to our knowledge of his potentialities as a practising architect.

It is when we turn to the books of designs that we find in J. M. Gandy something much more than ordinarily interesting.

[1] According to the RA catalogues he was concerned with altering houses at Chipping Norton and Ince, and designed something for the Duke of Newcastle at Clumber. At Liverpool he built a billiard room.

The two books were published very close together—in fact, in the same year, 1805. They are called, quite simply, *Designs for Cottages* and *The Rural Architect*, but their motive and contents are less conventional than their titles.

The first book contains a preface in which the problem of rural architecture is set forth; and it is set forth not merely as an aesthetic but as a social problem. A great many books of cottage designs were published about this time;[1] their aim was usually to deal with the appearance of the cottage, from the point of view of the tasteful landlord, rather than its convenience or its potential appeal to those who were to live in it. Gandy takes as his starting-point a memorandum published by the Board of Agriculture in 1804 in which certain standards of structure and accommodation are laid down. On this basis, he designs cottages ordinary enough in plan and arrangement but perfectly extraordinary in outward appearance and, at first sight, by no means prepossessing. They are, indeed, so extraordinary as to suggest that their author was not an architect at all, but an eccentric layman or even some self-educated man of the soil. Now Gandy was not only an architect, but a most sophisticated architect, as his drawings and his Phoenix Fire Office had already shown. So we are bound to conclude that the crudity, the extreme harshness of these little designs is perfectly deliberate. What can it mean?

There is one possible interpretation which cannot, I think, be far from the truth. It is possible that Gandy was consciously attempting to do in architecture what Wordsworth had, some years previously, done in poetry—to explode the gentility of

[1] Between 1800 and 1808, no fewer than 14 books of small houses and cottage designs made their appearance. The authors were D. Laing (1800), J. Plaw (1800 and 1802), R. Elsam (1803), J. M. Gandy (1805), J. Loudon (1806), J. Wood (reprint, 1806), E. Gyfford (1806), T. D. W. Dearn (1807), R. Lugar (1807), W. F. Pocock (1807) and C. A. Busby (1808).

architecture, to rediscover some of the virtues of 'humble and rustic life' and to express them in design. There is no direct evidence of this intention: Gandy's few surviving letters are mostly either about archaeology or his own personal troubles. But if we size up his position in the whole situation of the time, its thought and poetry, we shall find evidence of an imprecise but weighty kind.

Gandy, as we have seen, was born in 1771. It was a year more propitious for poetic than for architectural careers. Men of his generation grew up in an atmosphere of ideological dispute and invasion scares; they heard the news of the French Revolution just as they were old enough to understand what it meant. They were twenty-two when Britain went to war with revolutionary France, twenty-nine at the Peace of Amiens, and forty-four at Waterloo. They ran a hard course, coming too late to enjoy the aristocratic liberality of Chatham's time, and too early to play a full part in the epoch of *bourgeois* expansion after 1815. It was, moreover, a generation for which opportunities in the arts and professions came less easily than they had done in time past. There was, naturally, no great outcrop of patronage during the French wars. Men of ability were forced back upon their own resources—psychological as well as economic. There was too much to think about, too little to do. It was an age for poets rather than architects.

And so it proved. Wordsworth was born the year before Gandy, Walter Scott in the same year and Coleridge the year after; Southey and Lamb a very few years later: in certain respects a revolutionary generation, not devoid of a 'democratical' element, and carrying a century's poetic production on its shoulders. Wordsworth and Coleridge had crystallized their new theory of diction by 1798, the year of *Lyrical Ballads*. The vernacular was reinstated; the ballad-form rendered a medium for fantasy. In the north, Walter Scott, an aristocrat, far from democratical, rediscovered the Dorian mode of his own environment and used it to effect his own particular union of antiquarianism and poetry.

In architecture, the case was very different. The 'sixties and 'seventies saw the birth of not a single really successful man. The calendar offers us only Jeffrey Wyatt, in 1766, whose success as a practitioner did not start till he was nearly sixty; and a group of literary-antiquarian architects born around 1770–72, and including John Britton, the topographer, Heathcote Tatham and our present hero, J. M. Gandy.

This is, of course, what we should expect. Public architecture (the Bank, the London improvements, the new churches and so on) was in the hands of the generation born in the early 1750s and well launched by 1790: Nash, Soane, the elder Cockerell. A man born twenty years later had a poor chance. He would be articled somewhere about 1786. Before he was out of his articles the Revolution would have signalled its threat to European peace. In the years when he might expect to find his feet as a practitioner the first part of the French war would be in progress and the vista before an architectural beginner in the highest degree discouraging. And the inducements to desert architecture (as Turner, for instance, is said to have done) or to turn to scholarship or draughtsmanship or literature would be correspondingly large—at least to those with the talent to shine brilliantly in these somewhat unremunerative pursuits.

So Gandy, like others of this much tried generation, started out to be an architect, and, indeed, became an architect and practised as such, but left his mark chiefly as a creator of designs and compositions, an architectural draughtsman reflecting in his own medium something of Wordsworth, something, as we shall see, of the historicism of Sir Walter Scott and something, too, of the deeper romantic spirit of Coleridge.

Looking again at the cottage designs, it is possible to see Gandy as a frustrated Wordsworth of architecture. Observe how studiously every conventional detail is barred and how columns, when they do appear (as in Plate xxxi), are proto-typal, as though reverting to those timber originals whence the orders are supposed to have derived.[1] Observe the uncouth disposition of doors and windows and the grotesque accept-ance of the 'lean-to' (Plates xxxi and xxxii), the coarsely pro-jecting eaves and the squat chimneys. Certainly this is not the English cottage architecture we know—or that Gandy knew. But it is an interpretation of it (an interpretation, let us add, by a man who knew both the Italian landscape and the specially hard, vigorous vernacular of the English Lakes). Here is, in architectural terms, the 'plainer and more emphatic language'[2] which Wordsworth found in the country usage of his time (again, of course, the Lakes). Here is a protest against the Nash-Repton school of Cottage designers, against the Laings, Plaws and Elsams—and that genteel school of landscape which Wordsworth felt to be 'founded in false taste, false feeling and its effect disgusting in the highest degree'.[3]

For any personal communications between Wordsworth and Gandy there is no evidence. That Wordsworth knew Storrs Hall and was often its owner's guest is a pure coincidence. The poet very likely did not even so much as notice its archi-tecture; and we may be pretty sure that the two cottage books never attracted his notice for a moment.

[1] Compare the models illustrating this hypothesis in Sir John Soane's Museum.

[2] Introduction to *Lyrical Ballads*, 1801 ed.

[3] Letter to Sir George Beaumont, February 11th, 1806.

So much for the affinities of the cottage designs. Of their worth, what are we to say? Today they have a quite extraordinary, a sensational, fascination because of their directness, and their sharp prophecies of functionalism and cubism. They are the work of a very unusual mind and, I think, unique in their attempt to break clean away not only from academic classic standards but from the superficial romanticism of Gothic. Even Soane never took his experiments as far as this. Gandy must certainly be credited with having attempted a glimpse of something quite outside the world of architecture as he knew it. Had he been more his own master and less his own enemy, had he been supported instead of deserted by opportunity and patronage, who knows what strange adventure might have happened out of this vision?

As it is, the cottage-designs must be classed with Gandy's whole *opus* as a fantasist; and to the remaining and greater part of his life's work we must now direct our attention.

Many of Gandy's drawings exist, mostly in the possession of his descendants. Some thirty examples are at present known to me, apart from those at the Soane Museum, which being commissioned and directed for the purpose of exhibiting Soane's genius rather than Gandy's are the least important to our purpose. Of the known drawings, one of the best is a perspective of an *Imperial Palace*, designed about 1824 and now in the RIBA (Plate xxxiii). The Palace is shown as an Ionic building of indefinite extent, the order raised above the ground-storey. The drawing shows the entrance consisting of a fore-building carrying two circular tempiettos at its ends and prefaced by an open octagonal porch; this is covered by a low stepped pyramid with a sculptural group on the summit. Behind the main façade there is the hint of a great colonnaded drum.

The message in this composition is chiefly contained in the extravagance of the fore-building and the elaborate recessions and variations involved in its relation to the main block behind, such elaboration being rarely possible in actual building. The octagon porch is a unity in itself and so are the two tempiettos, but the tempiettos invert the characteristics of the porch: they shelter sculpture while the porch supports sculpture; they are circular, elegant and placed high, while the porch is octagonal, massive and placed low. The porch is the focal point of the picture and the eye returns to it, entering its shadowy interior to discover, at the entrance, the Doric theme from which the buttress-like projections develop. There is much play with the secondary Ionic order which is projected as a portico under each of the tempiettos and attended by Victories and ships' prows and a much elaborated plinth. There is much here which is pertinent to the musical analogy I suggested at the beginning of this essay: the play of architectural forms, unhindered by expediency, approaches the play of form in symphonic music.

Another extant fantasy is one of several compositions in which Gandy tried to objectify an architecture corresponding with the architectural allusions in *Paradise Lost*. The bathos inevitably consequent on such an attempt does not diminish the architectural lustre of these drawings, which is considerable. The *Pandemonium*, shown in 1805, delineates part of the 'high capital of Satan and his peers', a subterranean hall of the richest possible character, arched and vaulted and equipped with cornices of a diabolical order:

Built like a Temple, where pilasters round
Were set, and Doric pillars overlaid
With golden architrave; nor did there want

Cornice or frieze, with bossy sculptures graven:
The roof was fretted gold.

Gandy had projected a drawing on this text in Rome in 1796,
but the fascination exercised by the satanic theme goes farther
back and deeper into the artist's mind, for while on the high
seas on his way to Italy in 1794 he recorded a dream, which is,
I think, for several reasons worth quoting in full from his
Journal. The narrative is unpolished, but the substance of the
dream is a curious parallel to the substance of many of his pictures. Here is the document, nearly in full:

> I was upon a staircase, listening to a man and woman
> courting from a window. This woman was likewise my
> sweetheart. I was contemplating how to win her, when all of
> a sudden appeared an elderly man by my side, he came
> whispering in my ear the nearer way to gain her affection is
> by force and promised all he could to assist me in the attempt.
> I turned round to him, was making a reply to thank him for
> his trouble and for the rules and caution he was giving me,
> when he took me by the hand and clapping me on the
> shoulder said, I am your friend, come my lad, we will get
> through this business easy, so led me away and shew[ed] me
> a vast number of fine places and things, entertainments and
> presents he gave me etc.

At this point Gandy reads a moral into the dream, identifying
the elderly man with patronage and its tendency to pass from
encouragement to exploitation. He goes on:

> At last I discovered this man to be the Devil (I thought at
> first he was a fair looking man). This I was bold enough to
> charge him with and began to defy him. Then he immediately
> grasped me close, shut my eyes, and in his arms I was carried
> till I found my eyes were opened, that he had placed me in

125

Hell where he left me. I looked about to the right then to the left, and could find no passage where I might get out, but I was resolved to seek, therefore walked on and viewed the things around me—here I thought people was punished with the bad business of their lives, some was busy fighting killing each other, some was over the furnaces making all sorts of utensils for the luxuries of life, such as Glass, Gold, etc., others again on the left was dragging heavy cranes up to lift Foreign goods from ships . . . . But conceive Men, for I saw no Woman, were here in Hell torturing and racking their own brains continually, exactly the same as they was themselves tormenting them in their lives on earth before, which was the punishment inflicted on every individual.

In fact, this Hell was nothing but the everyday London which Gandy had just quitted, but enclosed 'under a low dungeon' and Hellishly sombre.

I saw a light, then again I was in total darkness and was groping my way, at last I saw daylight peep through a hole above me which appeared to be above a mile high. On my left hand I saw a room with the Devil drinking with Lawyers, Aldermen, etc., etc., etc., etc., but I passed these unnoticed and I surveyed this place some time and discovered that it sloped up to the top, which if I ascended, as I very easily could, there was a great many men on this Hill, and they seemed piling it up with bottles which the Devil and his companions had emptied, as a trophy of what feats they had performed, and were striving to reach heaven with them. I was now at the bottom, and taking a sudden run up them. I reached about half way, but the noise I made with my feet going up alarmed Satan, who saw me and was with me in a moment, when he began to abuse me and charge me with ingratitude, and said was this the return I made for all the favours he had done me and after so long a friendship and the kind offices he had done me, but said he 'I find you are like the rest of the World, never think of those that have done for your good, you must be certain I could have no interest in so doing, and yet you would run away from me.' With such like hypo-critical cant he ran on some time but says he 'I forgive you, come, I know you are dry.' Turning round his wand, the Bottles began to move round in a circle 'take a bottle of whatever you please and we will make it up again.' Me-thought I then knelt down, and looking up to Heaven de-sired he would give me a bottle of righteousness, immediately from out this ring flew a very small vial and fell to the bottom. I observed at the same time Satan was cast down and looked dejected and flew to his Companions directly. I jumped after the vial, and laid hold on the label, whereon I saw written discretion, this with thanks to him above, I went into the room where Satan sat carousing and hit him on the head with it, as I directly, as if inspired knew the use to put it to. I then saw pieces of the vial stick fast in his bald head which seemed to give him much pain. He grinned at me and did not seem inclined to go. I had said to him 'Come Sirrah, take me from this place, on Earth.' I hit him again and then the pain was intolerable to him, once more he took me gently by the hand and led me to the light of this world.

The dream reflects, quite simply, Gandy's resentment against patronage, a resentment evinced over and over again in his dealings with Soane who (generous man that he was) used to pay Gandy absurd fees for his drawings rather than offer money which would have been resentfully accepted or angrily declined.

But the subterranean setting, which might pass as merely incidental, is even more interesting in view of an obsession which reveals itself, as we shall see in a moment, in quite a number of the drawings. Gandy had a peculiar interest in caves: in his travel diary he notes particularly the caves of Gibraltar and the Roman catacombs. In the dream, the subterranean setting is clearly a symbol of his hampered and difficult position in life, groping at the foot of that great mountain of bottles which one cannot help identifying with the life at White's and the bibulous patronizing clientèle of Mr John Martindale who, dare one guess, was elderly and bald-headed like the Satan of the dream.

Gandy's life was, to a great extent, a struggle to emerge from the cave of poverty and dependence. Yet, the cave had also its attractions, for it comes constantly into the drawings, where however it is mysteriously illuminated or opens out into the sunshine. Gandy did also attempt to leave the cave and reach the heights—on canvas at least. There exists a very large oil-painting by him, probably identifiable with the *Gates of Heaven*, shown at the RA in 1832. It is a vast aerial perspective showing a succession of courts leading into a blaze of light. It is quite one of his worst productions; he was more at home in the cave.

But I am anticipating. After the *Pandemonium* of 1805, none of the existing drawings is particularly striking until we reach *The Tomb of Merlin* (Plate xxxiv), shown at the RA in 1815 and now in the RIBA. In 1816 Gandy wrote to Soane,[1] offering him this picture as a gift, 'as a mark of my esteem and gratitude'. Soane either did not accept the gift, did not receive it, or parted with it before his death. Gandy was in serious difficulties at the time and Soane, having recently given Mrs Gandy £20 for her children, probably felt disinclined to accept a valuable gift,

[1] A. T. Bolton, *Portrait of Sir John Soane*, 1927, p 230.

which might or might not be intended to efface the debt. Or Gandy may have failed to substantiate his offer. In any case, the picture became the property of Gandy's friend, Richard Westmacott. For many years it was exhibited on loan at the Victoria and Albert Museum but was eventually withdrawn, and remained in private possession till it was acquired by the RIBA from Mr P. A. Robson in 1941.

The Tomb of Merlin is perhaps the most characteristic of all Gandy's known productions, for it unites themes which had been haunting him for many years. He had shown *A Mausoleum* at the RA as far back as 1790, when he was a pupil at Wyatt's, *The Inside of a Mausoleum* in 1797, a *Sepulchral Chamber* in 1800, a *Subterranean Temple* in 1802 and *A Tomb as a Beacon* in 1804. His mind ran on obsequies and one of his last exhibits at the RA, in 1838, was a *Cast-iron Necropolis*. In the *Merlin* picture, Gandy, taking a passage in 'Orlando Furioso' (Sir John Harrington's translation) for his text, unites the ideas of a subterranean temple, a mausoleum and a tomb as a beacon. To the quotation, printed in the catalogue, Gandy added the following explanatory foot-note:

> This drawing is a composition from the school of Constantinople, where the adoption of early Christian emblems began, giving rise to a new style of architecture—*vide* Eusebius, and other ecclesiastical writers; also medals and a description of the temple of the Apostles, which held Constantine's tomb.

Gandy's scholarship was nearly as much an affair of the fancy as John Wood's, and Merlin's tomb-chamber is really a version of Anglo-Norman, with some reminiscences of Roslin Chapel (which Gandy had measured and drawn); while the tomb itself is a concoction from the symbolic architecture of Byzantine coinage. The conception of a great central tomb surrounded by other tombs derives from Constantine's Church of the Holy Apostles.

But the Ariosto text and the quasi-scholarship provide merely the scaffolding for this work of art, whose chief point is in the dramatic reversal of normal lighting. The tomb, instead of being lit from windows, is itself the source of light:

> The very marble was so clear and bright,
> That though the sun no light unto it gave,
> The tomb itself did brighten all the cave.

As a *tour de force* in water-colour, this enormous yellow-and-grey picture (it measures 2 ft. 6 in. by 4 ft. 3 in.) is most remarkable. A deep, dark foreground, littered with monuments, keeps the spectator at bay, creating a groping sense of frustration, relieved only where the rays of the tomb penetrate and where reflected light glows on the architectural detail. The idea and its execution recall the tenebrous romance of early Coleridge. Here is something of the atmosphere of 'Christabel', a poem always remembered for its curious lighting. Here, too, is some of the intricate archaeological romance of Walter Scott, a delighted if confused sense of 'period'.

At the Soane Museum, this fantasy of Gandy's which Soane either did not receive or soon parted with is, in a measure, realized. In 1824, Soane, having acquired the great alabaster sarcophagus of Seti I, had it erected in the well of the Museum under the central glass dome. Seen from below, through the low arches of the crypt, the translucent alabaster may be imagined to be refulgent and to be, in fact, the source from which the crypt is lighted. Was Soane's anxiety to acquire the sarcophagus perhaps stimulated by having seen, if not possessed, Gandy's picture?

After *The Tomb of Merlin* our knowledge of Gandy's academy exhibits is, through many years, limited to their titles; and tantalizing titles some of them are. There was a *Town Residence for the Duke of Wellington* (1816) designed to be set among villas and to accord with the (rejected) plan for Regent's Park by John White. There were *The Tomb of Agamemnon* and *The Mount of Congregation* (1818), Chinese and Oriental compositions, an *Approach to a Greek Town*[1] (1820), military and marine towers[2] and many other subjects, for the elucidation of which Gandy was sometimes permitted to occupy half a page or more of the RA catalogue. Then, beginning in 1824, there appeared the series of views of an *Imperial Palace for Sovereigns of the British Empire*, imagined to be in Hyde Park. To this series the drawing in the RIBA library, already mentioned, belongs. Its two companions are hardly as remarkable, but have some points of interest. In one of them, Gandy exploits the dramatic idea of a building entirely upheld by carved representations of male or female figures, acting as columns. Unfortunately, Gandy was peculiarly inexpert at drawing figures, a fact inauspicious for this particular project. The second drawing shows a courtyard of the palace, whose central block consists of two superposed temples—one Doric, the other Ionic, raised on an arcuated basement and approached by double flights of steps. Curved wings sweep round to side buildings in which caryatides are again introduced.

Aspects of the *Imperial Palace* appeared every year from 1824 to 1828—an ironic commentary on John Nash's hasty and ill-starred conversion of Buckingham House, proceeding during the same period. In 1831 and 1832 appeared two com-

[1] Engraved in *The Cabinet of Modern Art*, 1836, opp p 218.
[2] The 'Military Tower' may be identical with a drawing at the Victoria and Albert Museum.

positions inspired by Milton—the *Hall of Pandemonium*[1] and the *Gates of Heaven*;[2] in 1835, after the burning of the Houses of Parliament, came a *Sketch for New Senate Houses* in St James's Park.

In 1836, when he was 65, Gandy broached a terrific scheme which, had he lived to complete it, would have been one of the most imposing monuments of architectural draughtsmanship. It was nothing less than a pictorial survey in over 1,000 drawings of the whole of the world's architecture, demonstrating its 'divine origin' in nature and its various national developments throughout the world. In some ways, one cannot regret the demise of a scheme so preposterously out of scale with Gandy's qualifications as a scholar; the treatise which was to accompany it would certainly have been worthless. But the one surviving drawing (Plate XXXV) is something of a masterpiece. It was exhibited in 1838 as *Architecture: its Natural Model*. It remained in the artist's family till 1946 when a great-grandson, Mr Henry Gandy, presented it to the Soane Museum. The painting (water-colour 2 ft. 4 in. by 3 ft. 6 in.) represents a wild, mountainous, almost Arctic scene—the world after the subsidence of the flood. A careful scrutiny of the more distant mountains reveals Noah's Ark, stranded high on the very peak of Ararat. In the centre of the composition is a valley with a river, flowing towards the spectator, while all around are natural phenomena suggesting architectural forms. There is a 'Fingal's Cave'—nature's Gothic nave; there are alps, icebergs, glaciers, spire-like rocks, and a 'natural' bridge; proto-architectural forms emerge among the rocks and hills and the materials for a primitive architecture abound. Beavers, bees

[1] This was probably a picture in Dr Eric Gandy's possession which was destroyed in an air-raid in 1940 when several other pictures were destroyed or damaged.

[2] The oil-painting already referred to. It is in Dr Gandy's possession and was much damaged by a bomb.

and white ants are at work and in the foreground an orang-outang has constructed a hut in the entry of which his mate and offspring are visible. A palm tree, with a vine climbing up its trunk, suggests types of ornament; and the skeleton of a primitive reptile shows the serrated jaws which are the reputed origin of the saw.

Great technical skill has gone to the making of this picture— one of the last which Gandy exhibited. The mountain scene, with dispersing clouds and broken sunshine, is really admirable. But it is to be looked at less as a painting than as a record of an imaginative flight. Here, Gandy's thought has receded beyond architecture and beyond archaeology into a semi-biblical anthropology remote from factual evidence—a wild and beautiful excursion.

At the Academy of 1838, the *Natural Model* had as its sinister companion a *Cast-iron Necropolis*, which appears to have been in the nature of a cellular pyramid into which cylindrical corpse-containers could be inserted. Gandy had always been somewhat over-concerned with mortality and this was his last fling; after a few years of declining ability he himself was dead.

Joseph Gandy may never be placed very high among the artists of early 19th-century England; but in his own par-ticular kingdom—the kingdom of architectural fantasy— he reigns absolute. And that kingdom has its own unique constitution. This local sovereignty makes Gandy, in a sense, the companion if not the peer of Wordsworth, Coleridge and Walter Scott. Their work parallels his and sometimes touches it—as when Gandy, in 1807, showed Roslin Chapel as Scott had described it, two years before, in the 'Lay', glowing in the spectral light which presaged the death of the lovely Rosabelle. But there Gandy is an illustrator—an inspired one, perhaps, but still a worker at second hand. It is in his wholly independent creations that he is most admirable, and rises nearest to the level of his great contemporaries. The cottage designs, slight though they are, constitute a really extraordinary penetration of an architectural convention which, in 1805, was not by any means in decline. They are the work of an artist–critic not far removed in feeling from the Wordsworth of 'Michael' and 'Peter Bell'. Then, in the *Tomb of Merlin* and perhaps also in the *Origin* there is that Coleridgean echo which we have already observed.

Gandy need not be put down as an architect *manqué;* for, once launched on his career of draughtsmanship, he certainly did not use it as a mere means of advertising his professional abilities. His schemes for palaces and senate-houses were not only hopelessly unpractical but were exhibited, in most cases, after the public buildings concerned had been commissioned and even, in some cases, commenced. He was loyal to his chosen dominion and his designs are, as all architectural fantasies should be, ends in themselves. If one looks for an English Piranesi, one finds him in Gandy. He has no rival. John Martin, eighteen years younger, is the only possible candidate, and his architecture has little power in itself; stripped of the circumstantial storm and stress, it would be insipid. But Gandy was, first and last, an architect. With him it is the figures and the subject-matter which are insipid: as in the *Imperial Palace*, where after considerable acquaintance with the picture one may casually notice that the Sovereign is being driven up to the building in a coach and four. The spirit of early 19th century England is expressed with peculiar clarity in Gandy's work. He employed himself in that margin of territory which we observed at the beginning of this essay to be the special preserve of the architectural fantasist, and he employed himself in a way which makes the architecture of the romantic age speak as eloquently as its poets and painters.

VI

Viollet-le-Duc and the Rational
Point of View

THERE HAVE BEEN two supremely eminent theorists in the history of European architecture—Leon Battista Alberti and Eugène Viollet-le-Duc. They were successful for this reason. They constructed towers of thought—lighthouses, let us say—at points in history where such towers were very particularly needed. Alberti placed his tower at the point where the Brunelleschian renaissance was about to widen into the broad channel of the cinquecento; Viollet-le-Duc his at the point where the romantic movement of the early 19th century was passing into the age of criticism and materialism.

For us, today, Viollet-le-Duc is a figure of considerable importance because he is the last great theorist in the world of architecture, and the modern architect still leans heavily on verities which he expounded. How far he should continue to lean on them is a question I shall consider in another essay. Here, my purpose is to speak of the man himself and of his ideas in relation to the age in which he lived.

He was born in Paris in 1814.[1] His father was a civil servant—of no great eminence but with a pronounced taste for scholarship and the arts; he collected and studied French books of the 16th century and earlier, taking advantage of the dispersal of many private libraries at the revolution to build up what must have been a very noble collection. His wife, the future archi-

[1] The life of Viollet-le-Duc is admirably told in P. Gout's work already quoted on p 11.

tect's mother, was the daughter of a successful contractor (he had built the Odéon and the Hotel de Salm), a nervous, melancholy beauty who mellowed considerably when her husband was promoted to an official residence in the Tuileries. Her Friday salons were distinguished. Beyle (*alias* Stendhal) might be seen there; and Sainte-Beuve and a handful of clever young men who enjoyed their host's library as much as his company. At the Rue Chabanais, where the young Viollet-le-Duc was born, these parties were held on the first floor. Upstairs, on the fourth floor, lived Mme Viollet-le-Duc's brother, Eugène Delécluze. He, a bachelor, was at home on Sundays, from 2 to 5; his guests were exclusively male. Here one would meet the romantics, Prosper Mérimée among them; here conversation would run rather free. Delécluze himself was a painter in the mornings, a scholar in the evenings; he had been a pupil of David but preferred the pen to the brush and wrote art criticism for the *Journal des Débats*—presumably in the afternoons. He was a romantic, a liberal, and in all such things opposed to his loyalist brother-in-law, the civil servant downstairs. But they mixed and argued merrily: pro-romantic, anti-romantic; anti-Bourbon, pro-Bourbon. The only real cause of antagonism was that Mme Viollet-le-Duc would not receive, *au deuzième*, the lady who was Delécluze's frequent companion *au cinquieme*. Even that domestic stumbling-block, however, did not prevent Delécluze being entrusted by the Viollet-le-Duc couple with the education of their two sons, his nephews.

Eugène and his young brother were sent to a school at Fontenay, carefully selected by Delécluze for the rabid anticlerical republicanism of its head. Delécluze, irritated by the war of feminine nerves at the Rue Chabanais, likewise moved to Fontenay and supplemented the education of his nephews and some of their friends with long walks, lively readings and charades on two days in the week. To Eugène this kind of thing was preferable to school, where he was unhappy in the extreme —a sulky, ineffective rebel, equally resentful of work and games.

Eugène's disgust with institutions dates from this time. When he left school, nothing would induce him to pursue a conventional line of conduct. He followed his uncle in his strong radicalism and helped to build the barricades of July, 1830. He flatly refused to enter the Ecole des Beaux-Arts and be cast, as he said, in a mould; and from the social amusements of his age and class he retreated in horror after one *bal masqué* at the Odéon.

In 1832, when he was 18, his mother died. The shock—and it was a severe one—goaded him to furious absorption in work—reading, travelling, writing, sketching. He fell in love, but the girl's parents found him too young and he was dismissed. Again, he sought consolation in tramping about the country with a sketch-book. At nineteen, he fell in love once more, with a not specially remarkable young woman, whom he had adored as a little boy, and this time, after some months of parental hesitation, he married. About the same time he became Professor of Composition and Ornament at a small, independent Ecole de Dessein in Paris.

Then, in 1835, he went to Italy with one of his pupils, remaining there 17 months. He visited and drew everything and admired much, confessing himself disappointed, however, with the works of Palladio, Sansovino and Vignola ('They tried to discipline the Renaissance,' he wrote to Delécluze, 'and succeeded merely in flattening it'). On his return, he was decisively and irrevocably spell-bound by the architecture of medieval France. For the first time, apparently, he saw through the mere strangeness and romantic intricacy of its appeal to that essential logic of design of which he was to become the greatest exponent and on which he was to base a whole philosophy of architecture.

But he was still a man without opportunities and remained so until a movement which had been gathering strength for some years suddenly discovered in him its ablest and wisest protagonist. That movement concerned the scientific study and preservation of the monuments of medieval France. We must go back a year or two to describe its origin.

The pioneer in French medieval studies of this kind was Arcisse de Caumont who founded the *Société dès Antiquaires de Normandie* and published his great work on Norman architecture in 1830. His work was inspired by what had already been done in England, where Britton's *Cathedral Antiquities* had been appearing since 1814, where a work on Normandy itself had been published by Pugin and Le Keux, and where Thomas Rickman's *Attempt* to define the chronology of medieval styles was already more than ten years old. Following hard on de Caumont's work, in 1831, came Victor Hugo's *Notre Dame de Paris*, in which a great medieval building was made the hero of a novel, dominating the story with patriarchal grandeur, and making Gothic architecture touch the reader's imagination in a way it had never done before. Sainte-Beuve described the book as 'a beacon lit on the high towers'; and such it proved.

In this same year, 1831, Ludovic Vitet, one of the 'jeunes érudits' of Delécluze's Sunday salons, was appointed to the newly created post of Inspector-General of Ancient Monuments and in his first reports he drew attention to the decayed condition of France's medieval buildings. With that generosity towards the arts, characteristic of new and popular governments (the July Monarchy was then barely a year old), the Chambers voted money for preservation, entrusting the Direction des

Beaux-Arts (in the Ministry of the Interior) with its expenditure. Vitet was the responsible officer and for two years he pursued his task, quite alone. In 1833 he was succeeded by another habitué of Delécluze's Sundays, no less a man than Prosper Mérimée, remembered today rather as the author of *Carmen* than as an antiquary or a civil servant. Neither Vitet not Mérimée had any technical knowledge of building and the architects they employed were indifferently disposed to medieval work; but young Mérimée's enthusiasm surmounted all obstacles and valiant rescue-work was done. Then, at last, in 1837, the Service was placed on a broader bottom and the *Commission des Monuments Historiques* instituted. Vitet was a commissioner, Mérimée the secretary. In 1838 Viollet-le-Duc, then 24, was nominated 'auditeur-suppléant'; in 1840, he received instructions to report on the Abbey Church of Vézelay.

Vézelay, where Viollet-le-Duc took prompt and skilled action to avoid disaster, was his first restoration; but he only sprang to fame when, in 1845, in association with Lassus, he won the competition for restoring Notre Dame. By 1849 he was in constant request, serving on many commissions and committees and already wearing the ribbon of the Legion of Honour.

The remainder of Viollet-le-Duc's life-history is full of interest but has not sufficient bearing on the theme of this essay to be more than summarized. The literary works, which constitute him the greatest architectural theorist of modern times, all belong to the central period of his career, a period which coincided exactly with that of the Second Empire. Although a democrat, he not only did not find himself wholly opposed to the slippery dictatorship of Louis-Napoleon but even became personally associated with the court. The restoration of Pierrefonds was carried out for the Emperor; and at Compiègne he was relied upon as a sort of Inigo Jones, extemporizing contrivances for private theatricals and fêtes with infinite resource and universal applause. When at length the gimcrack Empire fell, in 1870, Viollet-le-Duc filled a *rôle* more like himself and as a Lieutenant-Colonel of Engineers played a conspicuous part in the fortifications of the City. During the Commune, he retired to Pierrefonds but emerged again during the first years of the Republic and, in 1875, was elected Deputy for Montmartre. By this time he was ardently republican, ardently anticlerical; he wrote continually for Left-wing papers and pressed those causes and antipathies which had absorbed him all his life. In 1879, in a house he had built for himself at Lausanne, he died.

Viollet-le-Duc's first great literary project began to be published in 1854, when he was 40. It was the famous *Dictionnaire Raisonnée de l'Architecture Française du XIe au XVIe Siècle*. It was published in instalments, the last number appearing seven years after the first. In 1858, he began a shorter work, a companion to the dictionary, dealing with furniture and equipment. In these two great works, although factual and descriptive in intention, his philosophy of architecture is implicit; in the *Entretiens sur l'Architecture*, published in 1863, it is explicit; while in the second series of *Entretiens* published after the war, in 1872, his ideas are further developed and applied in a number of his own designs. Viollet-le-Duc wrote much else—a memoir on the defence of Paris, a charming series of books on architecture for young people, a study of the architecture of Russia. But his principal legacy to architectural thought is contained in the two dictionaries and the lectures—most clearly of all in the first volume of the latter.

Now the theme which runs through the whole of Viollet-le-Duc's work is this. Architecture has to do mainly with the faculty of reasoning. Taste, properly understood, is simply unconscious reasoning. For the artist, however, unconscious reasoning is not enough. He must analyse what pleases him; he must be conscious of the logical process which lies behind the successful result. The architect's education must, therefore, proceed in two stages. First, he must learn to analyse the masterpieces of the past; then he must learn to make his own synthesis, serving the conditions and using the materials dictated by his age.

That is the kernel of Viollet-le-Duc's theory. It has, you notice, nothing specifically to do with Gothic architecture—or with Classic or any other architecture. Although it is a theory based on the conception that the architecture of the present must derive from the architecture of the past it dismisses at once any question of revivalism. The modern architect, says Viollet-le-Duc, must analyse the masterpieces of the past, reduce them to a process of argument, then apply the argument to his own problems. This is as different as can possibly be from the Gothic beliefs so ardently cherished by Viollet-le-Duc's English contemporaries—men like Pugin, Butterfield, Gilbert Scott, Street and Pearson. All of them were as deeply imbued with a love of Gothic architecture as was Viollet-le-Duc; but not one of them was man enough to *think his way through* the romantic attraction of style to a philosophic point of view applicable to all buildings at all times. The Englishmen built their Gothic churches, their Gothic schools, their Gothic houses, and within narrow limits they performed creditably. But the Frenchman, though he did build one or two Gothic buildings of an 'occasional' character, left a structure of thought upon which many of our own ideas of modern architecture are based.

How did Viollet-le-Duc arrive at this new basis for architectural development? How did he find his way to it? I think if we look back at the story of his early life we shall discover the answer. It begins with a fanatical hatred of dependence. That complicated ménage in the Rue Chabanais, with its divided loyalties, had an effect on young Eugène. It made him a rebel. Then there was the school which he hated and the treasured solace of the miniature houses he used to build during the holidays. Next, there was his mother's death and the obstructed love-match, both of which drove him back on himself, steeled his independence. By then, already up to his neck in architecture, it was inevitable that he had to find, in that sphere also, a point of view which was his own.

Independence of mind was absolutely essential to him—he confesses as much in his diary, and it was perhaps this ability to confess, this self-knowledge, which enabled him to direct and balance his energies so well. The enjoyment of independence is always enhanced by a consciousness of something to be independent *from*—it is stimulating to have an object of despite constantly in one's mind's eye. Now such an object Viollet-le-Duc did not lack for a moment—it was the Ecole des Beaux-Arts. From the day when he refused to be entered as a student to the day of his death he had the most absolute contempt for that historic and distinguished institution. Only on one occasion did he have dealings with it, and that occasion only increased his resentment—as well it might. It happened in 1863. The Government had appointed a commission to draft a new constitution for the Ecole, to regulate the expenditure of funds and, incidentally, to bring the curriculum up to date. Viollet-le-Duc chose this moment to write a series of articles outlining his own extremely radical ideas of how the architect's education should be conducted. He stood well with the Government and his programme was used to strengthen in detail their recommendations for the reorganization of the curriculum. But they went much farther. Over the heads of the Academicians they appointed the Ecole's critic himself as its Professor of History of Art and Aesthetics! The Academy was aghast; old Ingres was furious. And, unluckily, some tactlessly framed regulations regarding the Grand Prix de Rome lost any support which might have been forthcoming from the students. At the first lecture, hisses, boos, cat-calls and a shower of halfpennies greeted the Professor. The lecture proceeded, however, and six more lectures were given under the same conditions. Only a few attentive listeners in the front rows could hear what was said, but there was one occasion—a memorable occasion it must have been—when, during a lull in the storm, Viollet-le-Duc drew a parallel between the ability of the Greeks to give form and shape to their mythologies and the potential ability of the 19th century to express such concepts as the power of steam and electricity in an analogous way. For once, the audience was gripped and for a moment complete silence reigned, followed by applause. Perhaps in that solemn moment, modern architecture may be said to have been born. But in the long run, Viollet-le-Duc and the Ecole des Beaux-Arts could not agree. He resigned and, during the rest of his life, missed no opportunity of cudgelling academies in general and the Ecole des Beaux-Arts in particular. The Academy returned his hostility; and although, eventually, he was invited to stand for election to the Institut Français, with every possible chance of success, he felt that even those laurels had their academic thorns.

This unbending hostility to institutions, dating from his schooldays, might, in another man, be set down to envy or disappointment. In Viollet-le-Duc it was nothing of the kind. The sheer craving for independence—for seeing something which others could not see—doing something which others

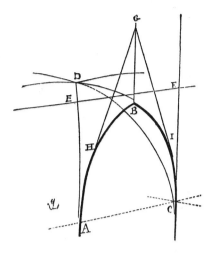

FIG. 10. The Sainte Chapelle, Paris. Diagram of detail shown on the
opposite page

could not do—came first. He had to discover architecture for
himself; he had to discover it in a form stronger and more vital
than what the academies had to offer and, above all, in a form
which he and nobody else had thought of. The mere adoption
of Gothic styles in place of Classic was not enough; that was
a mere idle preference in which his literary friends among the
romantics already gloried. But if that preference could be
logically interpreted—if it could be shown that Gothic architecture was not merely emotionally exciting but more intellectually satisfying than the architecture of the schools—then,
there was a cause to be embraced and a battle to be fought. The
journey to Italy was, consciously or unconsciously, a journey to
test the Gothic case. The respected and respectable architecture
of the ancients and of the Renaissance was patiently, judicially
studied—studied even with affection. But returning to France,
the case for Gothic—Gothic as an exemplar of rational archi-

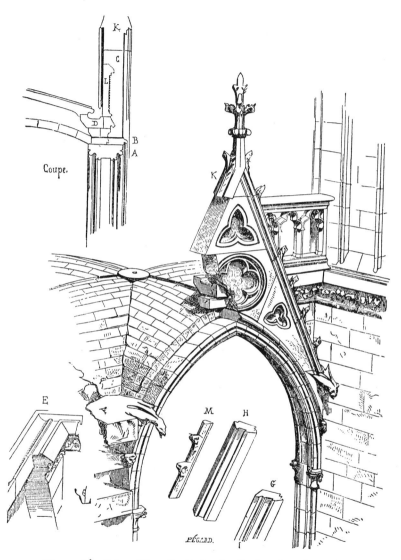

Coupe.

PÉGARD.

FIG. 11. The Sainte Chapelle, Paris: detail of vault and window-head. From Viollet-le-Duc's *Dictionnaire Raisonnée*

tecture—seemed overwhelming. From that moment he had two objects before him. First, the scientific exposition of Gothic. Second, abstracted from the first, the creation of a modern parallel.

Let us look at an example of Viollet-le-Duc's method. First let us go to the *Dictionnaire* and see his mind at work on analysis. In the course of the article on 'Construction', he illustrates the windows of the Sainte Chapelle in Paris (Fig. 11). Now each of these windows occupies the whole of the space between the adjacent buttresses and is surmounted by a pinnacled gable. Thinking in the terms expounded in my first essay, we should immediately see in this design a development of the *aedicule* motif. In this instance (comparable with the chancel windows of Troyes) the windows themselves have been considered as having a shrine-like character and gables have been placed over them in order to constitute each window a complete aedicule. The windows with their shafts and gables are, in fact, analogous to classical windows framed by decorative columns and pediment. But a stylistic approach such as this is foreign to Viollet-le-Duc's method. He regards the composition exclusively as the solution of a problem of equilibrium, and the steps in his argument may be summarized in this wise: 'The architect required as much light as possible; therefore he eliminated all superfluous masonry and made the wall-rib of his vault into a weight-bearing arch, coinciding with the window opening. The result of this was that the slight thrust of the cross-rib (AB) tended to push the apex of the wall-arch out of the vertical. To remedy this the architect decided to place a weight of masonry over the apex of the arch to stabilize it. Since it was precisely the apex of the arch and not its haunches which required stabilizing, this weight of masonry took a pyramidal form.' Hence the gables at the Sainte Chapelle. It is a neat explanation and none the less accurate because it entirely ignores the character of the design as a *motif*—as an aesthetic adventure.

That small and simple example epitomizes the method which Viollet-le-Duc employs throughout the *Dictionnaire*. Never for a moment does he relinquish the rational criterion. His brilliant ingenuity never deserts him, never leaves him at a loss for an explanation, and only the purely sculptural parts of Gothic architecture are actually admitted to be ornamental. The article on 'Construction', which I have quoted, is one of the longest and most significant. In the course of it he introduces a diagram (Fig. 12) explaining the equilibrium of the typical cathedral vault by exaggerating its elements, substituting for the sake of argument a thin cast-iron column for the nave pier and a timber shore for the flying buttress. The shorter articles are no less closely reasoned. Under 'Pinacle', the aisle pinnacles at Rheims are shown to be delicately differentiated counterpoises to the two tiers of flying buttresses. Under 'Profil', we are shown how the simplest string-courses are carefully calculated to throw the rain-water clear of the walls. Under 'Proportion', we are admitted to a remarkable theory of triangles, proposed as the basis of Gothic cathedral design and stability. And so on, through all the ten brilliant volumes.

Now, it must not be supposed for a moment that Viollet-le-Duc's analysis of Gothic arrives at a complete and final estimate of the style. Indeed, for us, its importance is precisely in the fact that it does not. The rationalism disclosed by Viollet belongs to the 19th century—not the 13th—and it is as a 19th-century performance that the *Dictionnaire* lives. As Viollet-le-Duc knew perfectly well, the process of design is not altogether a conscious process; in fact the very act of design itself—the logical synthesis of parts—is performed in the unconscious mind.

Thus, the creators of Gothic never proposed to themselves

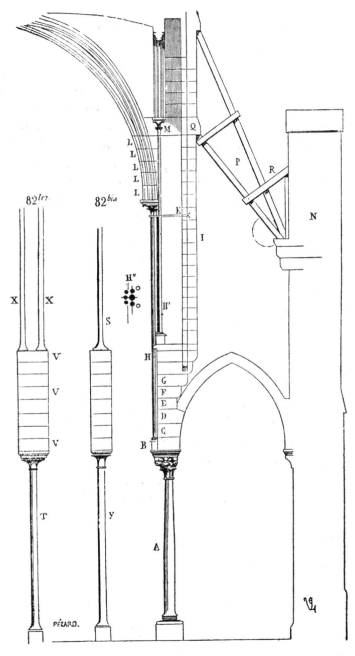

FIG. 12. Diagram from Viollet-le-Duc's *Dictionnaire Raisonnée*
(article on *Construction*)

that economy of structure which Viollet-le-Duc *abstracts* from their works. Their objective from generation to generation was the evolution of an idea—of many ideas—and although it is a fact that in the pursuit of those ideas they did produce some structural equations whose economic exactitude is remarkable, they did not produce anything in any way approximating to a rational architecture. For what do we mean by a rational architecture? We may mean two things. We may mean an architecture which aims at fulfilling certain specifiable functions with the nearest approximation to absolute efficiency and economy. Or we may mean an architecture which seeks to express its function dialectically—to offer a visible argument to the spectator. The first sort of architecture depends wholly on the extent to which function can be mathematically stated; the second sort depends on the architect's personal interpretation of function. The first sort is ruthless in its application of means to ends; the second sort adapts both means and ends to a game of its own. The first sort of architecture is, as a matter of fact, almost impossible of conception since the total requirements of a building can never be mathematically stated: it is the mythical 'functional' architecture of the day before yesterday. The second sort of architecture is a perfectly feasible one, the only proviso being that the function of the building be considered as of sufficient emotional interest to make this dialectical mode of expression significant.

Gothic architecture cannot, of course, pretend to correspond with our first sort. The function of a cathedral cannot possibly be expressed with precision, and function cannot, therefore, in this case, be the criterion by which it is judged. As for the second, which is, I think, the more proper meaning of 'rational' as applied to architecture, there is, to be sure, a certain *play of rationality* throughout the structure of a cathedral just as there is a play of rationality in the structure of medieval philosophy. A cathedral is a systematic aggregate—a *summa*. But that cannot be taken, either in the one case or the other, as a yardstick with which to measure the quality of the structure. It was, however, that play of rationality which appealed so enormously to Viollet-le-Duc and which, in his 19th-century mind, became merged with the other, materialistic, signification. So that he was led to the general conception of an architecture proceeding by a process of argument from the known terms of a problem to the unknown but discoverable solution. That was the idea which emerged from his Gothic studies and which, with all its inherent ambiguity, formed the foundation stone of modern architecture.

In the *Dictionnaire*, Viollet-le-Duc does not really prove a case and he does frequently damage it by hoisting the rational criterion where it is not wanted. But when we pass from the *Dictionnaire* to the *Entretiens* we find that the Gothic case is considered as proven. Evidence is then taken from other ancient styles in order to shift the whole argument from the particular to the general. Having shown as nearly as possible that Gothic architecture is rational architecture, Viollet proceeds to show that Greek, Roman and Byzantine are also, within their limits, rational architectures and, in fact, that all good architecture is rational architecture. It then only remains to show that the architecture of the 19th century, in order to be good, must be rational.

The *Entretiens* form, as I have indicated, the synthetical counterpart of the two analytical *Dictionnaires*. The first series of ten was published in 1863. They range through the history of architecture, not in the pedestrian manner of a text-book, but skilfully weaving the material of history round the grand theme which is always uppermost—the theme of reason as the criterion of all good architectural performance.

There is, however, much other speculation of great insight and value. The first lecture begins with a confession of faith in the emotional power of architecture. It is compared with music. Music can recall the serenity and grandeur of a sea-scape; so can poetry; so also, says Viollet, can architecture when it has occasion to give us long, unbroken, horizontal lines. Then he compares the emotional effect of a low broad crypt supported by squat columns with that of a soaring nave; he notes the physical reactions of a man in these two settings, thus foreshadowing the thesis elaborated a little later by Theodor Lipps in his theory of *Einfühlung*. Then he recalls how once, when he was a little boy, architecture and music became inexplicably identified as one medium. His old nurse had carried him into Notre Dame. It was very dark, but the sun was pouring in through the great rose of the south transept. Suddenly the organ started to play. For the little boy it was not the organ, but the rose window, which was producing the sound. The different lights in the window seemed actually to create the different sounds, some grave and resonant, others brilliant and sharp. The child was astonished to the point of fear; nor could his nurse persuade him out of the illusion and little Eugène, profoundly upset, had to be removed from the cathedral. Few writers have touched on this capacity of architecture to become 'alive' with sound, but it is, for most of us, a verifiable phenomenon. Have you not noticed how a bell-tower seems to become alive when the bells are ringing, like a magically great personage whose mind and voice merge in the music of the bells—or how the lines of an opera-house seem to vibrate and glow when the lights dim and the overture begins?

But the lecture soon leaves the arena of experience for that of creation. Here is Viollet-le-Duc describing how the artist's experience must be analysed and its contents put into reverse for the act of creation. This is, I think, the crux of his philosophy:

> Very often (perhaps always) the sentiment of taste is only involuntary reasoning, the terms of which escape us. To acquire taste is nothing but to accustom ourselves to the good and the beautiful; but to accustom ourselves to what is good we must know how to find it—we have got to choose. To make this choice we call to our aid the faculty of reasoning. We look at a building. Instantly we are charmed by it—we say 'what a lovely building'. But for an artist this instinctive judgment is not enough. He asks himself why it is beautiful and tries to analyse all those features of the building which charm him, so that he may be able to apply himself to synthesis when he comes to create in his turn.[1]

That taste is a matter of involuntary reasoning seems to me basically true. What does not seem valid in the statement just quoted is our implied ability to exercise a *rational* choice of 'good' buildings on which to form our taste. In fact, there is a contradiction here. Either taste is *unconscious* reasoning or it is arrived at through intermittent efforts of *conscious* reasoning, you cannot have it both ways. And Viollet-le-Duc's own life-long experience of Gothic architecture is the best illustration of how in fact a taste does become formed. His liking for Gothic was, in the first place, the contagious predilection of the eighteen-thirties—a romantic predilection engendered by the climate of his time. He later discovered, from that independent vantage-point in which life had placed him, that the reason why he liked Gothic was because it was a rational architecture in his own hybrid sense of that word. Now, although taste is involuntary reasoning, the terms of the argument are certainly not (in the case of architecture) those of structural performance.

[1] *Entretiens*. Lecture I, p 29.

Viollet-le-Duc's love of Gothic was one thing. His discovery of its structural efficiency was another. His early love of Gothic permeated his whole life, as it did that of so many artists of the 19th century. And in his case, it enabled him to construct a vast and elaborate theory of 'rational' architecture. But—and this is where we can see so much more clearly than Viollet—that structure cannot quite stand by itself. However perfectly the theory is articulated, it cannot be proved and it still does rest on the original predilection, the original involuntary reasoning which springs from deeper sources—sources exceedingly hard to analyse and into which Viollet himself does not inquire. There, perhaps, is the Achilles heel of Viollet-le-Duc. It is, in effect, a confusion, typical of the 19th century, between rationalism and materialism.

Today we see Viollet-le-Duc and his work as part of that world of historical criticism which was the splendour of 19th-century France. Like his near contemporary, Sainte-Beuve, Viollet-le-Duc has his roots in the romanticism of the eighteen-twenties and eighteen-thirties. But his achievement, in some ways not unlike Sainte-Beuve's, is the very antithesis of romanticism. He takes Gothic architecture to pieces with the same patient care and penetration which Sainte-Beuve exercises in his biographical studies. Viollet-le-Duc, however, goes much farther than the essayist. Having taken his subject to pieces, he starts to reconstruct it in different terms and in the context of contemporary life. It is rather as if a medieval historian, having dissected the principles of feudalism, had gone in for politics and put forward a programme of social and economic reconstruction on a model analogous to feudalism. Let me say at once that Viollet-le-Duc, who was politically conscious to an uncommon degree, would have been guilty of no such idiocy as this. Indeed, right at the beginning of his lectures he is at pains to assure us that there is no necessary connection between the quality of an art and the quality of the type of society which produced it (an opinion which our Mr Ruskin would scarcely have endorsed).

Nevertheless, Viollet's use of analogy in architecture does have the weaknesses one would expect from the use of that method in any field. And these weaknesses show as soon as he leaves the written word and begins to design. In the second volume of his lectures, he illustrates and describes several designs he has prepared in order to test and elucidate his theory. One (Fig. 13) is for a concert hall for 3,000 people; another is for a town house, another for a country house. He is very modest about these products of his own pencil and repeats many times that he makes no claim to having evolved anything new and that the designs are only given in order to indicate the kind of approach which the 19th-century architect should adopt. The designs are at once unattractive and fascinating. As one follows their author's description one sees that they are disciplined, daring, economical, ingenious. There is a reason for everything; geometry is paramount and ornament is admitted with nice discretion. But there is one thing missing. It is difficult to find the right word for it, but I think the word is *style*.

Probably Viollet-le-Duc, modest and self-critical as he was, would have admitted as much. He had a critic's flair for style in everything—in women, in cats (for whom he had a profound respect), in objects of everyday use. And he could sense style in a locomotive and a gun. But he knew as well as anybody that style cannot be produced by calculation or by taking infinite pains. He only believed that by the sincere and remorseless application of reason, style might be born. Here is what he says:

E. GUILLAUMOI.   MDCCCLXIV.

FIG. 13. Design for a Concert Hall in stone, iron and brick. From
Viollet-le-Duc's *Entretiens*

If we get into the habit of proceeding by the light of reason, if we erect a principle, the labour of composition is made possible, if not easy, for it follows an ordered, methodical march towards results which, if not masterpieces, are at least good respectable works—and capable of possessing style.[1]

'Capable of possessing style.' That is fair enough, and reflects the fundamental modesty and sincerity of the man, whose guiding star, through all his labours, was '*le respect absolu pour le vrai*'.

Viollet-le-Duc's designs are probably the least important aspect of his work, but as documents they are enormously illuminating. The 19th century had discovered iron as a structural material and Viollet was concerned to show how iron could be used with precisely the same economy and precision as stone and timber had been used in the Middle Ages. Thus, the roof of his concert-hall is a polyhedron constructed of iron members and the areas between the members are spanned by light iron ribs, with an infilling of brick. The whole idea is, quite evidently, a paraphrase of a Gothic vault. Then, the weight of the roof is taken partly by solid masonry and partly by iron columns whose weight is transferred to the walls by means of canted struts, held in place by iron ties which serve at the same time to support the gallery. Here again is a Gothic principle developed in a way which the enormous compressive strength of iron admitted for the first time.

It is all marvellously clever, but I think you will agree that the result (Fig. 13) is not very moving. It does lack style. It is rather like a language invented *ad hoc*; a sort of esperanto evolved from the salient characteristics of other languages but

[1] *Entretiens*. Lecture 6, p 191.

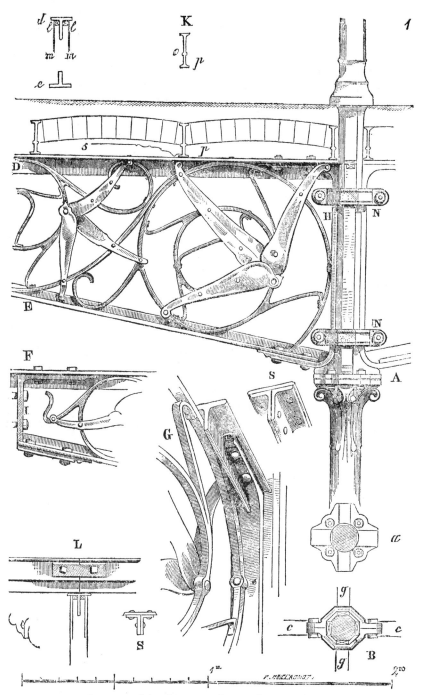

FIG. 14. Ornamental detail in cast and wrought iron. From Viollet-le-Duc's *Entretiens*

lacking the vital unity which any one language possesses. As in the composition of the building, so in the ornament (Fig. 14), Viollet gives us brilliant ingenuity and daring skill, but his foliations in cast iron are somehow just not quite the thing.

But these designs must be respected for what they are—demonstrations of how the rational theory *can* inflect contemporary design, not necessarily how it *should*. Viollet-le-Duc was afraid of nothing. Having mastered Gothic, formulated the most complete interpretation ever attempted, then built a corresponding aesthetic for his own times, he is still bold enough to take the final step and put his theory into practice. The vitality and scope of his genius commands unbounded admiration.

Of Viollet-le-Duc's influence on modern architecture I shall say something in another essay. I have devoted the whole of this to him because he is so much neglected. Yet he is, as I have said, the last great theorist of modern architecture. The integrity of his theory can be assailed, but although it is, I believe, now necessary to view it from a new angle and perhaps even to turn it quite upside-down, that does not diminish its value. Should anyone attempt to construct a theory of modern architecture in harmony with the conditions of thought prevailing today, he will discover no starting point so firm, no background so solid as that provided by Eugène Viollet-le-Duc.

VII

William Butterfield;

OR, THE GLORY OF UGLINESS

PEOPLE OF TASTE screw up their faces at the architecture of William Butterfield. Clergymen desperately whitewash his walls. Architects pay him respect distantly, having it on the authority of Beresford Pite, perhaps, or H. S. Goodhart-Rendel that he was a great man in his time. We are all diffident about that stern Anglican in steel-rimmed spectacles, whose fame earned him the Royal Gold Medal for Architecture, but whose aversion to public life was so intense that the Medal had to be carried to him privately by an envoy.

What is the truth about Butterfield? I believe I have asked myself that question for twenty years and still find it difficult to write down a clear and sensible explanation of the fascination he exercises. Here, however, is the attempt.

William Butterfield[1] was born in 1814, which makes him a contemporary within a year or two, one way or the other, of Dickens, Thackeray, the Brontës, George Eliot, Anthony Trollope and Robert Browning, in other words of that genera- tion of writers which produced the literary harvest of the 'forties and 'fifties. Among architects, his near contemporaries were Pugin, Gilbert Scott, G. E. Street, R. C. Carpenter and Benjamin Ferrey, in other words the 'hard core' of the Gothic

[1] The biographical information used in this article is derived from (i) Paul Waterhouse's article in the *Dictionary of National Biography*, (ii) W. R. Lethaby's *Philip Webb and his Work*, 1935, (iii) a paper by Mr Harry Red- fern read to the *Ecclesiological Society* and printed in *The Architect and Building News*, April 14, 1944, and (iv) a footnote in T. F. Bumpus, *London Churches* (classical and modern), p 268.

Revival. Ruskin was five years his junior. Born in London, the son of a chemist, Butterfield was articled at seventeen to a builder in Horseferry Road. The indenture was cancelled after three years, when Butterfield entered an office in Worcester, where, according to Paul Waterhouse, 'a sympathetic head clerk of archaeological tastes encouraged him in the study of English Church-building'. He was in London again by 1836, working in the office of Blackburn, an architect in Clement's Inn. None of his employers seems to have been of the slightest note and he was to all intents and purposes self-taught; though he did at this time acquire his intimate and affectionate knowledge of good, practical building.

Of his early adult life we know nothing, until he appears as the friend of three leading figures in the High Church movement of the 'forties—Benjamin Webb, J. M. Neale and A. J. Beresford-Hope. This High Church world was a somewhat frail vehicle of Victorian life, hitched to the wagon of inherited wealth and concerned, to a great extent, with the minutiae of religious observance which, seen in the context of 19th-century history, now seem childish in their unimportance. Webb, for instance, was a headlong champion of the adoption of the eastward position during the recital of the creed. Beresford-Hope, in the House of Commons, fought like a tiger for the rejection of the Deceased Wife's Sister Bill of 1859. It is only fair, however, to remember that those were the days when mobs broke the windows of known ritualists, and hooligans set their mongrels on surpliced choir-boys.

Anyway, Butterfield gave his loyalty to this movement absolutely. He contributed largely to *Instrumenta Ecclesiastica*, a book of approved designs for all sorts of things from cemetery chapels to fald-stools, published in 1847. For the whole of his life he was a devout adherent of the narrowest Anglicanism.

Church-building and worship were the whole content of his life. He built nearly a hundred churches, restored many others and his secular works (apart from vicarages) were confined to certain collegiate works at Oxford, two large houses, a hospital, and a few other things of small importance. For some fifty years he practised architecture, retiring towards the end of the century. In 1900, after a period of senility, during which the balance of his mind was imperfect, he died.

Mr Harry Redfern has described his appearance round about 1877. He was 'a slight figure, rather above medium height, with thin features, a high forehead and greying hair; side whiskers and round steel spectacles'. His dress 'consisted of a black cloth frock-coat and vest and grey trousers over immaculately polished shoes, a white linen shirt with collar à la Gladstone[1] and a loosely tied black bow'.

He was a life-long bachelor, cared for by a married couple, many years in his service. He was abstemious in all things, never smoked and, in his office, was a remote, inaccessible but courteous tyrant. His office was in Adelphi Terrace. The Adam room in which he worked was furnished, says Mr Redfern, with 'an old Turkey carpet and a few good pieces of late Georgian and early Victorian furniture', including horsehair covered chairs—a comfortable arm-chair for the client. No surroundings could be more inappropriate, you may say, for a medievalist. But, as I think we shall see, Butterfield was hardly a medievalist at all.

Butterfield's method of working was very remarkable. He possessed neither drawing-board nor T-square, his only instru-

---

[1] He was certainly Gladstonian in appearance. Only the other day I talked to a builder's foreman who remembered him as 'like nothing so much as Mr Gladstone'. The same informant told me how a site used to have to be tidied and swept when Butterfield was expected, 'as if it was the King'.

ments being a pair of folding compasses and a two-foot rule. Paul Waterhouse said he was a fine draughtsman, but Mr Redfern recalls how he used to make small and highly unattractive drawings of parts of a church and send them into the drawing-office to be developed, which was no easy task. Later he would revise and correct these office-made drawings to a fastidious degree and by a lengthy process of proposal, development and correction the design would emerge, the last corrections being made on the site. It should be added that his assistants were almost all hard-headed 'bread-and-butter' draughtsmen, arriving promptly at 9.45 and vanishing on the stroke of six. He only had three pupils—Henry Woodyer, Galsworthy Davie and, much later, Mr Redfern.

Thus we have before us the picture of a Victorian of the hardest, narrowest kind, unsoftened by any hint of humour or human irregularity. Here is none of Pugin's romantic glory, of Scott's paterfamilias geniality; of Street's high enthusiasm. Butterfield stood separate from these contemporaries of his, hardly knew them and mixed only with the high church clergy in the constricted social life he allowed himself in his afternoon visits to the Athenaeum.

His first work, 1842, was the Highbury Congregational Chapel at Bristol, an amateurish but by no means conventional design; his second was the little church at Coalpit Heath, Bristol, 1844, a solid workmanlike quasi-14th-century parish church with some shrewd hints at the future Butterfield, notably in the lych-gate. In the following year he designed the buildings for St Augustine's College, Canterbury, for his friend, Beresford-Hope. In 1849 he started work on the most famous of all his churches, All Saints, Margaret Street, begun to be built in 1850, structurally complete in 1855 and dedicated in 1859 (Plates XXXVII and XXXVIII). Another important church of this early period is St Matthias, Stoke Newington (Plate XXXVI), designed apparently within a year of All Saints and completed by 1853.

These early churches are the most important of Butterfield's work. But to understand them it is necessary to see them in the context of Gothic church-building between 1818 and 1848. Three phases must be distinguished:

1. The Gothic of the Commissioners' Churches, in many cases a cheap, but sometimes an extravagant, alternative to Greek. This Gothic, thin, wiry, decorative, 'late' and archaeologically incorrect, was in the 18th-century spirit. It came nearest to correctness in Barry's churches in Islington and Rickman's in Birmingham.

2. The personal Gothic achievement of A. W. Pugin. This was a miraculously fluent transcription of 14th-century Gothic adhering with automatic accuracy in planning, construction and detail to ancient models. More important, it gave birth in Pugin's mind to an architectural *philosophy*. This philosophy condemned all classical forms and held up Gothic as the only practical, as well as the only Christian form of architecture. Pugin became a Roman Catholic, so his personal contribution to Anglican church-building was *nil*.

3. The Gothic of the Ecclesiological Movement which had as its nucleus the Cambridge Camden Society, founded by Webb while an undergraduate, along with J. M. Neale, Beresford-Hope and the architect F. A. Paley. The ecclesiologists veered from *philosophy* to *dogma*. Their chief interest was in a liturgical orthodoxy which was to conform with the tenets of the English church under Andrewes and Laud. Rather illogically they went back much farther for their

architectural ideal and insisted on conformity with what they called the 'middle-pointed' phase of English Gothic—i.e. about 1320-50, excluding the Perpendicular as 'debased'.

The Camdenians had two favourite architects: R. C. Carpenter and William Butterfield. Carpenter, who was a convert from the 18th-century brand of Gothic, achieved a wonderful degree of antiquarian correctitude in his churches. St Mary Magdalene's, Munster Square, is a good example; no transcription could be more accomplished; no architecture, surely, more completely impersonal. The early churches of Benjamin Ferrey, F. A. Paley and J. L. Pearson are much of the same kind—graceful, reserved essays on the approved 14th-century theme.

It was against this background of conscientious self-effacement that All Saints gradually dawned. I say gradually, because the church was built very slowly and had exerted a widespread influence long before its dedication in 1859. It was in June, 1853, that readers of the *Builder* were treated to a whole page woodcut of the building and soon 'Mr Hope's Church' (as All Saints was rather improperly called) was the most discussed modern building in England. It is Butterfield's chief work; it was so to him and a portfolio of the working-drawings reclined always near his desk.

The smallness and inconvenience of the site are obvious. They were much deplored at the time of the building's completion; though I cannot help feeling that this tax on the young architect's ingenuity was productive of much originality and spurred him to break those rules which he enjoyed breaking and continued to break with unabated ferocity for the rest of his life. Those rules are rules of proportion, which Butterfield's contemporaries derived most conscientiously from medieval precedent. The site at Margaret Street might conceivably have accommodated a stunted version of a 'Decorated' parish church. Butterfield's church is, if you like, stunted, or rather, telescoped, but the curtailments are joyfully accepted and the church has the nobility of a saint in fetters. The short nave is of three huge bays, where I fancy that Carpenter, Wardell or Ferrey would have given us four, of much smaller calibre, in the hope of retaining a semblance of Gothic proportion. The height entailed by the width of bay is considerable and an ample clerestory rides on top, carrying a steep timber roof. But Butterfield goes farther and makes the short chancel even higher than the nave, its vaults springing far above the nave arches. For his tower he is forced to borrow the westernmost bay of the south aisle, but here again height compensates for ground-space and English precedent gives place to a sensational adaptation of the north German type. Finally, the single visible buttress of the south aisle is arbitrarily construed into a grand feature, on cathedral scale.

So much for the heterodoxy of composition, largely, perhaps, engendered by the site. Now for the handling. The chief materials are red bricks mixed with black bricks and stone to form bands and diapers. This, in 1849, was very startling indeed. Red brick was used, of course, in the 'forties, especially by those architects who cultivated the Elizabethan or Tudor revivals. But the true Gothic men clung to stone—Kentish Rag, with quoins and openings in Caen or Bath Stone. And in it he set those multiple black bands and hard, innocently crude diapers which made people wonder about All Saints as soon as the walls were breast-high and made them wonder still more when the bands climbed right to the summit of the tower and were echoed in the spire.

These bands were Butterfield's discovery—not Ruskin's—

and he must surely have been to Siena to discover them.[1] He must have imagined their reintroduction at least as early as 1849, and it was not till 1851 that the first volume of *Stones of Venice* appeared, explaining that colour bands were valuable for a variety of reasons which I do not think Butterfield would have guessed—as 'a kind of expression of the growth or age of the wall', as 'a symbol of the alternation of light and darkness' or 'in their suggestion of the natural courses of rocks, and beds of the earth itself'. Butterfield never thought in terms like these and I should be quite prepared to believe that he never bothered much with the *Stones of Venice*. Yet Butterfield's unwritten and Ruskin's written reasons had, I think, the same intuitive origin. These black bands are the Puritan answer to the sensuous beast-liness of what we now call 'texture'—they oppose sensibility; or again in Ruskin's words (borrowed from a different context) they are the 'noble grotesque' as against the 'ignoble grotesque' of rustication and of the kind of architecture which grows out of the drawing board and T-square.

The general style of All Saints is what was called by the Camdenians 'Middle Pointed' and for most of the details an English precedent can quite easily be found. But the precedents are not consistent and are selected and applied with a fanatical disregard for that decorative fluency which was already emerging in the 14th century. Butterfield loved the *awkwardness* inseparable from most early Gothic; he loved its strength and adolescence, its coltish negligence. He loved that his porch at All Saints should collide grotesquely with the wall of the Clergy House; he loved to clash the variableness of the pointed arch and to interrupt a rhythmical pattern in an agony

[1] Butterfield's travels are not recorded in any of the printed biographies, but I was recently assured by the daughter of one of his clients that 'he had been to Siena'.

of discord. This last device he carried, as we shall see, to ex-cruciating extremes.

The interior of All Saints (Plate xxxviii) shows Butterfield in all his rigour. The nave capitals are in a style borrowed from Dorchester, Oxon, a church he had recently restored; they are borrowed, obviously, for the special fullness and luxuriance of the stiff-leaf. The shafts are in the hardest, shiniest Aberdeen granite. The aisle walls are decorated in glazed bricks and Minton tiles, with mastic patterns inlaid in the jamb-stones of the windows. The nave spandrels and those of the chancel arch are crammed with geometrical designs in brick, stone and marble. There is no colour-*scheme*: merely a wonderfully childish belief that natural materials arranged in geometrical patterns are sure to be right. It is rather like the Pre-Raphaelite belief that if you copy everything you can see in a natural object on your canvas the result is sure to have some meaning, though you cannot know beforehand precisely what.

All Butterfield's churches are to a greater or less degree ugly. And in almost all there is power and originality transcending the ugliness. I *have* seen churches of Butterfield's which are not strikingly ugly and in which there is only a rather sickening coarseness in all the parts. But always the Butterfield personality is there—unmistakably there.

The ugliness in All Saints was recognized even by the most sympathetic critics at the time of its completion. The *Ecclesiologist*, the Camdenian organ, in a long and laudatory article, observed that the merits of 'force and power' had been 'carried to excess'. 'The foliage of capitals and string-courses . . . is often exaggerated in its coarse but honest originality . . . Curiously enough there is here to be observed the germ of the same of dread of beauty, not to say the same deliberate preference of ugliness, which so characterizes in fuller development the later paintings of Mr Millais and his followers.' The reference is, of course, to paintings like the *Carpenter's Shop* and *Lorenzo and Isabella* and the analogy, coming from a contemporary, is interesting. Butterfield was not a Pre-Raphaelite or anything like; I doubt if he thought painters quite respectable, and Millais's prodigal, facile talent was the very reverse of the uncouth obstinacy of the architect's. And yet in their different ways, Butterfield and the Brotherhood were the two great protesting forces in the visual arts, protesting against the tradition of taste by putting aside the fear of ugliness and believing in something beyond and more important than beauty or its antithesis. Millais threw overboard a fully-developed technique of composition, allowed his paintings to become formally meaningless *arabesques* into which a photographic finish introduced a strange, unearthly equivocation. Butterfield had, I think, no sense of composition to throw away. He was something of a primitive (which nobody could say of Millais!); but he, too, gives us an exaggerated insistence on detail which shocks in rather the same way as Millais's fantastic pursuit of finish.

All Saints, more than any other Butterfield church that I have seen, admits Italian influence and nowhere is this more obvious than in the sanctuary, with its great marble reredos, inset with panels painted by William Dyce, and in the traceried arches in the north and south chancel walls. The beauty of these arches, with their generous scale and full profiles, has often been remarked. Gerard Manley Hopkins, for instance, commented on their 'rich nobility' when he revisited the church in 1874,[1] finding it in some other respects less admirable than he had once thought it. But Hopkins, who was no great sympathizer with Gothic revivalism, recognized the power in Butterfield and

[1] *Notebooks of Gerard Manley Hopkins*, ed. H. House, 1937. Entry for June 12, 1874.

adds that not only the open arches of the chancel but 'the touching and passionate curves of the lilyings in the ironwork under the baptistery arch marked his genius to me as before'.

I said just now that we should find that Butterfield was not a medievalist and I think you will agree that All Saints shows not the slightest nostalgia for the Middle Ages. In a Pugin church the nostalgia is—nearly—everything; in a Butterfield church it is conspicuously absent. And a Butterfield 'restoration' is a quite ruthless affair of bringing a decayed fabric up to date, and (allowing for a certain reverence for the old as a fount of design) of giving it an all-Butterfield look. He was no medievalist. He was a Victorian builder, accepting with a queer literal-mindedness the conditions of his own time. He habitually used common red and black bricks or, as at Stoke Newington, London stocks. His rafters are pit-sawn timbers of ordinary scantling. He used luscious marbles when he had the chance, but he was perfectly happy with ordinary Birmingham tiles. He liked to build cheap and he held it a great thing to have built a church for under £250. On the practical side he was most painstaking; Halsey Ricardo has recorded that he even liked to have the curves of chimney flues set out full-size on the site.

An example of his love of the common Victorian building craft is provided by an answer he wrote, in the *Ecclesiologist*, to somebody who had criticized his stalls at Dorchester. They said that certain corbels were merely 'glued on' to the frame. Butterfield replied by a patient reference to the common practice of gluing the brackets which stiffen the junction of riser and tread in an ordinary domestic stair. It did not occur to him that such risers were unseen; if the use of glue was good carpentry practice there was nothing wrong in gluing a moulded corbel on to Gothic stalls.

Butterfield's idiosyncrasies lasted him all his life. The gawky builder-like roof at St Augustine's College Library, Canterbury (1845) is echoed in the roof of St Augustine's Church, Queen's Gate (1870–76). The criss-cross framing of the partitions in the one is echoed in the criss-cross diaper of the other. These and other idiosyncrasies occur over and over again but always in different relationships. It is not the details, but the use of them which never fails to surprise and impress. At the church of St Matthias, Stoke Newington (1851–53; Plate XXXVI), we find a strange topsy-turvydom—clerestory windows in the aisles, aisle windows in the clerestory, a transept gable flung up to the top of the tower and a west window split in two by a buttress riding on a porch. At St Alban's, Holborn (1859–63; Plate XXXIX) there is again a saddle-back tower, this time at the west end. The stair-turret, traditionally an angle-feature, is thrust violently up the centre of it, rather, I think, in the spirit of the grand solitary buttress at All Saints. Butterfield gloried in a duality. Internally, this tower yields itself to the church, providing with the two transeptal wings a vestibule of extraordinary nobility. At Babbacombe (1867–74; Plate XLI) there is a nave of the strangest kind with a wagon roof through which little stone dormers are allowed to peep. The chancel of the same church is one of the architect's most alarming and ferocious adventures. Nowhere else does his favourite stridency—criss-cross *versus* segment—strike such a terrible note. And then there is Keble College, where, in the Chapel (Plate XL), we find echoes of many earlier buildings—the grand buttress of All Saints, for instance, and the shallow west transepts of St Alban's. Of the main quadrangle, built between 1867 and 1870, Eastlake observed that 'the details are refined and artistic in design'—curious epithets to apply to Butterfield, but certainly true of Keble in relation to his earlier buildings. There is even a kind of sweetness in the handling, and the brick diapers are distributed with taste, if not with discretion. The Chapel is gloriously adventurous in its proportions and altogether one one of the architect's most easily acceptable works—though still, I believe, rather strong meat for the delicate appetites of Oxford.

Butterfield went on building churches till 1891–2, the date of the little church of St Augustine at Bournemouth, which has the same tricks and also much of the same power as the earlier buildings. But Butterfield in the 'nineties is already an anachronism. He had delivered his message long before and English church architecture had fallen into the gentle hands of Mr Bodley.

The essential Butterfield belongs to those critical years 1845–65, in which the 18th-century rule of taste was finally broken. In architecture, Butterfield is the great symbol of that sense of revulsion and liberation which permeated English art and letters in those years. Out of this context he is indeed difficult to estimate. Within it he is conspicuous as one of its most remarkable witnesses. It is just a century ago that his first important work was done and I think it is time for us to correct our perspective of the Early Victorian scene, more especially where architecture is concerned. Butterfield was a creator of the same stature as Dickens and Emily Brontë; and although the collision of either of these names with his is, at first sight, grotesque, there is something to be learnt from the experiment. The relationship of *Wuthering Heights* to the Waverley novels is not unlike the relationship of All Saints, Margaret Street, to the Houses of Parliament. In both transitions, conventionally romantic luggage goes by the board. Both Emily Brontë and William Butterfield seem to be trying above all to escape from *taste*. To make a Montoni live in Yorkshire, to make a whole novel out of the characterization of sadists and weaklings was

Miss Brontë's way; Butterfield's was to drag the Gothic Revival from its pedestal of scholarship and gentility and recreate it in a builder's yard. Both artists are working at two removes from life. Butterfield attacks architecture not as building, but as Gothic-architecture-as-building. Miss Brontë attacks the novel not as an interpretation of life but as an interpretation of the Gothic novel touching her own experience of life. In these instances the Gothic Revival is no more remote from life than the Victorian novel.

To suggest comparisons between architects and writers is risky at any time and if I go on to say that the inartistic verbosity with which Charles Dickens hammers out his characters always strikes, in me, the same chord as do the copious devices which Butterfield requires for his effects, I may very well be accused of careless talk. But in Dickens the 'aesthetic' appeal of hardness and cruelty is evident both in the choice of his material and in its handling and, without carrying a very ambiguous parallel any farther, I think there is no escaping the general conclusion that during the middle decades of the 19th century there was a singular attraction on the part of some painters, architects and writers towards ugliness. They deliberately set their aim wide of the mark of organic unity and trampled ahead with a sense of adventure and power and perhaps of curiosity —'to see what would happen'. To describe their aim would be to attempt more than they themselves could do. 'Truthfulness to Nature' was the kind of phrase which some of them liked to employ and in architecture this could and did mean a great deal more than arbitrary combinations of natural materials and the use of organic ornament. It meant that if the convenient arrangement of a building suggested a violent duality or a formal discord, the duality and the discord could be accepted as right. But that after all is the mere rationalization of a desire and the truth is that these people wanted, needed, craved ugliness. The architects found something of what they wanted in the Middle Ages, which the romantic proclivities of a century had bequeathed them. The use of the pointed arch is in itself amply suggestive of discordant relationship; and the sheer gaucherie of much early Gothic—resulting from the localized vision and rule-of-thumb practice of the masonic craft—is an inexhaustible source for those in search of thoroughly uncomfortable relationships. Whence came this inclination for ugliness? It might plausibly be argued that it represents a surgence of that hard *bourgeois* Puritanism half-hidden in the 18th century which had never expressed itself emotionally but at last seized the opportunity to do so; and did so most significantly, perhaps, in literature but also in the architecture associated with the Oxford movement in the Church of England. Such a thesis needs considerable testing. But I think that if the social and environmental origins of a number of the personalities concerned are examined much evidence can be found to support it. The phase did not last very long. Quite suddenly, around 1870, taste was again established, though on a very different plane, with church architecture rapidly receding from the conspicuous place it had occupied for thirty years.

To sum up. The first glory of Butterfield is, to me, his utter ruthlessness. How he hated 'taste'! And how right he was! Just imagine yourself living in late Georgian London—yes, *living* in it, not just reading about it or enjoying the melancholy of its time-washed fragments. Imagine a city in which every street is a Gower Street, in which the 'great' buildings are by smooth Mr Wilkins, dull Mr Smirke or facetious Mr Nash. Imagine the unbearable oppressiveness of a landscape in which such architecture represents the emotional ceiling. That is the London—already faded, but scarcely altered—to which a man born in

1814 grows up. To such a man, being by nature an architect, the Pugin revelation comes when he is about 23; and across the hideous streets, the flaccid stucco, the flimsy railings and the six or seven million chimney-pots he sees the vision of an architecture which is hard, muscular, fearless, contemptuous alike of the drawing-room and the drawing-board—which is full of everything which the architecture around him negates.

That is the emotional setting, felt then by nearly every young architect who could see beyond his T-square. But William Butterfield in this setting is unique. He is an innocent. He avoids and fears the crowd—especially the architects. He loves and clings to the Church, and to churchmen, among whom he is the architect—*their* architect, an architect among churchmen, not an architect among architects.

Narrowly, looking neither to right nor left, he makes his way forward. He knows how to build—he is no studio man; he can command on the site. First he is the modest, watchful apprentice of the 14th century; he wins men's approval and his own confidence. He is armed—and his imagination is free. In this imagination there is something of the *fauve*, something of the contemptuous joy of distortion and destruction. And in All Saints, right in the heart of joyless London, he is able, at 34, to deal his most tremendous blow.

At this point a strange thing happens. The *fauvisme* in Butterfield releases something else—a sense of form, yes—even something very like taste, but on a quite new plane. From the hardness and ruthlessness of All Saints emerges that noble elegance which makes it, in some ways, the most moving building of the century.

Butterfield's sense of form is inextricably confused with his sense of protestantism. All his architecture protests; and the trouble about our appreciation of him today is that we do not quite understand what he was protesting about. How can we see what Butterfield saw in a brand-new, stubbily moulded Early English shaft and capital? To us its hardness and coarseness are dull. To him its hardness and coarseness were a deeply sincere protest against whatever was wiry, soft and genteel. Of course, we shall learn in time; it only remains for the Victorian perspective to become a little more distant and a little sharper and we shall over-admire Butterfield as easily as we over-admire Wren, Adam and Soane. Or shall we? I cannot help hoping that Butterfield will always be a tough nut.

I have said that, to me, the first glory of Butterfield is his ruthlessness. The second glory is a wonderful, childish inventiveness. He was, I repeat, an innocent. His sense of composition was perfectly naïve, and resulted in things as surprising and memorable as the west ends of the Stoke Newington and Holborn churches, the nave-chancel relationship at All Saints and the curiously-formed sanctuary at Babbacombe. In decoration, too, he was often a real primitive with his zigzags and circles and crudely coloured geometry. His painted roofs are like huge, ingenious toys from a giant's nursery.

Lastly, one word more about Butterfield's 'ugliness'. It seems absolutely deliberate—even systematic: a calculated assault on the sensuous qualities latent in the simplest building-forms. Deliberately he contrives dualities; deliberately he clashes a diaper with the extrados of an arch; deliberately he fractures the raking line of a gable or the curve of a wind-brace. Is it possible, I wonder, to parallel this purposeful sadism in the whole history of architecture? Its cause I have already suggested as lying in a pietistic revulsion from the sensuousness of the classical tradition and of the first phases of the Gothic Revival. But what of its effect? The answer to that question must lie with the individual observer and the theory he chooses to hold as to

values in the arts. If you are a professed and absolute humanist
—well, there is an end of it. If not, and if the value of a work of
art is, for you, inseparable from its position in time, the ugliness
in Butterfield becomes an essential part of a *situation* which must
be evaluated as a whole. When Butterfield's churches were
new it was easy—and exciting—to feel the rightness of these
hammerblows against 'taste'; fifty years later it was impossible
—the situation had passed out of focus; now it is again possible
because we can look at the Victorian world from our own
through the spy-glass of understanding.

Today, we live in an age of taste or, at least, an age eager to
become such. Butterfield frowns upon us from the eighteen-
fifties. Taste is the smiling surface of a lake whose depths are
great, impenetrable and cold. At unpredictable moments the
waters divide, the smooth surface vanishes and the depths are
revealed. But only for a moment and the storm leaves nothing
but ripples on the fresh, icy surface. Butterfield reminds us of
this as we go along Margaret Street, or Queen's Gate, or the
Gray's Inn Road or stand in the red umbrage of Keble.

VIII

Architecture, Painting
and Le Corbusier

IF YOU had been in Paris in 1863, you might have been aware of two mild sensations in the world of art. One of these arose out of a situation I have described in another essay: a certain M. Viollet-le-Duc had been appointed to a chair at the Ecole des Beaux-Arts and his lectures had been received in a most unfriendly fashion, partly because the new Professor had been instituted in an untraditional way and partly because the content of the lectures was an uncompromising attack on accepted methods of teaching architecture. I suggested, however, that the lectures had a certain historic importance and that from an incident in one of them one might (poetically, perhaps) date the birth of the modern movement in architecture.

The other sensation of Paris, 1863, concerned not architecture but painting and is better known. It was the Salon des Refusés. The jury of the Salon d'Automne had been uncommonly strict and, perhaps, more than usually conventional. A great many rejected painters were bitter in their disappointment, to such an extent that Napoleon III, always ready to act the liberal in matters remote from statecraft, was induced to command that a separate Salon should be held, in the Palais de l'Industrie, where the rejected painters should have the opportunity of submitting their works to the judgment of the public. It was at this Salon des Refusés that the works of Manet, Pissarro and Monet first came under public notice. The public, however, was not impressed. Affronted by the naked model in Manet's *Déjeuner sur l'herbe* and wholly contemptuous of the efforts of Pissarro and Monet, people assured each other that the rejected paintings were no better than they should be and that the jury had acted very properly in securing their exclusion.

Now these two incidents were, of course, totally unrelated. One does not know what Viollet-le-Duc thought of the *Déjeuner sur l'herbe*—or if he ever saw it; nor whether Manet had ever opened the pages of the *Dictionnaires Raisonnées*. Nor does it much matter. Viollet-le-Duc was then nearly 50; the painters I have mentioned were in their twenties. They and the great architect lived in very different worlds. But all the same, those two episodes, lying parallel with each other in the identical year 1863, can be shown, in the light of subsequent history, to have a certain connection with each other. Both are records of protest; both are records of failure though in both cases failure was eventually turned into success. Viollet-le-Duc's lectures, as we have already seen, provided a reasoned programme of architectural revolution—the first which had been formulated for four hundred years. The paintings of the impressionists, on the other hand, raised the curtain on a long drama of unreason in the world of vision—the drama which reached its climax just before the first world war, but is still, as we approach the middle of the 20th century, unfolding itself in episodes of an inflammatory character.

Viollet-le-Duc and modern painting are the two great forces which have contributed to the creation of the more advanced and novel architecture of today. It is difficult—and it would be false—to compare them, because one cannot compare a man with a movement. One cannot compare the Eiffel Tower and the Seine. Viollet-le-Duc stands four-square in the eighteen-sixties, an intellectual giant whose shadow reaches to 1914 and beyond. The impressionists were beginners—pioneers; they and two generations of painters following them, widening and deepening their discoveries, made a tradition of modern painting which has flowed from achievement to achievement, like the widening course of a river. And yet neither man nor movement can be left out of account in an attempt to estimate modern architecture. So I shall try, in this paper, to show how these two major influences made their contributions to the history of modern architecture and how they eventually came to be reflected together in the work of the most remarkable of living architects—Le Corbusier.

The history of modern painting is usually held to begin with the impressionists and it may be said that they and Viollet-le-Duc had at least this much in common—they were determined realists. Viollet wanted architecture to conform with the conditions imposed by modern scientific discovery; he was ready to use cast-iron and to use it in forms appropriate to industrial production, with precision and economy. The impressionists were equally anxious to be hard-boiled—to meet the challenge of Science. Pissarro got hold of the spectroscopic theories of Helmholtz and Drude and, with Monet, applied them to the business of painting—at least to the extent of being determined *plein-airistes* and arranging their palettes in conformity with the doctrines of vision which Science had placed at their disposal. But there all similarity ends. Viollet's designs were intellectual solutions overshadowed all the time by the analogy with Gothic. Pissarro and Monet were intuitive artists of a younger generation, and if dabbling in optics gave them a stimulus and a bent that is all it did.

The influence of Impressionism on architecture was, of course, absolutely nothing and we must follow the consequences of the movement a long way before we can understand exactly how painting comes into the story at all. If the Salon des Refusés of 1863 is one milestone in the history of painting, the

Salon d'Automne of 1905 is the next. In that interval of 42 years much had happened in the narrow, unadvertised world of advanced painting. Impressionism had bloomed—a beautiful, shapeless flower. Then Seurat had lived and died, leaving the world his half-dozen masterpieces, austere contradictions of the impressionist contempt for formal design. Gauguin and Van Gogh had fled from Impressionism in quite other directions—Gauguin to a primitivism inspired by Japanese prints and the peasant art of Brittany; Van Gogh to the kingdom of his own imagination. And all the time the greatest man of them all, Paul Cézanne, had been working through his long, lonely career trying, as he said, to make out of impressionism something solid, 'like the art of the museums'. Cézanne's working life almost exactly fills the space between those two milestones of 1863 and 1905. Curiously, the official who appointed Viollet-le-Duc to his chair at the Beaux-Arts was the same M. de Nieuwekercke to whom young Cézanne addressed rude letters which were never answered. The year 1905 was the last of Cézanne's life.

What Cézanne achieved is told in his canvases and can be expressed in no verbal equivalent. One can say, perhaps, that he rehabilitated the art of painting as an art of construction and design and not merely as an art of description. Although a landscape of Cézanne's may take its origin in some Provençal scene—often trivial and commonplace enough—the life and strength of the finished work is wholly in itself; it is a complete fabric of paint-on-canvas, of brushstrokes following, reinforcing, counterpointing each other and mastering the area of canvas which Cézanne has set out to conquer.

Cézanne died in 1906, still practically unrecognized; but a memorial exhibition was held in 1907 and the man's full stature began gradually to dawn on the world. By then a new generation surveyed the scene. In 1905 Henri Matisse was 26; Pablo Picasso 24; Georges Braque 23. It was Matisse who led the *fauve* group who showed in the salon of that year. The label was well chosen, for the period of destructive violence in the arts had begun in earnest and the next six years were to see everything happen which shocked then and still shocks the man in the street who wanders off his beat into a modern picture gallery. I believe it would have surprised many visitors to the recent (1946) Picasso exhibition in London to know that nothing which they saw there exceeded the violent ugliness of the *Ladies of Avignon*, which Picasso painted in 1906; and it is certainly curious to reflect now that when that picture was painted, we—or our fathers—lived in a frock-coated, Edwardian world, innocent of total war, astonished by steam-cars and by aeroplanes which sustained themselves in the air for two minutes.

In 1908, the influence of Negro sculpture displaced the earlier archaisms of Gauguin and in that year, too, Matisse looked at a landscape by Braque and noticed that it resolved itself into forms with sharp edges arranged in a sort of crystalline geometry. He made some disparaging remark about 'les petits cubes'. The expression stuck. Cubism had been invented and named.[1] Picasso developed his 'analytical cubism', building up portraits as angular, crystalline structures; and the first cubist sculpture appeared. Obviously, painting as an art of representation was suffering complete transformation. In 1910, 1911 and 1912, the separate influences of the pioneers began to coalesce in the Ecole de Paris, with not only Picasso and Braque but Léger, Gris, Marcoussis, la Fresnaye, Picabia and Marcel Du-

---

[1] For a clear and systematic account of the history of modern painting, see *Cubism and Abstract Art*, published by the N.Y. Museum of Modern Art, 1936.

champs all making their distinct contributions to the new art of abstraction. In other countries, movements of similar ferocity sprang into life at this time. 1909 is the year of the first Futurist manifesto in Italy—a document which has all the clamour of the Fascism it heralded. And in Munich, in 1911, Kandinsky painted his first purely abstract composition. Finally, in 1913, Malevich in Russia invented Suprematism, establishing, as he said 'the supremacy of pure feeling or perception'. One of his paintings consisted of nothing but a white rectangle on a white ground.

So, by the outbreak of the first world war, painting can be said to have broken completely free from its obligation to represent a scene, an object, a person or an anecdote. It had become, in the hands of a few men, here and there, purely a matter of the organization of form and colour, with or without reference to the visible world. It had undertaken vast new responsibilities; and, obviously, in this condition of unfettered freedom it was liable to exert its influence on much that was outside the traditional sphere of the painter's work—on decoration, on industrial design and on architecture. A mysteriously active world of *form* had emerged from the old categories of representation and style. It was a release of power—a destructive release. Creation through destruction is characteristic of much of this phase of art. Picasso has said[1] of his own work, 'a picture used to be a sum of additions; in my case a picture is a sum of destructions.' And again, 'when you begin a picture you often make some pretty discoveries. You must be on guard against these. Destroy the thing, do it over several times.' To which, however, the painter adds this: 'In each destruction of a beautiful discovery, the artist does not really suppress it, but rather transforms it, condenses it, makes it more substantial.'

[1] In A. H. Barr, *Picasso: Fifty Years of his Art*, 1946.

A room full of Picassos is a room full of ruins. Each painting is the destruction, the devastation, not only of appearance but of the charms incidental to the representation of appearance on canvas. Through all this destruction emerges the artist's complete and absolute possession of form. It is strange and, perhaps, inexplicable how necessary is the ugliness of Picasso; but evidently there is no other course for him to take. He must start with appearance—a nude on a sofa or a woman in a queer hat —then he must tear it apart, interchange and dissolve its elements until the canvas is mastered wholly and entirely by the form-colour equation, the fragments of actuality—ludicrous and brutal in their dismembered disarray—being brought into complete subjection to this equation. But the most dissonant and alarming canvas by Picasso is not so very far removed from the gentler, but no less revolutionary art of Cézanne. The great eruption in the arts, whose premonitory stirrings go back to 1863, whose fire and smoke issued in 1906–1912 and whose intense heat is still illuminating and fusing the arts of our time, is all one prolonged act—an act of which we have not yet, perhaps, seen the end.

Now, before we consider how the art of architecture became subjected to the disruptive forces emanating from the world of painting we must go back for a moment to where we began, with Viollet-le-Duc and his teachings. Even before he died, in 1879, he was honoured throughout Europe as the most compelling of architectural thinkers. English architects awarded him their highest honour—the Royal Gold Medal—in 1864. Ruskin said[1] bitterly of the *Dictionnaire*—'I ought to have written that book.' But England, deep in the sentiment of her Gothic Revival, thought of the great Frenchman rather as an expositor of Gothic than as an innovator who was to lead the

[1] Sir Sydney Cockerell, *Friends of a Lifetime*, 1940.

world away from the styles. On the Continent it was different. The intellectual novelties of the *Entretiens* exercised enormous fascination, especially to the generation of the 'nineties—the generation, that is, born about 1860 and grown up to a *fin-de-siècle* restlessness and sense of adventure. It was not so much in France, however, as in the Low Countries, that the message of Viollet-le-Duc was appreciated and made the spring-board of adventure. In Holland, H. P. Berlage wrote about a 'pure art of utility' which was to be '*the* art of the 20th century' and when he built the Exchange at Amsterdam (1898–1903) it followed, in a personal and local way, the principles exposed in the *Entretiens*. In Belgium, in 1893, another young architect, Victor Horta, launched a very curious architecture of his own, quickly christened 'Art Nouveau'. That shallow and long-outmoded style, which inflected Continental art and manufactures for about a decade, owed much to Viollet, in its sense of innovation if not in its forms; and the house which Horta built in Brussels in 1893 most certainly has Viollet for its godfather.[1] But Horta was determined to give his new architecture the thing which Viollet's own designs so conspicuously lacked—style. And to do so, he borrowed, according to Pevsner, a form of curvilinear decoration from a source which is important to our theme—namely, from contemporary painting. It was not, to be sure, the kind of painting we have been discussing just now, but a side-issue of English Pre-Raphaelitism, the decorative and symbolistic work of the Dutch painter, Toorup. Horta interpreted the Viollet idea in terms of the swirling etheriality of Toorup.

[1] For this part of the story see Nikolaus Pevsner's valuable *Pioneers of the Modern Movement from William Morris to Walter Gropius*, 1936. Curiously Pevsner does not mention Viollet-le-Duc and says, for instance, that Victor Horta's *art nouveau* 'appeared . . . without any visible architectural premisses'.

Neither Berlage nor Horta exercised a very penetrating influence on the future of architecture. Both accepted Viollet-le-Duc's challenge and answered it in their own way. But their results did not lead on to the further development of style and they remain strictly limited and personal solutions of the grand problem of how to create a reasonable and characteristic architecture for the 19th-20th centuries.

But in the early years of the present century another architect took up the same old challenge and this time with somewhat greater effect. The name of this architect was Auguste Perret. He was born in 1873—seventy-four years ago—and is today the most distinguished of living French architects. His first important work was a block of flats in the Rue Franklin, Paris, built in 1903—and built of reinforced concrete. Viollet-le-Duc, you remember, had thought of the modern arsenal of materials as consisting chiefly of cast-iron, masonry, brick and timber—an arsenal still half-medieval but lacking the homogeneity of that great age of masonry construction. Reinforced concrete was developed in the last two decades of the 19th century and does offer a new homogeneity—that is to say, it combines the compressive strength of cast-iron with the tensile stress of steel; and thus an entire building can be satisfactorily conceived in this one material. Perret's block of flats has little about it to suggest the medieval analogy implicit in the Viollet-le-Duc point of view; but a garage he built in 1905 (Plate XLIX) contains, framed in a concrete opening, a huge rose-window of iron. That, however, is the last link, for in nearly all his subsequent buildings, Perret is inspired not so much by Gothic precedent as by the simple canon of the classical styles. He has found that the frame-and-panel construction appropriate to reinforced concrete suggests a diagrammatic interpretation of classical orders. His Mobilier National (Plate

XLVIII) is classical in composition and most of his later works have rudimentary orders and are crowned by heavy projecting cornices. Important exceptions are his churches, where a Gothic model is followed and the idea of the traceried window ingeniously, if quaintly, interpreted by the filling of wall-panels with pre-cast concrete blocks, pierced to form a decorative design.

Perret is a real follower of Viollet-le-Duc and the first, it seems to me, who has succeeded completely in making an architectural language to fit the terms of the theory. He has succeeded partly because he has the advantage of working in a homogeneous material and partly because he has discarded the burden of Gothic analogy and availed himself of the rhythms of the classic styles. Of the degree of his success there can be no doubt; his pupils and admirers have spread his style all over France and the French colonies. Blocks of flats, schools, hospitals, government buildings bear witness to the adaptability of Perret's style in many parts of the world.[1] It has become one of the great innovating styles of our time.

One of the styles—but only one; and there are many people who will say that Perret has really done nothing more than interpret the French academic tradition in a manner appropriate to modern planning requirements and the use of modern materials. Even if those are his limits they are honourable enough. But the same critics would go on to say that the real revolution in modern architecture only happened when another architect, 15 years younger than Perret, appeared on the scene and in a few breath-taking designs, executed in the early nineteen-twenties, destroyed every vestige of analogy with the past and introduced an architecture as powerful and independ-

[1] *Art Présent*, No 1, 1946, contains a review of Perret's work and that of his followers.

ent in its forms as the paintings of the Cézanne-Picasso tradition. The name of that architect is, of course, Le Corbusier.

Edouard Jeanneret, who later borrowed his grandmother's name of Le Corbusier,[1] was born in La Chaux-de-Fonds near Geneva, Switzerland, in 1887. His father was a craftsman in enamel and a nature-lover; his mother was musical. He went to the local art school at Chaux-de-Fonds where, under the influence of L'Epplatennier, he built a villa with Art Nouveau decorations in 1900. After a visit to Italy he went to Vienna and saw something of Hoffmann's work and teaching. At Paris, in 1908, he saw Matisse's paintings at the Salon des Independents, and discovered Cézanne. He went into Perret's office and was there for over a year. In 1910–11 he went to Germany and was for five months with Peter Behrens—a man whose work in some respects parallels that of Perret. Then he went off to Greece, the Balkans and Rome, returning eventually to Chaux-de-Fonds, where he remained for most of the war. It was in 1916 that he built his first important house there—decidedly in the Perret manner. In 1917, on a sudden impulse, he returned to Paris and in the following year met Amedée Ozenfant. With Ozenfant he initiated the painting movement known as Purism—a movement whose products are, I believe, limited to the canvases of its two founders.[2]

[1] Maximilien Gauthier, *Le Corbusier; ou l'architecture au service de l'homme*, 1944, gives an account of the architect's career. For his works see the series of monographs published by Girsberger, Zurich.

[2] Purism is explained in *L'Esprit Nouveau*, No 4, Jan., 1921. It insists on the importance of logic in creative art. Logic is 'an instrument of control and, for the man who has the power of invention, a guide to discovery. It controls and corrects the sometimes fantastic progress of intuition'. Cubism is criticized for creating 'arbitrary and fantastical forms', e.g. a square pipe, painted so because it must establish relationships with a match-box. Cubism shows 'a lack of research in the choice of themes', and needs purification: hence *le Purisme*.

Le Corbusier's first important building after the war was the studio residence he built for Ozenfant in Paris in 1922. In the following year he published his famous book *Vers une Architecture*.[1] Probably the most influential architectural book of its generation, its contents adds remarkably little to what Viollet-le-Duc said in his lectures exactly sixty years before. The beauty of the machine, the importance of geometrical control in the creation of design, the stupidity of academic tradition, the lessons of the past in precision and logic—all these are topics which Viollet-le-Duc had dealt with. But in Le Corbusier the emphasis is, of course, very different. He is able to put the car, the air-plane and the liner in the foreground of the picture; he insists far more vehemently on the way in which engineering has leapt ahead of architecture and he coins the phrase 'la maison—une machine a habiter'. His technique, too, is lighter and faster, adapted to an age of headlines and headlights. And there is one subject he deals with at some length which would have been perfectly strange to his great precursor—the subject of factory-built houses.

Between 1922 and 1927, Le Corbusier built those buildings which, more even than his book, made the world take notice of his name. They included, besides the Ozenfant studio, some houses in Auteuil, working-class housing at Pessac, the Cook house at Boulogne-sur-Seine (1926) and the Villa at Garches (1927). When these buildings were illustrated in the art and architectural magazines of the world, they caused considerable bewilderment and widespread misunderstanding. To most of us, then, it seemed as if Le Corbusier was deliberately cultivating every perversion and every discord which utilitarian design in steel and concrete had introduced into building. He

[1] It had already appeared as articles in *L'Esprit Nouveau*, starting October, 1920.

flouted the appearance of stability; he allowed huge windows to approach within a few inches of the corner of a building; he even used that unspeakable product of factory-design, the 'north-light', with its cruel saw-tooth silhouette. It was generally supposed that this kind of architecture must be an expression of sheer utilitarianism—a challenge to architecture rather than a contribution to architecture. The word 'functionalism' was freely used to express this point of view.

But it was impossible, at the same time, to deny these buildings a certain artistry—a perverse poetry of their own; it was impossible to deny that the designs were *felt*; to deny, in fact, that they possessed 'style'. And to those who were familiar with what was going on in the world of painting it was evident where this poetry, this 'style', came from. Le Corbusier's architecture was seen to be in the nature of an extension of the abstract painter's vision. It was, indeed, the same vision, with the same devastating perception and the same fierce love of destruction and distortion, but all directed into the design of buildings instead of the making of paintings and sculptures. Le Corbusier, of course, hoisted the old banner of functional efficiency and has brandished it much in his writings. But in his hands it has always been a mere verbal weapon, clearing the common-place and the second-hand out of the path of his imagination. Just as Picasso's work is, as he has said, a sum of destructions, so, in a sense, is Le Corbusier's; for to him the obvious solution of a problem, however charming, cannot possibly be the right solution. Just as in a painting by Picasso, Braque or Léger the appearance of a thing is torn to pieces, broken into bits and reconstituted in a ridiculous jig-saw which has, nevertheless, a perfect logic of its own, so a building by Le Corbusier is a ruthless dismemberment of the building *programme* and a reconstitution on a plane where the unexpected always, unfailingly, happens. Herein is Le Corbusier's poetry—or his wit. He sees the reverse logic of every situation. He sees that what appears absurd is perhaps only more profoundly true than what appears to make sense. His architecture is full of a glorious, exciting contrariness—a contrariness which is never affectation because it invariably is a solution of a hard and fundamental problem of use.

This is an age which has rediscovered nonsense—or, perhaps, which has discovered that only a hair's breadth divides the nonsense of Lewis Carroll or Itma from the imagery of Shakespeare or the modulations in a Beethoven sonata. I cordially agree with Mr Wyndham Lewis who has said in a recent article[1] that a great deal of Picasso is 'just witty nonsense—and none the worse for that'. Much of Le Corbusier is 'witty nonsense', though on that plane of seriousness which an architect who is spending rather large sums of somebody else's money must necessarily perform. I hardly think we can explain this nonsense by reference to particular examples, because nonsense is really inexplicable. When Tommy Handley says that he can't afford to dress shabbily and the Colonel observes 'Chablis?— a glorious wine—I don't mind if I do', it is really not practicable to inquire why several million people throw their heads back and make a crowing noise like a six-months-old baby. But Le Corbusier's nonsense is rather of this order—sudden, irresistible. One can, perhaps, illustrate his topsy-turvydom by imagining a conversational encounter with the man. In the course of it we observe, naïvely enough, that 'the house stands in the garden', to which Le Corbusier replies, 'no, the garden stands in the house', proving his assertion by an executed design in which this is, in fact, the case. We suggest that 'a building is, in principle, four walls with windows for light and air'

[1] *The Pavilion*, ed. Myfanwy Evans, 1946.

and he replies that 'on the contrary, a building may just as well be four windows, with walls for privacy and shade'. We put it to him as axiomatic that a park is a space for recreation in a town and he replies, 'not at all; in the future the park will not be in the town but the town in the park. Work, after all, is an incident in life; life is not an incident in work'. In details of house-planning, too, we find this passion for opposites. To take one example: we habitually think of a chimney-breast as an excrescence from the wall of a room; so Le Corbusier gives us a room which is loosely arranged round a free-standing chimney-breast. And—one last example—Le Corbusier is the great apostle of fresh air, so what does he do but advocate that (in certain cases) all windows shall be hermetically sealed—so that mechanically freshened air can be pumped in.

This witty, sublime-nonsensical approach to architectural design is Le Corbusier's very own, personal and inimitable possession. Many architects borrow from him; which means that they borrow his combinations of forms—novel, exciting and infectious—which have emerged in the course of his adventures in design. But this borrowing is meaningless—often nothing more than witless and inapposite quotation. It is impossible, alas, to design like Le Corbusier unless one happens to be Le Corbusier.

It would be difficult to say just how much Le Corbusier's development as an architect has owed to his association with modern painting, but it seems to me that some of his plans have, in themselves, something of the quality of an abstract painting or drawing. The plan of a building is, as every architect knows, the key to its success or failure as a work of art: the whole building as an organism is implicit in its plan. Le Corbusier has underlined this in his writings, where he speaks often of *le plan générateur*. And if we look at the plan of one of his most original and admired works—the Pavillon Suisse (Plate XLII), in the Cité

Universitaire at Paris—we see a pattern which has a nervous, delicate beauty of its own, apart from the three-dimensional structure which it implies. If we compare it with a Picasso drawing (Plate XLIII), we shall recognize similarities in the tensions of the curves and in those grotesque discords which, by playing a headlong game of never quite cancelling each other out, give the drawing—and the plan—an explosive, fascinating beauty.

No doubt Picasso has influenced Le Corbusier. But only in the sense that the architect found something in the painter's vision which helped to amplify his own. For Le Corbusier has a curious faculty of seeing practically everything as architecture, and it is no more astonishing that he should see a Picasso drawing as a potential plan than that he should see the upper works of a liner as a potential country-house or—to recall again his most celebrated aphorism—a house as a machine.

The question of the *influence* of modern painting on modern architecture is not so important as the historical truth that Le Corbusier, the architect, has shared the same vision as some of the cubist and abstract painters. In his work, the intellectual concept of a modern style, first propounded by Viollet-le-Duc and later interpreted by—among others—Auguste Perret, has been divested of its importance and reduced to a mere verbal equation. Le Corbusier has effected nothing less than a re-valuation of architecture itself. He has found fragments of real architecture lying around outside the rather unreal category of which 'architecture' is the traditional label. He has found architecture in the worlds of engineering, of shipbuilding, of industrial construction, of aircraft design. What has enabled him to bring these fragments together and fuse them into buildings possessing style is his own personal vision—the vision which is his as well as Picasso's and Braque's and Léger's—the vision of the modern school of painting.

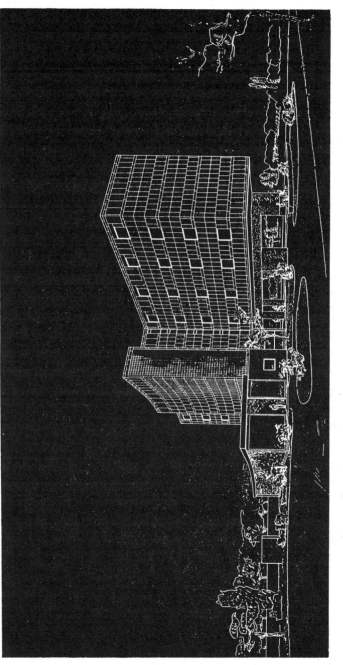

FIG. 15. The Pavillon Suisse, Cité Universitaire, Paris. By Le Corbusier. See also the plan, Plate XLII

It would be wrong to give the impression that Le Corbusier is the only architect whose development has been closely involved with the other visual arts. Thus, in Holland, the group of artists who, after the first World War, became associated under the title 'de Stijl' included several architects. The group worked in collaboration and it really is sometimes possible to be uncertain whether one is looking at an abstract painting by Mondrian or a plan by J. J. P. Oud![1] This Dutch off-shoot of the cubist tradition shows us the closest possible collaboration between painters and architects—both working on exactly similar lines and endeavouring to reach the utmost purity of form both in two and three dimensions. We find here nothing of Le Corbusier's extravagant wit, but on the contrary, a sober Puritanism striving for impersonality and that criterion of 'pure perception' already envisaged by Malevich in his white rectangle on a white ground.

This collaboration between painters and architects cannot, I think, be paralleled at any time in the past. In 15th-century Italy the architects assisted the painters with their architectural settings; and in the Baroque age the painters and sculptors joined hands with the architects in creating illusory, cloud-capped superstructures to their churches. But only in our own day has the art of painting opened up a world of form which has subsequently been explored by architects to their own great advantage. It is often said that today architecture and the other arts do not collaborate—that painters and sculptors no longer adorn the works of the architects as they did in the past. That is, in one sense, true; but in another sense—which I hope I have made explicit—collaboration between the arts has never been so richly productive as it has in the last thirty years.

[1] See the juxtaposition in *Cubism and Abstract Art*.

IX

The Mischievous Analogy

IT IS widely believed that we have a Modern Architecture—an architecture as distinct from, say, classical architecture as classical is from Gothic or Gothic from Byzantine: an architecture which belongs to our time and could belong to no other. In this essay I propose to examine this belief rather narrowly, to test it and to see if anything useful comes out of the stirring about of some accepted ideas.

We believe that we have a Modern Architecture. Why? Chiefly because we want to believe it. We have wanted to believe it for something over a hundred years. In 1847, Professor Donaldson, speaking to some young men at the opening meeting of the Architectural Association, said:

> The great question is, are we to have an architecture of our period, a distinct, individual, palpable style of the 19th century?

This rhetorical question has been asked hundreds of times since then and answered in hundreds of ways and in hundreds of buildings—some of them very queer buildings. But what a curious question! No other century but the 19th would have asked it. No century would have asked it in which men were not overshadowed and overborne by the past. For the question can only exist in relation to the past. It springs from an analogy. The questioner ranges the historic styles in his mind, then measures up the 19th century against them. He finds the century copying the Greek, the Roman, the Gothic. This will not do. The history form is improperly filled in. Under *19th century, architectural style of,* there must be a distinct and appropriate entry.

We now feel—after a hundred years of trying—that something like an adequate entry, distinct and appropriate, has been found. We have our Modern Architecture. We can trace its history back into the 19th century and show from how many sources it came, how each contribution was woven into the general theme and how, even as far back as 1911, there were enough buildings in the world possessing a sort of kinship of modernity to make it true to say that if the 19th century had failed to answer Professor Donaldson's question, the 20th century had succeeded.

Today we have got our Modern Architecture and very soon it will be absolutely inescapable. It has the loyalty of the young; it is established, with different degrees of firmness, in every school of architecture in the country. Soon it will not be Modern Architecture any longer. It will just be Architecture.

So the time has probably come to ask not merely where this Architecture has come from but what it is. At the moment it can show no theoretical basis whatever, beyond a handful of generalisations borrowed (unknowingly, very often, and at fifteenth hand) from Viollet-le-Duc, and a number of clichés which could be applied equally to most other styles of architecture. Perhaps we had better start our examination of Modern Architecture by looking at a group of these generalizations and clichés. Here are some of them. Modern architecture arises from *an accurate analysis of the needs of modern society* and represents *the logical solution of the problem of shelter* achieved by the *direct application of means to ends;* it *expresses the spirit of the machine age;* it is the *architecture of industrial living*. It is based on *a study of scientific resources* and *an exploitation of new materials*. Finally, it is *organic*.

Taken at their face value, such phrases as these are, shall we say, uninteresting. They tell us just nothing. Yet to the people who have coined and used them during the past thirty years they have meant much. In fact, although they do not tell us anything about Modern Architecture, they do tell us something about the Modern Architect. They tell us this: that he has, for some reason or another, stepped out of his *rôle*, taken a look at the scene around him and then become obsessed with the importance not of architecture, but of the *relation* of architecture to other things. This is exactly what has happened. The architect has walked out of himself, rather like a second personality is seen to walk out of the first in a psychological film. He has (to pursue this metaphor for a moment) left the first personality at the drawing board and taken the second (the 'live' personality) on a world-tour of contemporary life— scientific research, sociology, psychology, engineering, the arts and a great many other things. Returning to the drawing-board he finds the first personality embarrassing and profoundly unattractive. There he stubbornly sits, smelling slightly of 'the styles'. So the second personality sits down beside him and painfully guides his hand.

This distortion of the architect's attitude to his art is a portentous fact in the architectural scene today. The reasons behind it are important; even more important are its results. Both need investigation.

Ever since the days when Donaldson asked his question at the Architectural Association, architects have been obsessed by a sense of inadequacy. I believe it started from two discoveries both made just about a century ago—both made (significantly enough) just about the time that aristocratic patronage was, relinquishing its hold on the arts and the architectural profession had to stand on its own feet. The first discovery was this: that architecture was almost entirely an affair of *copying*—copying either the Greek, the Roman, the Gothic, the Italian or even the Indian and the Chinese. Many Early Victorian architects felt acutely uncomfortable about this and expressed their feelings strongly in articles and discussions. But faced with the problem of creating a genuine architecture owing nothing to 'the styles' they were completely impotent. There were only two things they could do. One was to mix the styles together in the hope that something new would emerge out of the resulting pudding. The other was to choose a style as a starting-point, to believe in it very hard and trust to the future to weave something contemporary out of it. On the whole, the stupider architects tried mixing (with preposterous results); the wiser stuck more or less closely to their styles—Middle Pointed, Early French, Venetian Gothic, *Cinquecento* or later, 'Queen Anne'—and produced some remarkable buildings which have an involuntary Victorian twist which we are beginning to find interesting. Anyway, in this matter of trying to produce an architecture not wholly derived from a past style, we find one important cause of the architect's obsession of inadequacy.

The other cause was—the engineer. This, too, began to have its effects about a hundred years ago. At the time of the Great Exhibition, architects had to confess that some of the most original structures of the day were the work not of architects but of engineers. The Exhibition building itself, the work of a gardener, had been preferred to any of the designs submitted by architects. Bridges, railway structures, markets, industrial buildings, disappeared one by one from the architect's grasp and were dexterously and efficiently handled by engineers. Even if the results were ugly, they were what was required; and they were results which architects, because of the limitations of their traditional training, *could not give*.

These two causes, in combination, pressed very hard on the architect's self-esteem. On the one hand, he saw himself as a kind of dealer in styles, with no genuine wares of his own to dispose of; on the other hand he saw the purely practical reasons for his existence being undermined by members of a new and flourishing profession. His sense of guilt became intolerable and it eventually drove him to the self-desertion which I have tried to describe.

All this is clearly written in the history of English architecture of the last hundred years. Events on the Continent tell much the same story, and Viollet-le-Duc's interpretation of Gothic as a challenge to the architect to give up the styles and become a pure artist-constructor, was the first great attempt in any country to meet the situation. The attempt consisted, fundamentally, in the substitution of *analogy* for *imitation*. Viollet-le-Duc's rationalism did not succeed, any more than the English fumbling with styles. But it did make a much greater intellectual stir; it did create an atmosphere of urgency—of *imminent* solution—in which the generations following him had to do some hard thinking. Hard thinking, under pressure of an uneasy conscience, gradually distorted the architect's attitude to his art. And this distortion is more marked today than it has ever been.

And now, as to the results of this distortion. If a man's interest in his wife is in her abilities as a cook, a hostess, a housekeeper, a nurse and a mother, rather than in her personality, it is probable that the wife (assuming her to be wholly amenable to her husband) will become a dull, lack-lustre person. If architects are more interested in the relationship of buildings to a social and scientific context than in the buildings themselves, it is probable that the buildings will become dull, empty and unattractive to all except the architect. And this, of course, is what has happened. The most successful buildings of the pre-1939 period were buildings of an almost purely *diagrammatic* character. They were successful, in relation to the great mass of confused architecture around them, because they did clearly state a relationship between architecture and life. Sometimes, it is true, this statement has been made with so much wit, sensibility and resource that the buildings do have a certain vivid reality of their own. But running through the whole of modern architecture one is aware of this curious reservation that it is not architecture but the *relation* of architecture to everything else which has been the architect's concern; that he has not sufficient confidence in his own art to believe that it can be anything more than a neat prose account of this or that situation—a correct answer to a rather complicated examination question.

Now, it is obvious that this distortion of the architect's attitude has, during the past thirty years, been not only inevitable but of high importance. It has nearly got rid of the intolerable burden of 'the styles'. It has restored the architect's confidence in the worthiness of his profession *vis-à-vis* that of the engineer. But, on the other hand, the distortion remains a distortion. There is an uncomfortable tension in the modern architect's point of view. He still stands off-centre, designing diagrammatically, staking a claim for architecture rather than producing architecture, hugging the mythical coast of 'functionalism' and the 'calculated' result. And he has, at the moment, no alternative. For one thing, he is working in an age of extreme poverty—that alone is enough to confirm the distortion as far into the future as one can see. For another thing (of perhaps greater psychological force) he is terrified that if he should return to his normal attitude, if he should concentrate again on the exposition and elaboration of purely architectural values, he would commit the terrible sin of creating 'a style'. Of this possibility he has an unmitigated horror.

This horror of 'a style' is curious. It arises from a too vivid but too thoughtless sense of analogy. Always at the back of the architect's mind are those fatal categories of the examination room—Egyptian, Greek, Roman, Byzantine, Romanesque, Gothic, Renaissance—categories of death. To create a 'Modern' style would be to inter one more corpse in this Pantheon of the text-books, to submit to a tyranny leading to the certain extinction of all hope in the future of architecture. So, while there is, as I said at the beginning, a general belief that a Modern Architecture does exist, there is also a widespread and inhibiting fear that it will become 'a style', if the architect yields himself too freely to his time-honoured task of making buildings which are eloquent and dramatic, buildings which are heightened expressions of their function and not merely crisp statements of it.

That is the present *impasse*. On the one hand, the architect is beginning to feel that more is expected of his works than nice definitions of the relation between building and life; on the other, he dreads relaxing into that old self, that first personality —the man concentrating on ART at the drawing-board. He knows that if he concentrates on ART he will produce a STYLE. And that, his conscience informs him, would be to stultify the purpose he has had at heart for so long—to make an architecture loved and honoured by his contemporaries.

Now what is the solution? First of all, I must state my absolute belief that no problem in the arts can ever be solved in words but only in the creation of new designs. The most a critic can do—and it is a not wholly unimportant job—is to sort out those ageing ideas which get encrusted round past creative achievement and clog the proper exercise of the imagination in changing times. At the present moment there is a terrible clutter of such ideas lying around. Most of them belong to the nineteen-twenties—some are older. The best of them did service in winning the acceptance of certain concepts which, at this date, nobody wants to argue about. During the last seven years nothing new has happened in architecture—in fact, *nothing* has happened. And yet the world is a good deal older, and perhaps even a little wiser; and when we start to build again, we shall find that the language in which we used to talk about architecture when the first 'modern' buildings appeared in this country, is not only ugly and trite but embodies ideas which, from being useful aids to communication between architects and the public, have become positive obstructions to further progress.

The ideas which I want to assail are really a group of ideas, which come under the general head of the *misuse of analogy*. If you have read the essay on Viollet-le-Duc you will realize what I am aiming at and how far back this particular kind of wrong-headedness goes. Not that it was wrong-headedness at the beginning. Far from it. Viollet-le-Duc, more than any one man, levered architecture out of the academicism, grown thoughtless and unwholesome, of the early 19th century. And the lever he used was analogy. The whole of his thought was in the form of analogy; most of his designs are in the nature of paraphrases; his principles are principles he had discovered, or thought he had discovered, in Gothic architecture. I have not, I think, left any room for doubt as to the importance of the man's career. But does this mean that we, today, should continue to attach any importance to historical analogy in thinking about the architecture of tomorrow? I believe not. And yet, how long is the shadow cast by Viollet-le-Duc! There are people who will feel dissatisfied with contemporary architecture so long as it fails to produce anything strictly comparable to Greek temples or Gothic cathedrals. I have heard it hopefully said that the cathedral of the 20th century is the school or the hospital or the power-station, as if such things could bear any conceivable relation to buildings in which the utilization of space was the very last consideration in the world—buildings which were built as abstract monuments to objectify and render conspicuous certain collective ideas which could be communicated in no other way. It is surely certain that we shall not build cathedrals or anything remotely analogous.[1] A power-station may be as vividly striking in mass and silhouette as Durham Cathedral, but it would be childish to attempt to elaborate or 'heighten' it to the degree required by a religious building—or to pretend that it signifies anything more profound than the provision of that necessary power which in the past was provided by a large quantity of firewood and many thousands of horses. The power-station is not the 20th-century cathedral. It is the 20th-century power-station—*nothing more and nothing less than that.*

We must accept, willingly and without self-pity, the fact that architecture today cannot be monumental. Reason it thus. Monumental architecture begins with the temple. The temple is a building of more-than-human scale, built to house a more-than-human personage—a God. The temple is a building whose scale is deliberately increased beyond the ordinary scale of human needs to express the idea of something greater than humanity. Monumentality begins, as I have said, with the temple; but it does not end there. It has always been one of man's greatest and most devastating temptations to borrow the attributes of God. Monumentality in architecture is one of those attributes and it has only been appropriated by man in his more recent history. It has been appropriated for the

---

[1] This statement is, I am aware, quite untrue. We *shall* build cathedrals and they *will* be strictly analogous to medieval cathedrals—hence their utter unimportance either as architecture or as expressions of religious life.

palaces of kings, emperors, dukes and very rich gentlemen; later for the palaces of corporations and institutions; later still for the premises (call them palaces if you must) of large commercial organizations. In all these cases it is principally the architecture of temples which has been used—in other words classical architecture. For classical architecture, with its system of applied and interrelated orders, offers the most facile system for the enlargement of scale in a building applied to specific human purposes.

Today, to endeavour to be monumental is to be untrue to our own times. Except for churches and certain other very exceptional things, the kind of buildings we need have no aptitude to the monumental. Houses, blocks of flats, schools, libraries, hospitals, offices, administrative buildings—none of these in their modern form are susceptible of that grand increase of scale which is the essence of monumentality. Even theatres and great halls seem entirely to have lost that character of being places of formal assembly which would warrant their being conceived on monumental lines. The fact is that the whole idea of formal assembly in public has withered; and with it has gone the need for an architecture reflecting that collective sentiment which goes with the love of formal assembly. Today wherever we go and whatever we do, we go and act as individuals. If we go to the theatre we demand a comfortable seat, an uninterrupted view of the stage and room to manoeuvre at the bar in the interval—and nothing else except a certain sense of amenity. We do not demand to be canopied under a golden dome, with floral pendants, and nymphs riding in a painted heaven. At the town hall, where, if we go at all, we usually go to complain about something, we demand courteous attention and expeditious service; we do not really care to be reminded by the grand staircase of the majesty and greatness of Mr

Mayor. Of course, some of us may think that these things are nice. Perhaps they are. But they are no longer of the slightest importance. And to pretend that they are or can be important is to enforce an analogy which has no natural force of its own.

Now, this loss of the natural impulse to monumentality should not be a matter for regret. It is a perfectly natural reflection of the change which is taking place in the whole character of western culture. All those things which suggested and supported monumentality are in dissolution. The corporate or social importance of religion was one of them. The sense of the dominance of a class—of the exclusive possession of certain privileges by certain groups of people—was another. The prestige and competitive ambition of commercial corporations was another. Monumentality in architecture is a form of affirmation; and affirmations are usually made by the few to impress the many. Today the few are becoming increasingly merged in the many and there are no groups within the community (possibly excepting the churches) who are anxious to express their corporate identities by gestures as costly and conspicuous as the erection of monumental buildings. In the present trend of things it seems highly improbable that even great commercial corporations—banks, insurance companies, multiple stores— will wish to impose themselves on the public attention as they did between the wars, by building enormous classical palaces enriched with symbolic sculpture.

The social history of our times seems to be moving simultaneously in two opposite directions. On the one hand there is a drastic flattening out of society, a reduction to uniformity in opportunity and reward based on an old conception of social justice which is only now beginning to beget its full realization. On the other hand, there is the enhanced evaluation of the individual and his life and it is in this direction that we must look for the fruitful development of modern architecture. The point where architecture chiefly touches the individual is in his home. The home is, today, no less the stronghold of the individual than it was in Victorian times. In one important respect it is, more than it has ever been in history, the place where a person's cultural life is centred. I mean because of the development in the past 25 years of radio entertainment. Today a man is as well, and nearly as fully, entertained at his fireside as he can be in halls and theatres; and when television has reached the technical perfection which it presumably will, it seems to me inevitable that radio entertainment will dominate the cultural life of our time. This is an enormously imposing fact. Today the art of the musician and the poet, the wisdom of the philosopher and the scientist are laid on to our homes, along with the water-supply and electricity. Tomorrow the art of the painter, the sculptor and the architect will be exhibited, demonstrated and enjoyed in millions of homes. Now, obviously, if observation, taste and interest in the arts are to be encouraged in this way, almost the first reaction of the public will be a renewed interest in the design of the home itself— the auditorium of the listener and the viewer. Already there are unmistakable signs—the interminable queues, for instance, which waited outside the South Kensington Museum in 1946 to see an exhibition of industrial design. One cannot help linking such a symptom as this with the fact that these people have acquired the habit of being entertained through the ether. The new public which has taken Mozart and Tschaikowsky, Stravinsky and Ravel to its heart, which has endorsed the propriety of that solemn and not universally audible enterprise, the Third Programme, is not, I imagine, going to be content always to receive its entertainment against a lack-lustre background of negligently proportioned rooms and indifferently designed furniture. It is in the home that it will most readily follow the lead of the architect and designer.

To talk about the home as a centre of architectural interest seems tragically absurd today, when to have the use of a weather-tight and commodious apartment obsolete in form, character and equipment is as much as anybody dare expect. Still, I believe that the dwelling-place of the individual and the family is the clue to architectural evolution in a democracy; assuming, of course, that our interpretation of democracy is one which insists on the cultivation of the individual within the grand framework of society. That framework being, inevitably, the desperately colourless one of equality and uniformity, the life of the individual must be enriched and coloured to the greatest possible degree—and architecture must play its part in this process. The home, whether it is a house or a flat, constructed *in situ* or in a factory, must be the chief creation of the architects of this age.

From this follows an important consequence. If we give primacy to the individual dwelling in our view of the architectural future it follows that we are giving primacy to human scale in the category of architectural values, and I think it is right that we should do so. Human scale should control all our buildings—with deviations exactly measured to the use of the buildings—deviations within a narrow range of scale allowing for much subtlety of design. Obviously we are going to build many very large buildings and I am not suggesting for a moment that these should be the object of less enthusiasm, study or care than domestic buildings. On the contrary, in the conditions of frightful overcrowding in which we live, there may be more and earlier opportunities in public than in private architecture. But our public architecture—schools and universities,

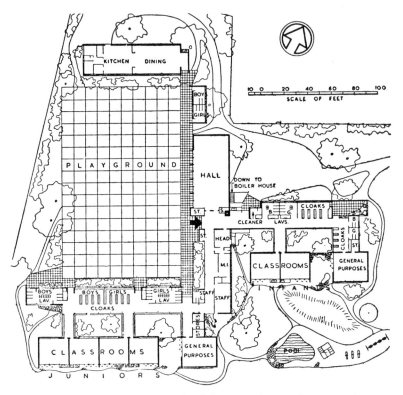

FIG. 16. Junior and Infant School for Ormesby, Yorks. By Denis
Clarke-Hall

hospitals and clinics, libraries, theatres, administrative buildings,
should, I think, be studied on the same plane as the house and
with the same concentration on the individual human being—
on human scale. In big building programmes today there is
a tendency entirely in accord with this precept—a tendency to
break down the programme into its components and to express these components separately in the plan. Thus the old-
style hospital—a great, gaunt block of architecture—has become the hospital city, in which not only is each department

a separate unit, but each ward in each department is quite clearly articulated. Again, in schools, there is a tendency for class-rooms to be virtually separate buildings linked by a corridor, a principle resulting in a plan like the one illustrated on the opposite page (Fig. 16).

All that I have been saying is designed to contradict the wrong and misleading idea—entirely derived from the loose application of analogy to past epochs—that architecture must necessarily take a monumental and dramatic place in the fabric of a civilization. It may do so—or it may not. In our own age it is perfectly reasonable that it should not. Architecture is no longer required to give symbolic cohesion to society. Cohesion is now maintained by new methods of communication. The chief function of architecture now is to bring a sense of dignity, refinement, subtlety, gaiety, to all the places where we live and work—to bring out the values which are latent everywhere in the measured enclosure of space. A beginning has been made in the creation of such an architecture, but only a beginning.

So much for that species of analogy which induces an artificial craving for the monumental where conditions do not dictate the monumental. Now, there is a second analogy which is productive of much confused thought at the present time—the analogy of 'styles' or 'idioms' or 'vernaculars'. As I pointed out at the beginning of this essay we have been in search of 'a contemporary style' for a hundred years, and something of the sort now seems imminent if not actual. But on the other hand, architects have lately become afflicted with an intense horror either of 'inventing a style' or 'working in a style'. Confusion is intensified by an itch—very infectious in some quarters—to have a 'national style'—an English modernity all our own.

The questions of contemporaneous uniformity of style and

of national or local variety of style are not really so difficult. Recently, there was held in London an exhibition of Swiss architecture (Plates XLIV to XLVII). Nearly all of it was what is usually termed 'modern in character', but this character was by no means always the same. The variations reflected very nicely Switzerland's geographical position and three-fold cultural loyalties. One could group most of the exhibits under four or five heads. There were buildings deriving directly from Perret and from Le Corbusier; there were buildings belonging to the Italian School which stems from Sant' Elia and Futurism; there were buildings influenced by Gropius and the Germany of the nineteen-twenties. Behind nearly every building one could discern, clearly or dimly, not so much a nation as a name—the name of one of the innovators of the past thirty years. Inquiring a little more closely one found, of course, that French-speaking Swiss architects (Plate XLIV) had gravitated to Paris and Perret; that German-speaking architects (Plate XLV) had had contacts with Gropius and his group; and that Italian-speaking architects (Plate XLVI) had necessarily come under the influence of Italian Futurism. But these linguistic loyalties were not clear-cut and there were strong cross-currents originating purely and simply in an attraction to a personal achievement—principally, in this instance, that of Le Corbusier (Plate XLVII). The lesson of that exhibition seemed to me to be this. Architectural change occurs as the result of the irregular and incalculable incidence of men of genius—innovators.[1] These men—involuntarily, very often—create schools, like pebbles dropped into a pond make rings. Obviously, these schools are likely to form in the immediate neighbourhood of the master—hence we get something

[1] I know that this statement runs contrary to the now fashionable opinion that great men are the product of their age and environment. Controversy on the point should be left to those who believe that any one interpretation of history can enclose all historical truth.

approximating to 'national' schools of architecture, propagated by the pupils and admirers of one or two or three men. But the influence of one man can extend much farther than his own country and, here again, the prodigious revolution in 20th-century communication is of paramount importance. Neither the Alps nor the Atlantic are, today, boundaries of architectural style and if the innovations of an architect in, say, Turin are sufficiently striking they may be found on the drawing-boards of New York in no time at all.

The whole question of style today depends—as it has always done—on personal leadership. Once this fact is recognized, the problems of a 'universal style' and a 'national style' become quite unreal. Also, the recognition of this fact enables us to be on our guard against the dangers of uncultivated hero-worship. Our own architecture, between the wars, is strewn with trib-utes—often grotesque and feeble in the extreme—to the geni-uses of our time; to our own Sir John Burnet and Sir Edwin Lutyens, to Ostberg of Stockholm, to Dudok of Hilversum, to Le Corbusier and half a dozen others. These tributes are often mere whims of fashion, a wholly uncritical infection. The illustrated professional Press is often blamed for the dissemina-tion of alien fashions since periodicals are apt to thrive on novelty and disseminate it for its own sake. But the cure for the contagions of fashion is not less knowledge of its sources but more; and I believe that a necessary part of an architect's mental equipment is a deep acquaintance with the architectural history of his own times. Perhaps I may have indicated in the last two essays—on Viollet-le-Duc and Le Corbusier—the kind of recent-historical study which is valuable to the architect. It is valuable because it enables him to understand the varieties which the architecture of his time offers. He will see that there can be no question of *a* modern manner but that contemporary architecture is a texture of many styles—all in the last resort personal styles. Out of this texture the architect will involuntarily choose threads akin to his own temperament; but let him first examine the texture of yesterday and the day before and not idly surrender to the name on which the printer's ink is still wet.

The term 'vernacular' enjoys considerable popularity. It implies a generalization. A 'vernacular' is an intuitive discipline in language or the arts, widely shared in any given historic period. It is conceived to have been a good thing in the past and therefore, by analogy, a worthy objective at the present. 'A vernacular architecture' of today is sought. The word is really in the nature of an apology for inadequate knowledge of the workings of the past periods concerned. We speak of a 'Georgian vernacular' when we find that certain rules of expression were adopted throughout England in the 18th century. whereas we are ignorant of the precise means by which these rules came to be accepted. In so far as we do succeed in plotting architectural history we cease to have occasion to use the word 'vernacular'. Its use by historians is a confession of ignorance. Its use in relation to contemporary architecture is absurd. As an objective it is a chimera.

As for a 'National style' of architecture for this or any other country, the answer is clear. If our schools of architecture produce one single innovator of real power and originality we *may* possibly have in due course a style which *may*, if you wish, be called National. But there is no guarantee even then; for remember that one of the most original native architects of the last half-century—Charles Rennie Mackintosh of Glasgow— was noticed only in Vienna and Holland and wholly ignored in his own land. Remember also that the little Dutch town of Hilversum, with its town hall and schools by W. M. Dudok, has probably coloured recent English architecture more strongly than it has coloured any building work in and around the Netherlands. Thus arbitrary and unpredictable are the currents of style in this age of immediate and multiple communications. I think you will agree that the application of historical analogy to this matter of styles—national or international—is as fruitful a source of wrong-thinking as one could hope not to find.

There are several other directions in which historical analogy is working mischief. The doctrine of 'new age—new materials' is one which has certainly passed the meridian of its usefulness. As a rough weapon against the façade mentality of the nineteen-twenties it was serviceable and it may still do useful journalistic skirmishing in the backwoods of Philistia. But it contains little truth of ageless value and becomes altogether absurd as soon as we ask ourselves how long a material remains 'new'. Steel and reinforced concrete, for instance, have been in general use for some forty and sixty years respectively and the next generation of architects is not likely to experience any considerable sensation of novelty in employing them, though it is probable that they will find them no less convenient than we do now. Technological progress has really very little to do with advances in architectural design and it is by no means true that the 'new materials' of our time have changed architecture; it would be more accurate to say that a generation vitally anxious to rationalize its feeling for revolutionary design grasped the doctrine as a challenging and exciting one. The *myth* of new materials, derived from historical evaluations, has had a greater effect on architecture than any technological change in itself.

The architect's relation to the materials at his disposal can, at any time, be a productive or an unproductive relationship. It may be that a productive and happy relationship is found most often when a strong will-to-form has to struggle with a relatively intractable vocabulary of means. History books, taking their readings from the *faits accomplis* of the historic periods teach the reverse; and the student accordingly starts his career with the belief that the refinement of the Parthenon developed in some mysterious way out of Pentelic marble and that the limestone of central France facilitated the taut profiles and thin supports of the Gothic cathedral. Some such argument can, of course, be upheld; but there is the mischief—with adequate historical research, almost any argument can be upheld! The Greek or Gothic situation can be studied from many points of view. None may be wholly right—or wholly wrong. But a generalization deriving from any one of them is quite certainly wrong.

The doctrine of 'new materials' can be given a rest. It is plain common sense for the architect to avail himself of every technological advance which comes within reach; but his use of methods and materials must necessarily be empirical and the enthronement of a material because it is 'of the 20th century' or 'of our time' or 'scientific' is pure nonsense.

It is sometimes said that engineering science has created 'new forms'—that more and newer forms will be created and that the future of architecture hangs on this process. The truth is that there is no such thing as a 'new form', that architecture, in any case, is not an affair of forms but of the relations of forms, and that if anybody is to innovate in architecture it can only be the architect. He is the determinant of the use of forms—that is the one function of which he cannot possibly divest himself.

There is still one further aspect of architecture where historical analogy has wrought indescribable confusion—that is in the matter of *ornament*. The question 'ornament or no ornament' is dominated by the fact that, nearly always in the past, architecture has developed ornamental systems and that these systems provide the most convenient way of distinguishing one architectural style from another. Modern architecture has consciously eschewed ornament. Adolf Loos, in 1913, insisted that ornament was a criminal waste of wealth and a symptom of degeneracy and his point of view has been endorsed with puritanical zeal during the past thirty years by every architect who considered himself as contributing to the furtherance of his art. This fear of ornament is part of the protestantism of modern architecture; it contains a sense of fending off some insidious evil. Loos struck the appropriate note in equating *ornament* with *crime.*

Architecture has, with some difficulty, liberated itself from ornament, but it has not liberated itself from the fear of ornament. The idea of ornament still hangs in the air, ready to infect us, to destroy the integrity of our work if it comes too near. The spirit of analogy bids it approach; the same spirit of analogy keeps it at bay because the architecture of today is to be 'the architecture without ornament', in contradistinction to its predecessors. Either way, we are obsessed by the looming *fact* of ornament.

But, after all, what is this problem of ornament? Does it really exist? Have we ever asked ourselves exactly what ornament means?

Now, the ornament of the historic periods consists broadly of two totally distinct things. First, surface modulation. Second, what I have called elsewhere (and shall continue to call, until I can think of a better expression) *subjunctive architecture.* The meaning of surface modulation is obvious: it signifies pattern, diapers, decorative revetements. The meaning of subjunctive architecture needs explanation. Roughly, I intend that expression to cover all those many types of ornament which originate in the notion, 'as if'. Most architectural ornaments which originate in the copying of natural forms come within this category of the subjunctive; so does ornament originating in the copying into one material of structural features originally evolved in another; so does the use of developed architectural forms for decorative or associational reasons. In all these cases the original incentive has about it the desire to act *as if* something were otherwise than it is. The primitive idea of the leafy capital was to make the beam above it seem *as if* so nearly air-borne that leaves would support it; the mutules and triglyphs of the Greek Doric are wrought *as if* a timber structure had magically taken on a strange homogeneity, weight and permanence; the applied pilasters and pediment framing an opening are, similarly, a conventional pretence: it is *as if* the opening were a shrine. This last example leads on to the whole subject of aedicular architecture which I dealt with in the first essay in this book. This is, from beginning to end, the architecture of *as if*—an entirely subjunctive architecture.

My only purpose in stating this definition is to make clear a natural division in the subject of ornament. Surface modulation is one thing; subjunctive architecture is another. Modern architecture has completely eliminated the subjunctive. But in doing so it has tried, in spite of itself, to eliminate also the problem of surface modulation. This problem cannot be eliminated. It can be whittled down to a question of 'texture'; but the dividing line between 'texture' and surface ornament is very hard to draw. In this matter, modern architecture is still fluid, still uneasy. Surface has not been mastered. And I suspect that the problem is not, as has so often been stated, the purely technological one of finding adequate materials, adequate finishes, revetements which 'weather well'. It seems to me at least possible that the problem of surface remains unsolved simply because architects in their anxiety to get rid of the clogging, cloying legacy of the subjunctive, have surrendered themselves too blindly to Adolph Loos' Puritan all-exclusive thesis—a thesis which classed together and condemned two totally different considerations—calling them both by the same name, 'ornament'.

I am not 'recommending' ornament to the modern architect; how he is going to solve the problem of surface is for him and for him only to decide. I am only concerned to show that the concept 'ornament' includes not one but at least two distinct considerations. That these should be lumped together and condemned together seems neither intelligent nor profitable. My own feeling is that whereas 'the subjunctive' is something of which architecture has divested itself with genuine relief and advantage, the modulation of surface is still a teasing and embarrassing problem which cannot be solved in a negative way and demands that change-round from negative to positive, from subtraction to addition which, indeed, not only this but many problems of architectural design seem to demand.

I have devoted most of this essay to attacking a mode of thought which, although it has served a vital purpose in the thinking out and establishment of the modern movement, is now mischievous and confusing. We have our Modern Architecture and, as I said earlier on, it will soon not be Modern Architecture any more but simply Architecture. The time has come when we can knock away the awkward fabric of analogy and study our architecture as a living thing, considering not whether we are filling in the history form correctly, not whether we are producing things to compare with the Parthenon or Chartres Cathedral, but whether the architecture we are making is or is not adding something to the experience of living. That is the only test that is worth anything. Therein is the architect's only absolute and imperishable reason for surviving; for, disappointing in this, the rest of his responsibilities could now all too easily be sapped by planners, structural engineers, industrial designers and interior decorators. The architect must no longer stand outside himself, merely out-lining and defining architecture. Reverting to the metaphor which I used at the beginning, the first and second personalities must re-unite, not by the regression of the second (live) person-ality into the first but by the drawing of the first into the second. It is time for the architect to take a new and more positive view of his functions, to learn to study not merely minimum re-quirements, but maximum possibilities; to learn not only how to economize space but how to be extravagant with it; to study the overtones of architecture and the geometrical discipline of space as space: to learn not only to use space but to play with space.

Is it too soon to think about architecture in this fashion? I believe not; for we are likely to arrive in a decade at one of those crises in architecture which occur with singular regu-larity every thirty years or so—in fact, once in every genera-tion. If the 'functionalism' crisis can be dated at 1927, the next critical year will be round about 1957. This gives us less than ten years to remember how to build at all, after the ghastly wilderness of 1939 and after; ten years, too, to prepare the approach for a wider, more adventurous conception of the meaning and possibilities of architecture. In 1957 one, rather weary, generation will be building as it would like to have built in 1927–37; but desire always rides ahead of practice and the springing thought of 1957 will be different. What it will be like I do not know; all I have tried to do here is to clear away leaves—or perhaps even less than that: to show that leaves which some still seem to think are young are in fact yellowing and will fall at a shake of the bough.

X
The Past in the Future

ALBERTI, describing an ideal town, declared that, if any Roman ruins existed upon the site, they ought to be preserved. That must be one of the first recorded pleas for preservation on strictly 'cultural' grounds. Often, in more ancient times, buildings have been preserved for political or religious reasons —reasons of prestige; but Alberti's recommendation, of about 1450, has motives identical with those which prompted our own Ancient Monuments Act of 1912. Decayed and obsolete structures are to be preserved because they are sources of wonder and interest to the artist and historian and to those elements in the contemporary mind to which art and history minister.

Preservation has been held a worthy thing by some few people in every generation since Alberti. Today, a large part of public opinion endorses its propriety; and in the Town and Country Planning Act of 1944, steps were taken towards preservation on a scale more systematic and comprehensive than any country has at any time proposed.

The subject is, however, subtle and delicate, susceptible of fatuity, hypocrisy, sentimentality of the ugliest sort and downright obstructionism. In its worst form preservation may be a resentful fumbling, a refusal to understand the living shape of things or to give things shape. In its best form it is a mark of civilization such as few nations have aspired to show. It illustrates in a concrete way our power to embrace human achievement wherever and whenever it has reached an honourable level; and our lively curiosity about and sympathy with the long flow of human history of which we are only the momentary fringe.

The theory and practice of preservation have grown up alongside the habit of objective, scientific thought. In this country they date from the days when Fellows of the Royal Society were often Fellows of the Society of Antiquaries and when a county historian thought it the most natural thing to include descriptions of prehistoric remains and a new waterworks between the covers of the same book. Today, buildings share the protection of that paramount duty felt by every nation, and overriding the strongest currents of modern barbarism, to preserve its works of art from destruction in war. With a strangely deep sense of the values involved, every belligerent in the last conflict endeavoured to protect its ancient monuments, or those parts of them which by any means of human ingenuity could be protected from explosives and fire. Certainly, John Vanbrugh was right when, in a letter[1] to the Duchess of Marlborough dated June 11, 1709, pleading for the preservation of Woodstock Manor, he wrote:

'There is perhaps no one thing, which the most Polite part of Mankind have more universally agreed in; than the Vallue they have ever set upon the Remains of distant Times. Nor amongst the Severall kinds of those Antiquitys, are there any so much regarded, as those of Buildings; Some for their Magnificence, or Curious Workmanship; And others; as they move more lively and pleasing Reflections (than History without their Aid can do) on the Persons who have Inhabited them; On the Remarkable things which have been transacted in them, Or the extraordinary Occasions of Erecting them.'

Perhaps Vanbrugh exaggerated a little: I do not think people have ever set a *greater* value on buildings than on pictures or

[1] Printed in *The Complete Works of Sir John Vanbrugh*, 1928, Vol 4, p 29.

literature. But these latter are less hard to preserve. A local authority does not have to define the public usefulness of Hooker's *Ecclesiastical Polity* or the novels of Mrs Humphry Ward before deciding to build a public library. Nor does the building of a concert hall hang on the ability of Orlando Gibbons or Sir John Stainer to recommend themselves to the public ear. Their works will remain in print whether they are heard or not.

But old buildings are different. Like divorced wives they cost money to maintain. They are often dreadfully in the way. And the protection of one may exact as much sacrifice from the community as the preservation of a thousand pictures, books or musical scores. In their case only, we are brought face to face with decisions on values. And these values are complicated.

Complicated as they are, they can be sorted out and here, to start with, is a rough list of types of buildings which may in certain circumstances deserve protection.:

1. The building which is a work of art: the product of a distinct and outstanding creative mind.
2. The building which is not a distinct creation in this sense but possesses in a pronounced form the characteristic virtues of the school of design which produced it.
3. The building which, of no great artistic merit, is either of significant antiquity or a composition of fragmentary beauties welded together in the course of time.
4. The building which has been the scene of great events or the labours of great men.
5. The building whose only virtue is that in a bleak tract of modernity it alone gives depth in time.

Obviously, several quite different basic kinds of values are involved in all these cases. They could be grouped under two heads—aesthetic and literary. Literary values (by which I mean those associated with history and a sense of continuity) are never absent from an old building. Neither are aesthetic values. But aesthetic values, unlike literary values, are not enhanced with the passage of time. They can only be accurately assessed in relation to their time and through their time in relation to all time. They are susceptible of strict comparative analysis. More precious and concrete, therefore, I have placed them at the head of my list of valid grounds for preserving buildings.

When is a building a work of art? I do not think there is much difficulty about that question if we remember that no artistic product is an isolable thing. Refer the building to the individual or school which produced it. Compare it with other buildings from the same hand or source. If these stand out as a group exemplifying in a conspicuous way the genius of an age, the building you are concerned with stands a good chance of being worth considering as a very precious object. If, in addition, the building is among the principal works of a man of acknowledged genius, an innovator, a leader, well then you have what can, I think, be placed in the first and principal category of buildings deserving protection. I admit, of course, that the conditions suggested here are open to various interpretations. You and I may have equally clear-cut but not identical views as to who are the really great figures in English architecture; and some critics may take the view that each and every building, whether by a great man or not, should be assessed objectively on its merits. This, however, is quite certain to lead to endless altercation. Aesthetic judgments supported by historical analysis are more stable and lasting. My own list of the great English architects from Wren onwards would consist, besides Sir Christopher, of Hawksmore, Vanbrugh, Gibbs, Robert Adam, Chambers, the younger Dance, Soane, C. R. Cockerell,

Pugin, Butterfield, Lutyens, and perhaps one or two more. I am prepared to consider applications on behalf of other candidates, but I believe that any building by any of these men is as likely to be stamped with original genius as, say, a satire by Swift, a painting by Reynolds, Romney or Blake, or a poem by Gerard Manly Hopkins. They were architects who took minute pains with their work; all of them possessed phenomenal imaginations; all were acknowledged leaders in their time.

The work of art cannot, of course, always be historically certificated. There are medieval buildings which exhibit skill and originality in a high degree but to which no individual's name can be satisfactorily attached. And yet the personal skill is there and it is perhaps only lack of research and comparative analysis which makes it impossible to use the names of medieval masons as freely as we do those of professional architects at a later date. But in medieval buildings the problem, so far as preservation is concerned, is not acute, for their antiquity alone usually places them securely in some other category than my first.

Now a word or two about my second category—buildings whose virtues are the routine virtues of a widespread school of architecture. The obvious example is the Queen Anne or Georgian house. These survive in their hundreds, perhaps thousands, and any region of town or country would be poorer if all were swept away. But here preservation must be selective, co-ordinated. And one of the things I would stress is that preservation in general is only valuable when it *is* co-ordinated and related to a plan of positive development. The planned survival of old structures can enrich a town enormously. An unplanned snatching of isolated buildings from unplanned development will result in pathetic patchworks of obsolescence. I shall have more to say in a moment on the possibilities of systematic preservation as part of urban planning.

It is curious how, in almost every town or large village, there are one, or perhaps two, houses which stand out as the unquestionable candidates for preservation. Inquiry into the history of such houses usually leads us to some peak of local prosperity represented in an individual success-story or a notable mayoralty, and the employment of the best available talent in a mature local school of craftsmanship. Here has been a confluence of circumstances, crystallizing in a structure where the quality of an epoch is gathered, so that it stands clear above the average of its own day. The house cannot be said to be of great significance as a work of art, but it is a little eminence in the art of its time. It belongs very much to its locality: and for that very reason it is a building which the visitor carries away in his memory. Today, its prestige is perhaps maintained as the house of a medical practitioner; or it is in the hands of a firm of solicitors. Or it may be empty and 'threatened', in which case its preservation now devolves upon the community. It is not usually difficult to find a use for these houses, but it is wise to wait till the right user comes along and not to let the place be turned over to the first club or institution which can pay a rent. Houses of this sort, with their traditional prestige, often serve to stimulate initiative and to bring to birth the kind of organization which will use them wisely and well.

Thirdly, there is the building which is an accretion of beauties rather than a meritorious unity in itself. The small medieval parish church is typical. Our old parish churches are all local pantheons, consecrated museums which are in the highest degree worth preserving. They are incomparable treasure-houses of history and art. Every square foot illustrates and annotates. There is the primitive structure itself, the work perhaps of five consecutive centuries, each of which has left its curious imprint; the Saxon quoining, the Norman enrichment,

the varieties of tracery and moulding, the mass dials and masons' marks, the effigies and brasses, the screens and bench-ends;
the ineffaceable scars of the Reformation and the new harvest
of Renaissance craftsmanship, the arabesqued pulpit, startling
'waxwork' effigies of the early 1600s, theatrical baroque
memorials of Queen Anne's time, delicate marble tablets of the
Regency; then the Victorian accretions, the brass altar cross,
the tiled chancel, the two-manual organ with Hosanna painted
across the pipes. And lastly the memorials, often so crude but
always so eloquent, of the warfare of our own time. Many
countries possess churches as fine and finer than ours. But no
country has fitted its churches with such vividly detailed witnesses of parish life. I do not think anything more need be said
of these buildings for I doubt whether anybody will ever wish
to deny them protection.

My fourth category, however, introduces far more question-
able elements. To what extent should we respect the purely
literary and associative values which a building acquires through
having been the habitation or resort of great men? Look at
some of the past results of this curious practice. I am glad that in
this country (excluding Scotland) we have never given way to
the craze for preserving birthplaces, usually the least significant
structures in any man's life (incidentally, the increasing use of
hospitals and maternity homes should solve this problem absolutely for future generations). But there are many houses
which have been preserved because great men lived and worked
in them. There are Hogarth's House at Chiswick, Keats's
House at Hampstead, Wesley's House in City Road, Carlyle's
House at Chelsea, Lord Leighton's House near Holland Park,
Dr Johnson's Houses in London and Lichfield, and many
others. These have all been made into museums, and pleasant
enough places they are; though it should be observed that they

are show-places exclusively for strangers and never visited by the townsfolk who pay for them.

I think the best reason for preserving the house of a great man is when the house has itself been an object of the man's creative work—as in the case of Sir John Soane's incomparable museum. Where, as often happens, a great man has been totally indiffer-ent to his own or anybody else's architectural surroundings it seems rather inconsequent to preserve his house. Take the case of Keats. The villa where he lived in Hampstead is a decent Regency house, one of a pair; but I do not suppose that Keats ever thought of it as anything but just—well, a house. The fact that it was the scene of his intolerably unhappy affair with Miss Brawne gives it what is called, in the jargon of the guide-books, 'literary interest'. So the house has become a museum, with a blue plaque, a notice board and a Council fence; the street, which Keats knew as John Street, is now, in deference, Keats Grove, and the area having become dedicated to literature, a library has been squeezed in alongside the house. It is pretty, but wrong. If I were allowed to stick yet one more inscription on this preserve it would, I think, bear these words, written by Keats just after visiting Burns' cottage at Alloway:

'Cant! Cant! Cant! It is enough to give a Spirit the guts-ache.'

I believe we should preserve the houses of great men only when architecture comes into the picture *as* architecture; and chiefly when this architecture is itself eloquent of the mind which inhabitated it. Abbotsford: yes. Garrick's Villa at Hamp-ton: yes. Scott's birthplace: no. Garrick's birthplace: no.

The last of my five types of architecture which may merit preservation is the humble building—farmhouse, barn, cottage, dovecot—which may give a flush of historic colour to a rather

monotonous district. Here are few difficulties and many opportunities. The 'continuity value' of so simple a thing, even, as an
old brick wall, when it can be gracefully dovetailed into a plan,
is considerable. But preservation of this kind is much on a level
with the protection of trees, a pleasant asset of which the skilful
town-planner who knows his site and thinks beyond his drawing-board will naturally avail himself.

I have tried to identify, in a general way, some of the values
involved in this matter of preservation. Now let use see how
these values can be protected in the formulation of reconstruction programmes.

Many of our towns—the towns which one hopes we are
going to replan—possess what is usually referred to by town-
planners as the 'historic centre'. This consists of an astonishing
lamination of architecture which would take a whole library of
Mumfords to analyse in detail. The 'matrix' is medieval and
a few Tudor gables jut out in the High Street; the one where
Cromwell is conclusively proved not to have slept is an antique
shop; another is the Nell Gwynne Cakery. These are the much-
photographed 'old bits'. The remainder of the High Street is
70 per cent Georgian—I should, perhaps, say 35 per cent,
because the shopfronts have eaten up half the façades and sash-
windows peer over the enormous flashing facias of the chain
stores—that commercial regiment which has given the British
Isles a perfectly standardized (and perfectly hideous) shopping
street. The Bull Hotel breaks into this crude hash with a bland
stucco façade masking an interior which smells like a cinema
and is furnished to match. Somewhere off the High Street is the
old Parish Church, safe in its acre of graveyard; around it are
pleasant houses and the former Grammar-school, obsolete
since its occupants migrated in Jubilee year. Crossing the High
Street we find St Peter's Church, which was given a horrible

skin of ashlar in 1840 and is a problem alike to traffic and the Church authorities. Follow St Peter's Street and you come to Monkgate with its two adjacent almshouses—one medieval, the other, whose site is for sale, late Georgian. The survivor is still what it has always been, a refuge for twelve decayed paupers. They wear blue gowns on Sundays and grumble all the week.

In the Market Place you find the Town Hall, wrongly attributed to Wren, but preserved on the strength of his fame and standing gracefully on its sixteen brick arches. Opposite is the Greek Doric Corn Exchange, now operating as the Exchange Cinema and fiercely daubed to out-stare its towering rival, the 1931 Regal.

Now back to the High Street and down Union Street into Albion Place. This, with George Crescent and Trafalgar Row, is the brass-plate quarter: doctors, architects and lawyers have taken over the houses from a defunct local aristocracy. The architecture is highly esteemed and fairly well maintained.

For the rest, there are the older back streets, wobbly mixtures of Stuart and Georgian, and the horrible vermilion rows in which the 'historic centre' merges with successive rings of more or less hideous suburbia.

This is the picture of the 'historic centre' of a thriving English town, and it is not altogether a satisfactory picture. It is a distressing fact, but to enjoy the bloom of untouched antiquity you must go to a town which is not thriving; a town dependent on a stagnant agriculture, where the great stores do not think it worth while to cash in, where land values are low and rebuilding offers no attraction.

Now, this 'historic centre'; what is to be done with it? Some will wish to protect it as a whole, because of its romantic intricacy, its impregnation with history. They will resent interference with the twist of St Peter's Street, where you look

through Bobbin's Court to a timbered gable; they will point
our the high antiquity of each site, to Dickens' familiarity with
this or that view, to the association of this or that house with
Nelson or Wordsworth or Wilberforce; they will emphasize
the distinguished 'character' of George Street or Albion Place.
I sympathize with their sentiments, but I submit that they form
no basis whatever for preservation.

It is impossible to preserve the 'character' of a place when the
life in that place has completely changed. This feeling for
'character' is evanescent, intangible, 'literary'; it can be fixed in
the shape and rhythm of words, but not in the stones of
buildings. Here is what I mean. You come to a strange town on
a lovely, persuasive sunlit evening. You stroll down streets
where you know nobody, where nobody knows you. You are
charmed by the timeless, stationary semblance of it all. You
are soothed by apparent stability. You notice only the things
you like. In a street of Georgian houses you picture respectable,
well-to-do families living lives not very different from what
their ancestors lived—perhaps in the same houses. The picture
is partly true. The large old houses and the comfortable middle-
class menage are still there. But as a whole, the picture is a fake.
It is changing. The large old houses become untenanted, are
made into offices or flats. The old families break up and live in
urban flats and rural cottages. The 'character' of the place—
the bloom of a certain kind of life lived in certain surroundings
—is a thing that you cannot fix.

The moral is: do not try to preserve what you cannot preserve—'character'. Aim at the things which have the permanent
values of architectural order and real artistic quality. They are
often worth preserving not only for their own sake but as parts
of a town highly adaptable to certain phases of modern life.
Almost every town, for instance, has a quarter laid out in

Georgian times and comprising the best individual houses, streets, crescents or squares. One finds professional men naturally gravitating to this area: it is quiet, well-planted, and the houses are roomy and light. In any plan for reconstruction it may well be considered as an *enclave* of professional life.

The most notable examples of the 'professional *enclave*' are, of course, the Inns of Court in London. They were built as such and still serve their purpose remarkably well. Where they have been damaged by bombing, I cannot see that much would be gained either by replanning them or rebuilding them on substantially different architectural lines. I say this in spite of the fact that little of the architecture in these places is of very high quality, being, with certain exceptions, routine carpenters' work of the 17th and 18th centuries.

Now why should not every big town have its Temple, its 'professional *enclave*'? They are there ready made—the George Squares and Albion Places and Church Rows. They should be acquired by the Local Authority, protected from invasion, and leased to proper tenants. This would be a perfectly economic proposition, and I understand that in York something of the sort is being done in the case of individual houses and groups of houses. But the beauty of the scheme would only be fully realized if it formed part of a thoroughly sound and comprehensive development plan.

Returning to some other aspects of the 'historic centre', I think we should agree that where radical replanning is possible general sentiments regarding historic associations should not be allowed to be an obstruction. They are, as I have said, in any case fugitive. There remains, however, the problem of isolated buildings of special importance: churches, almshouses, private houses of special beauty—which come right into the middle of an area which can be, and ought to be, cleared. The question of churches I shall come to in a moment. Alms-houses are difficult since they occupy large sites and belong to a system of public administration very remote from our own. Some of these buildings make at least as good living places as most Oxford colleges, and I do not see why, with judicious alteration, they should not continue to serve their original pur-pose of sheltering people without families who wish to live in the centre of the town. Almshouses are also eligible as museums (where a museum is really needed; the Geffrye Museum in Kingsland Road is a good example) or as the offices of local archaeological and other societies; and in rare cases may be preserved for their intrinsic beauty as 'show-places'. Alms-houses are apt to be extremely obstructive and at Coventry the city architect has come up against this problem in his recon-struction plan. Ford's Hospital is one of the most interesting timber buildings in the country, a Lilliputian palace with a long narrow courtyard of tiny lodgings. It has been bombed and now looks rather as if Gulliver had tripped over it. But framed structures, whether timber or steel, are not easily annihilated by blast, and the thing could be pieced together. However, in the new plan for Coventry, Ford's Hospital comes plumb in the way of an essential traffic artery. The architect has two alterna-tives—either to divert his road, leading it round on either side of an island, with Ford's on the island, or to put the hospital on a lorry and deliver it at Coventry's museum centre at Bond's Hospital where it could be rebuilt to form part of the existing Gothic group.

Now, antiquaries hate old buildings being moved; and there is some sense in this in so far as the beauty of a building as a document naturally extends to its siting and topographical relationships. It is true, certainly, that Ford's Hospital on an-other site becomes merely a specimen of woodwork. And yet we cannot, surely, perpetuate an obsolete town-plan for the sake of one ancient and rather beautiful building. Ford's Hospital preserved on an island, moored midstream in a torrent of Ford vans, seems to me a bad compromise. Obviously, a sacrifice of certain values is forced on us and the hospital may have to be moved.

The prolongation of Coventry's medieval life is an anomaly of a century's standing and it is interesting to recall the remarks of an American who saw the place in 1855: 'We . . . wandered wearily up into the city, and took another look at its bustling streets, in which there seems to be a good emblem of what England itself really is—with a great deal of antiquity in it, and which is now chiefly a modification of the old. The new things are based and supported on the sturdy old things, and often limited and impeded by them; but this antiquity is so massive that there seems to be no means of getting rid of it without tearing society to pieces.' A process which Mr Nathaniel Hawthorne did not live to see.

And now the problems connected with churches. The question of what is going to happen to churches is closely bound up with what is going to happen to the Church. Let us face some facts. Church-going is no longer considered to be a social duty by any class of the population. It is a practice confined to minorities represented in all classes, but there is no longer any universal consent as to its importance. The part played by the Churches in the national life is considerable but it is effective outside rather than inside the fabrics, which become more and more historical symbols and less and less essential meeting places. Women's institutes, boys' clubs and all sorts of local organizations may thrive under the shadow of a church; but the Sunday congregations may still be very thin indeed. A certain amount of reorganization within the Church of

England is inevitable: there will be an attempt to get rid of the weaker units in its structure by merging them into larger and more effectively staffed units, better related to the present distribution of the population. Any move in this direction will result in large numbers of churches becoming superfluous and the Church will wish to disencumber itself of their upkeep and, where convenient, dispose of their sites.

The question what to do with unwanted churches cannot be burked simply by protests against the Establishment from those who never enter a church except to enjoy its architecture, peruse its monuments and experience that sense of the confluence of past and present which becomes so real in these lonely, evocative buildings. The Church has its work to do and for this work it may not need all the churches it has inherited from the past. What is to be done with them?

The country parish churches are the least problematic. Most of them are regularly used; few are likely to form obstructions to planning. There are, however, those often beautiful derelicts, built by Georgian squires, half to their own vanity, half for the spiritual benefit of a minute congregation of agricultural tenants, now quite deserted; enchanting, melancholy and locked. These present acute problems.

In the towns there is a higher proportion of unnecessary churches, owing to the outward shift or change in character of the population. These are the churches built under private Acts in the 18th century and under the Church Buildings Acts of the 19th: enormous rectangular, galleried structures. Sometimes architecturally good, sometimes not. Many of these, I have no doubt, will have to be removed sooner or later. The important thing is that the best of them in each area should be scheduled as architectural valuables and, unless there is overwhelming evidence for their removal on town-planning grounds, preserved. They could, I suggest, be secularized and placed in the hands of a commission charged with leasing them for appropriate purposes and preventing incompetent alteration and disfigurement. One must admit that the number of such churches which could be satisfactorily used would be small: but in some cases they would make good halls or might be fitted up as branch libraries. Their architecture is, as a rule, curiously independent of their function. They were sharply criticized for this when they were built, but this original sin renders them reasonably adaptable for modern and secular purposes.

Conspicuous in the category of unwanted churches are the London City churches of Wren, for the safety of which architects and antiquaries have been keeping up a running battle for thirty years. About one-half of the thirty churches surviving in 1939 were destroyed or gutted during the war and, as a result, the whole problem has become much more acute, as it is now no longer a matter simply of preserving churches but of rebuilding—or protecting—ruins. The Bishop's Committee, set up to consider this matter, has produced a sensible and conservative compromise. But detailed decisions have yet to be reached. Assuming that, intact Wren churches being now somewhat scarce (there are but 16 out of an original 53), the survivors will be left undisturbed, it remains to determine what shall be done with the ruins. Demolition apart, there seem to be three possible courses:

1. To rebuild the fabric loyally to its original form.
2. To improvise a new church, incorporating what remains of the old structure.
3. To leave and protect the ruin as it stands.

The first course is extremely difficult and could not possibly be carried out to the letter. The structure might be reproduced with fair accuracy, but the craftsmanship in stone, wood and plaster would present great difficulties. Moreover, allowance would have to be made for the many alterations carried out between Wren's time and 1939. Furthermore, the City churches hardly qualify as works of art in the strict sense defined at the beginning of this essay. They are not complete, unadulterate products of a single mind, but conglomerates of craftsmen's work conforming to the general 'model', given (or approved) by Wren. There would be an element of fatuity in reproducing grotesque details and ugly relationships simply because they had existed before.

The second proposition is more to the point and probably the most universally acceptable. Its success will depend wholly on the ability of the architects employed.

The third proposition is controversial, involving the very large question of the deliberate retention and protection of ruined structures. As this question involves principles affecting many buildings besides the City churches and touches on some neglected aspects of architectural aesthetics perhaps we should follow it a little farther.

The admiration of ruins is generally supposed to be 'sentimental'; that is, it is supposed to stir the kind of emotion which the author of *The Old Curiosity Shop* would like us to feel in following the pathetic career of Little Nell. Little Nell was good and beautiful and the world used her very badly. The reader feels for her, fiction though she be. An admirable building which has been burnt or battered or left to decay is supposed to arouse a sentiment akin to this—a literary sentiment: a sentiment of vicarious suffering. There is no doubt that ruins may have this effect. The effect may, indeed, be very real, especially when the person affected has had a deep personal love for the building, arising from associations rather than the building's form; it will be deeper if it cannot be shared, or glorified, as in the case of war-damage. That effect—in which the building is as strictly symbolic as a character in fiction—may be called sentiment. When the feeling is widely shared and takes on a conventional form, so that it comes to be induced or cultivated, it becomes sentimentality.

But is the general appeal of ruins solely or even principally an affair of sentiment or sentimentality? I believe not. It is, in origin, an aesthetic appeal, though it may be, and very often is, interpreted in sentimental terms. There are good reasons why the aesthetic effect of a ruined building is often greater than that of the building intact and in use. For one thing, the building has been liberated from certain restrictions. The psychological barrier between 'spectator' and 'user' has been demolished; the building is free—everybody's building, nobody's building. The barrier between 'outside' and 'inside' has likewise been destroyed; space flows through the building; the interior is seen through the glassless windows and breaches in the walls. The building has become comprehensible as a single whole—no longer an *exterior* plus one or more *interiors* but a single combination of planes in recession, full of mystery and surprise, movement behind movement; and since it retains all the while the character of architecture—a structure designed for use—it suggests its own participation in life: a fantastic participation. The doors and windows in a ruined building accent the drama of human movement, of through-going, out-looking and raise it to a transcendental plane.

This being so, one is tempted to argue that an artificial, purpose-made ruin should have the same effect, or even a better effect than the genuinely accidental product. And so it well may; but in the sham ruin we come against a psychological obstacle. For it seems that we need to have the reassurance of accidental creation in order to set at rest the mechanism of 'why' and 'why not' which comes into motion when we look long at a building. A sham ruin challenges criticism; we begin to criticize it as a work of art and to ask ourselves whether such and such a thing might not have been better done. The accidental ruin is, up to a point, a work of nature; we accept the approximations, the hints and suggestions, and freely conjure our own interpretations.

The preservation of ruins shares some of the disadvantages of the making of sham ruins. Once a ruin is preserved, the ruination seems no longer a work of pure accident. The 'owner' comes back into the picture, especially if he fences the site and still more if he charges an admission fee. And the ruin is inevitably modified by repair and maintenance. Nevertheless, to protect a ruin is a perfectly warrantable procedure, under certain conditions. The first of these is that the building must have possessed real value of its own, artistic or historic or both, and retain sufficient evidence of this value. The second is that the state of ruin must be such as to contribute its own peculiar qualities. Thus, a building which has simply had its roof burnt and windows broken is usually perfectly uninteresting as a ruin; it demands to be re-roofed. A building which has become a chaotic and meaningless heap of masonry is likewise valueless; it demands to be removed. The ruin to be respected is the one where the accidents of assault or decay have conduced towards those spatial, three-dimensional qualities which I have tried to describe but which could never be encompassed in a formula.

The theory and practice of ruins deserves to be understood, because it sometimes offers an imaginative solution to problems of preservation otherwise overshadowed by formidable questions of reconstruction, user and maintenance. Some few of the Wren churches might plausibly be dealt with in this way—even if only as a temporary measure. Time tests a ruin in more ways than one, and a future generation will be perfectly at liberty to restore or demolish as it deems fit. Meanwhile, the thing can be enjoyed. The art of preserving ruins is a kind of play-acting and must be approached in that spirit. But it is a mistake to suppose it mere sentimentality. It is—as play-acting should be—an affair of taste and imagination. Ill done, it is ridiculous. Well done, it is an extravagance which costs extremely little.

Inevitably, the more intense and dramatic effects of ruination are purely transient. When a flying-bomb destroyed the west end of William Burges' church of St Faith, Stoke Newington (Frontispiece), a spectacle of incredible grandeur was created out of a church of very moderate artistic stature. It became a torso—the fragment of something infinitely magnificent. The remote apse was patinaed with sunlight sprayed through open rafters; and the west wall had been torn aside just sufficiently for the noble and still fresh interior to gain by contrast with its rough-hewn shell. Nothing could have been more moving—and nothing less stable. The ruin of St Faith's will remain a fine thing until it is removed; but the brilliance of the first revelation has gone for ever.

So far, I have discussed only town problems, which are, as a rule, more pressing and more troublesome. But I must say a word or two about preservation in the country. It is necessary to face the fact that the extent of preservation in any given district will depend on the kind of life which takes root there. Thus, in a small 'unspoilt' town which becomes a centre of vigorous local industry, preservation will have to be sparse and selective. On the other hand, a town like, say, Rye or Winchelsea, whose face is its fortune, may legitimately be protected almost street by street. If agriculture should become once again a lively and prosperous industry, more new and fewer old farm buildings and cottages will be needed. Our habit of regarding the 18th-century rural scene as the essential aspect of the English countryside will have to be very much modified; but it is probable that in any widespread agricultural planning vast numbers of reconditioned buildings will in any case be retained on economic grounds and it should be the community's business to see that a little extra money is found, here and there, for reconditioning buildings of special merit which might otherwise go under.

In the country as in the towns solid architectural merit should be the passport to protection. We must not deceive ourselves into believing that we can preserve the poetical effects of things by preserving the things themselves. Backwardness and squalor are essential to much that is strangely beautiful in the country as it now stands. Why, the ancient labourer, his back round-arched, his body gnarled and twisted by rheumatism, himself contributes a rococo touch of considerable pathos and beauty. Yet, we cannot preserve him; and few of us are sufficiently cynical in our enjoyment of the curious to wish to preserve his disease. The beauties of decay and dissolution can be seized by the painter and the poet and made into something new and permanent. But decay laughs in the face of the man who, to steal its beauty, would arrest it.

The preservation movement has at this moment (1947) gathered extraordinary momentum. This is partly due to the attention which bombs so sharply draw to ancient buildings. But the bombing which, in this country, destroyed not many more good things than had been lost to the pickaxe between the wars, served merely as a rallying call to a generation which was discovering that an 'ancient' building and a 'late' or 'modern' building are, if separated by time, not otherwise divorced, being both, potentially at least, works of art; and that for some preposterous reason buildings not recognized as 'ancient' were afforded no protection under the law, however great their artistic worth. The Georgian period, having receded in time sufficiently for the charms of advanced obsolescence to blur distinctions of quality, was marked out as the neglected heritage and an intelligentsia often puzzled and perhaps sometimes a little bored by the truly ancient, erected the Georgian standard. A 'Georgian Group' emerged, first consorting rather impishly with William Morris's grand old Society for the Protection of Ancient Buildings and then floating off by itself on a career as brilliant and beribboned as Lunardi's balloon. The SPAB and the Georgian Group are organs of public opinion. Their influence, combined with that of official bodies and departments concerned with Antiquities and the Arts, has proved sufficiently strong to cause Parliament to place on the Statute Book provisions for the listing and, up to a point, the protection of valuable buildings of all periods throughout the country.

That this burden should be shouldered by the State is admirable. But it is attended by certain dangers. We must always remember the mixed and more or less imponderable nature of the values involved. The desire to preserve is irrational; however clearly we may suceed in objectifying the values involved, the motive is a deep psychological one, beyond our present means of analysing the mind of a civilization. This being so, preservation by legislation is valid only so long as it retains the constant and earnest sanction of a minority of the electorate, as well as the tolerance of the majority. Dictatorship in preservation, unlike, say, dictatorship in the matter of water-supply or efficient refuse-disposal (wherein we desire dictatorship, silent and absolute), may easily become a kind of national ritual, an inglorious fetishism. A building preserved by the State for the nation inevitably becomes an object of prestige, and prestige is a terribly potent anaesthetic where the arts are concerned. No building should ever be deliberately preserved unless it is judged to be capable of matching that prestige by its own intrinsic power to move what Vanbrugh called 'lively and pleasing reflections'—and to move by virtue of its worth as a work of art or of significant antiquity.

As a preserver of buildings the State should be reluctant and critical, subject always to rather angry pressure from below but prompt, firm and open-handed in support of proven causes. A wide margin of old buildings may properly be left to the goodwill of owners and tenants, the public spirit of groups and societies, and the discretion of planning authorities. Within that margin there will be tiresome breakages, but it is the testing ground of good faith and of the lively, insistent interest in architecture without which preservation is sterile.

In the enormous picture of a developing and changing civilization this matter of the preservation of buildings may seem a detail almost trivial and barely relevant. Yet it has its importance. The future of civilization depends, I believe, largely on our observation and interpretation of the natural history of our species; and the study of species includes the study of habitat. 'Study', however, is too precise and academic a word. Each generation establishes broad and scarcely definable relationships with history, deriving from them a sense of equilibrium in time. In several essays in this book I have tried to show the nature of those relationships at certain moments in the past and in one essay I have assailed a mode of thought which seems to me a sure way of getting them wrong in the present. Such relationships, largely unconscious, are more than the sum of incidental experiences. In observing and studying the past, if we do it with realism and ardour and avoid the vanity of supposing that there are any specific formulas to be learnt from it, we refresh the spirit of present creativeness. But how can we do so in architecture, without the visible, tangible witnesses of past usage and invention? Preservation, therefore, has its place; not easily defined but already sanctioned by the opinion of some few centuries. There is 'no one thing which the most Polite part of Mankind have more universally agreed in'. As the centuries pass and the nations slaughter each other among each others' sandbagged monuments, Vanbrugh's over-emphasis diminishes towards a matter of fact.

I. The classical form of aedicule, illustrated in a 1st-century AD painting at Pompeii. *See p 4*

II. Restoration of the Temple of Bacchus at Baalbek. *See p 4.* (From Krencker, von Lüpke and Winnefeld, *Baalbek*)

III. 1st-century AD wall-painting at Pompeii. The general composition and main sub-divisions and the elongated character of its architecture bear comparison with the porch at Chartres, illustrated opposite. *See p 7*

IV. CHARTRES CATHEDRAL: south porch (completed *c*1250). Here, as in the Pompeian painting opposite, figures are introduced in miniature shrines which constitute the main features of the composition. *See p* 7

V. NOTRE DAME, PARIS: view from south transept. *See p* 14. (From L. Gonse, *L'Art Gothique)*

VI. ST URBAIN, TROYES: south side of choir (late 13th c). *See p* 18 *and compare also the diagrams of the Sainte Chapelle, Paris, pp* 144 *and* 145

VII. Detail from the buttresses OI RHEIMS CATHEDRAL. showing enlarged and diminished versions of the aedicule. (From L. Gonse, *L'Art Gothique*)

VIII. **AMIENS** CATHEDRAL: lower part of west front (1220–1240). *See p* 20. (From Arthur Gardner, *French Church Architecture*)

IX. S ANDREA, MANTUA: west front. L. B. Alberti, 1472. *See p 41*   (*Photo: Alinari*)

X. S FRANCESCO, RIMINI. L. B. Alberti, 1446–57. *See p 40*   (*Photo: Anderson*)

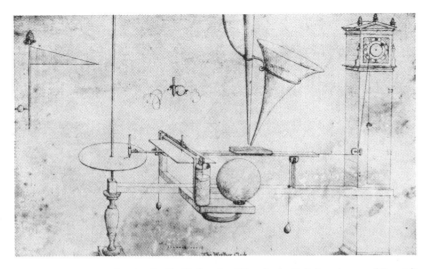

XI. A weather-clock: drawing by Sir Christopher Wren in the 'heir-loom' copy of *Parentalia* (RIBA Library). *See p 60*

XII. SHELDONIAN THEATRE, OXFORD. Sir Christopher Wren, 1663–69. (D. Loggan, *Oxonia Illustrata*, 1669.) *See p 64*

XIII. ST PAUL'S CATHEDRAL: pre-fire design, 1666 (All Souls, Oxford). *See p 72*

XIV. ST PAUL'S CATHEDRAL: the 'Model' design, 1673 (All Souls, Oxford). *See p 75*

XV. ST PAUL'S CATHEDRAL: the 'Warrant' design, 1675 (All Souls, Oxford). *See p 75*

XVI. ST PAUL'S CATHEDRAL: section through north transept (All Souls, Oxford). *See p 78*

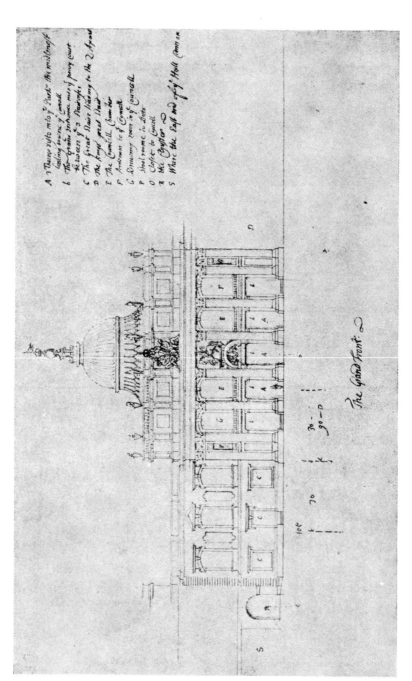

XVII. HAMPTON COURT PALACE: drawing in Wren's hand, 1689 (Soane Muscum). *See p 84*

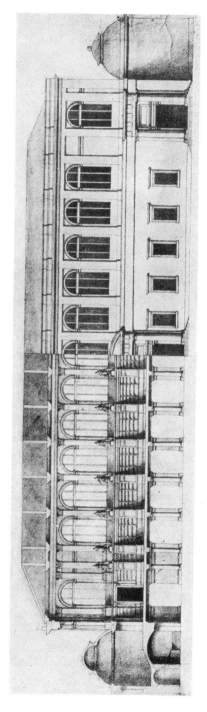

XVIII. TRINITY COLLEGE LIBRARY, CAMBRIDGE: Sir Christopher Wren, 1676–84 (All Souls, Oxford). *See p 85*

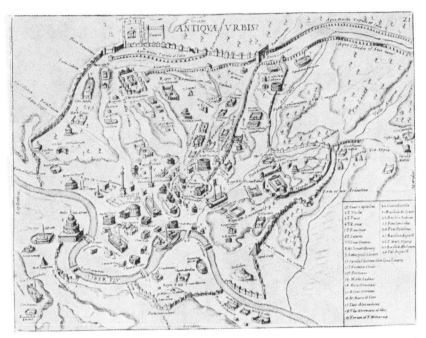

XIX. Bird's-eye view of ancient Rome (From J. Laurus, *Antiquae Urbis Splendor*, 1612). See p 98

XX. First design for Wanstead House, Essex, by Colin Campbell (From *Vitruvius Britannicus*, 1715). See p 92n

XXI. GROSVENOR SQUARE, LONDON, showing Edward Shepherd's houses on the left (Engraving after E. Dayes, 1789). *See p 91*

XXII. QUEEN SQUARE, BATH, by John Wood, the elder, 1729–36 (Engraving after T. Malton, 1784). *See p 91*

XXIII. THE CIRCUS, BATH, in relation to the Colosseum, Rome (Soane Museum). *See p* 100

XXIV. THE CIRCUS, BATH: detail. John Wood, the elder, 1754: continued and completed by his son. *See p* 100

XXV. THE ROYAL CRESCENT, BATH. John Wood, the younger, 1767–71. *See p* 100
(Photo: N.B.R.)

XXVI. LINDSAY HOUSE, LINCOLN'S INN FIELDS. Attributed to Inigo Jones. (From *Vitruvius Britannicus*, 1715.) *See p* 101

XXVII. THE CRESCENT, BUXTON. John Carr, of York, 1779–81. *See p* 107

(Photo: N. B. R.)

XXVIII. Houses in COVENT GARDEN. Inigo Jones, 1631–5. (From *Vitruvius Britannicus*, 1715.)
See p 107

XXIX. BEDFORD CIRCUS, EXETER: laid out c1780. See p 106 (Photo: Aerofilms)

XXX. ROYAL CRESCENT, BRIGHTON: built 1789. See p 108 (Photo: N. B. R.)

XXXI. 'A small Public House on or near a High Road.' Plate from *Designs for Rural Buildings* by J. M. Gandy, 1805. *See p* 122

XXXII. 'A Shepherd's Cottage, and Convenience.' Plate from *Designs for Rural Buildings* by J. M. Gandy, 1805. *See p* 122

XXXIII. 'An Imperial Palace for Sovereigns of the British Empire'; watercolour by J. M. Gandy *(RIBA Library). See p* 123

XXXIV. 'The Tomb of Merlin'; watercolour, by J. M. Gandy (*RIBA Library*). *See p 128*

xxxv. 'Architecture; its natural model' by J. M. Gandy (*Soane Museum*). *See p* 132

XXXVI. ST MATTHIAS, STOKE NEWINGTON. William Butterfield, 1850–52. *See p* **163**

XXXVII. ALL SAINTS, MAR-GARET STREET. William Butterfield, 1849–59. *See p* 162

XXXVIII. ALL SAINTS, MARGARET STREET: interior. William Butterfield, 1849–59. *See p 167*
(Photo: Alex Corbett)

XXXIX. ST ALBAN'S, HOLBORN. William Butterfield, 1859–62. (From the *Builder*.) *See p 170*

XL. KEBLE COLLEGE CHAPEL, OXFORD. William Butterfield, 1873–6. *See p* 170
(Photo: Country Life)

XLI. ALL SAINTS, BABBACOMBE, DEVON. William Butterfield, 1873. *See p* 170
(Photo: N. B. R.)

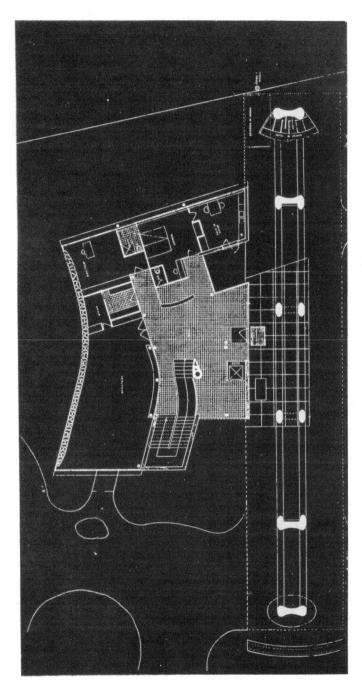

XLIII. PAVILLON SUISSE, Cite Universitaire, Paris. Le Corbusier, 1930–32. *See p* 191

XLIII. Picasso: 'Arlequin', 1914, pencil-drawing. (*Collection George Melly.*) *See p 192*

XLIV. FRIBOURG UNIVERSITY. F. Dumas and D. Honegger, 1938–41. *See p* 210

XLV. CONGRESS HALL AND TERRACE, ZURICH. M. E. Haefli, W. M. Moser and R. Steiger 1939. *See p* 210

XLVI. CANTONAL LIBRARY, LUGANO. C. & R. Tami, 1940–41. *See p* 210

XLVII. APARTMENT HOUSE, BASLE. O. & W. Senn, 1935. *See p* 210

XLVIII. MOBILIER NATIONAL, PARIS. Auguste Perret, 1933. *See p* 185

XLIX. GARAGE, RUE PONTHIEU, PARIS. Auguste Perret, 1905–6. *See p* 185

INDEX

ABRAHAM, POL, 15

ADAM, ROBERT, 114

aedes, 3

aedicula, 3; classical usage of, 3

AEDICULE, antiquity of, 3; architectural use of, 4; Byzantine Empire, 8; Carolingian renaissance, 8; Cathedrals, aedicular architecture, 14-6; decorative feature, 5; fantasy of the aedicule, 7; Gothic, use in, 12; key to Gothic, 16, 22; Gothic mouldings, 17-8; Hellenistic and Roman architecture, 4; Indian architecture, 3; pointed arch and the aedicule, 14; Pompeii, wall painting, pl. 1; porches, aedicular architecture of, 20-1; ribbed vault, 14-5; Romanesque architecture, 8-10, 12, 20; shrine, aedicule as, 4, 18, 20; stained glass, 18; statues, setting for, 4-5; 20-1; temple architecture, 5; thirteenth century, 18; unit of design, 27-8; windows, aedicule motif in, 146, 216

AESTHETIC THEORY, Wren's, 79-80; aesthetic values, two groups, 80

AESTHETICS of architecture, 1, 11, 12, 28; vaulting rib, 15; Alberti on, 35-6

ALBERTI, LEON BATTISTA, *De Re Aedificatoria Libri Decem*, c. 1450, 33 *et seq*.; life of Alberti, 33-4; estimate of his work, 35-6; architectural works, 40-2, pls. IX, X; Alberti and Colonna compared, 46-50; Alberti and Viollet-le-Duc compared, 135; preservation of ruins, 219

ALLAN, SIR WILLIAM, 116

ALLEN, RALPH, 95-6

AMIENS, 14, 20, pl. VIII

AMSTERDAM, Exchange, 184

ANCIENT MONUMENTS ACT, 1912, 219

ANCONA, 41

ANDREWS, LANCELOT, 54

ANGOULÈME, 20

ARAB ART, 12

ARCADE, 10; *l'homme arcade*, 10; Norman arcading, 11n

ARCADED WEST FRONTS, 8

ARCH, pointed arch in Gothic, 12-13, 173; from Arab art, 12; in Romanesque, 12; pointed arch, adoption of in Gothic, 13; fantasy of, 13, 16; arch as a shrine, 18; round arch, 9, 12-3, 16

ARCHITECTS, 1771-1815 age for poets rather than architects, 120; in 'sixties and 'seventies, 121; architects and writers compared, 172; architectural profession, development of, 62, 197; attitude of modern architects, 197, 200; feeling of inadequacy, 197-8; effect of the engineer, 198-200; distortion of architect's attitude, 199-200

ARCHITECTURE

Aedicular architecture, 4-21, 27-8, 146, 216; Aesthetics, 1, 11-2; vaulting rib, 15; Alberti on, 35-6; Analogy, misuse of, 202; Art of architecture: independent existence, 111; chained and fettered, 111; special attributes of, 112; developed and restricted art, 112-3; a building as a work of art, 222; knowledge and practice of, 62-3; Architect's education, 141; new basis for architecture, 141-2

Classical architecture: contribution of Alberti and Colonna, 47; popular attitude to, 48-9; rules of, 49; Cultural changes, effect on architecture, 205, 209

Designs, creation of new, 201; Development of architecture, 3

Emotional power of architecture, 151; Engineer and industrial architecture, 198; Engineering science and new forms, 214; English architecture, great figures in, 222-3

Fantasy, 6-7; fantastic architecture, 111; scale and form, 111; architectural fantasies, 113; combination of architect and graphic artist, 113-4; Italian fantasies, 114; Gandy's work in architectural fantasy, 133-4; French architecture, Louis XIV, 69; Function of architecture, 209; Functionalism, 149, 200, 217; functionalism, utilitarianism, 188-9

Gothic. *See* Gothic

Home, architecture of, 206-7; Human scale in architectural values, 207

Intellect and imagination, 51; Italian Renaissance, 31

Life, architecture and, 200-1, 217

Materials: effect of on architecture,